DATE DUE

DE 23 '94		
OC 17 '95		
NO 18 '97		
DE 9 '97		
SE 16 '98		
AG 2 '99		
OC 20 '99		
NO 15 '99		
MY 22 '02 FE 13		

DEMCO 38-296

EVERYTHING A WORKING MOTHER NEEDS TO KNOW*

*about pregnancy rights,
maternity leave,
and making
her career work for her

 • •

EVERYTHING A WORKING MOTHER NEEDS TO KNOW•

•about pregnancy rights,
maternity leave,
and making
her career work for her

ANNE C. WEISBERG
and
CAROL A. BUCKLER

MAIN STREET BOOKS

DOUBLEDAY
New York   London   Toronto   Sydney   Auckland

PUBLISHED BY DOUBLEDAY
a division of Bantam Doubleday Dell Publishing Group, Inc.
1540 Broadway, New York, New York 10036

MAIN STREET BOOKS, DOUBLEDAY, and the portrayal of a building with a
tree are trademarks of Doubleday, a division of Bantam Doubleday Dell
Publishing Group, Inc.

"A Checklist of Essential Questions to Ask when Seeking Good Child
Care," Child Care Action Campaign's Information Guide #19. Modified and
reprinted with permission from the Child Care Action Campaign, New York,
New York.

"Summary of State Parental, Family, or Medical Leave Legislation,"
Families and Work Institute, April 1993. Reprinted with permission from
the Families and Work Institute, New York, New York.

Library of Congress Cataloging-in-Publication Data

Weisberg, Anne C.
    Everything a working mother needs to know about pregnancy rights,
maternity leave, and making her career work for her / Anne C.
Weisberg and Carol A. Buckler. — 1st ed.
        p.   cm.
    Includes bibliographical references.
    1. Mothers—Employment—United States.   2. Pregnant women—
Employment—United States.   3. Maternity leave—United States.
4. Child care—United States.   I. Buckler, Carol A.   II. Title.
HD6055.2.U6W45   1994
331.4'4—dc20   93-27207
                                                                          CIP
ISBN 0-385-47288-9
ISBN 0-385-42410-8 (pbk.)

To my mother
ACW

To Rob, Sarah, and Sam
CAB

ACKNOWLEDGMENTS

We are both lawyers by trade; this book is our first nonlegal writing project. Anne did most of the research and initial writing; Carol reviewed and edited Anne's work, and did some of the research and writing. Together, we shared not simply the production of this book, but a mission to speak honestly and openly to working mothers, whose real, day-to-day issues are often forgotten in the debate over whether mothers should be in the workplace. We hope this book fulfills that mission.

We are indebted to many people for helping to create this book. To begin with, we would like to thank Ellen Archer, director of publicity at Doubleday, for believing in the book before we did. We would also like to thank our editor at Doubleday, Casey Fuetsch, for her constant encouragement and constructive criticism.

We are grateful to all the people we interviewed for sharing their stories with us. Their personal experiences enrich the book in a unique way, and their willingness to talk with us reinforces our belief that working mothers are eager to be heard. In almost all cases, we used the real names of the people whom we interviewed; we note in the text where we have changed a name.

In addition to the interviews, we did a significant amount of research to gather statistics, analyze trends, and confirm our experience and the experience of the people we interviewed. We have drawn on a wide range of material, including anecdotes and experiences described in newspaper and magazine articles. We were helped in our research by several energetic and resourceful research assistants: Rhonda Cooper, James Gillespie, Grace Hackmeier, Elizabeth Haussler, and Elissa Kaplan. To them, we owe a big thanks. Without them, the book would not have been as thorough as it is. Any mistakes or misinterpretations of the research material, however, are solely our responsibility. We also thank Arthur D. Buckler for sharing his professional insights and expertise with us.

Finally, we owe special thanks to the law firm where we met. The firm was always supportive of us, even as it struggled to respond to our needs as working mothers. We are grateful to everyone at the firm for making that effort. Their willingness to explore new arrangements sets an example that we hope others will follow.

ACW and CAB

My personal thanks go first to my husband, Don, for encouraging me to follow my dream. My thanks go second to my children, Sarah, Matthew, and Rachel, for the lessons they teach me and the joy they give me every day. They are my inspiration.

I dedicate this book to my mother who, as a wonderful mother and distinguished architect, provided me with an unsurpassable role model for all of life.

ACW

First, I thank my parents, M. L. Buckler and Joan Buckler, who have always encouraged me to believe in myself. I also thank my husband, Robert Muffly, on whom I count for both clear-eyed realism and loving support, and for a laugh when I most need it. Finally, I thank my children, Sarah and Sam, for the questions they ask and the love we share.

CAB

CONTENTS

Chapter 8
ALTERNATIVE WORK ARRANGEMENTS 140

INTRODUCTION

How This Book Came to Be

When Anne got out of law school, she was already four months' pregnant. People gave her a good-natured warning: "You don't know what you're in for: Having children is going to change your life." Anne would think about how having children might affect her personal life, her marriage, her sense of self. But she didn't think about how having children would impact another important dimension of her life: her work. She assumed that if she worked hard and well, she would be treated as anyone else would be who did the same. It never occurred to her that having children would affect significantly how colleagues perceived her or judged her potential. Two children and five years of professional work later, Anne wished someone had prepared her for being a mother in the workplace.

Carol didn't get pregnant until she had been working as a lawyer for three years. She had had plenty of time to ponder the effect of children on her career, but she did not have plenty of answers, or even people whom she could ask.

The two of us met as colleagues at a small environmental law firm in New York City. Anne started working at the firm while Carol was on her first maternity leave. Other lawyers told Carol, "You're really going to like Anne; she has a baby, too." Fortunately, we did become friends, developing a bond as the only lawyers at the firm who were also mothers. We didn't simply supply each other with information about pediatricians or child care. Equally important in our friendship was sharing the daily challenges of combining work* and family without worrying about sending the wrong message. Anne could talk with Carol about having to be in court while her daughter was home with a bad flu; Carol could tell Anne about scheduling a client meeting around the nursery school teacher's conference.

As more and more of our friends and colleagues became pregnant, they would come to us asking for information on maternity leave policies, or seeking support for the decision to go back to work. We realized that working mothers needed a book that dealt with their experience in the workplace.

Why This Book

There are countless books on how to take care of our minds and bodies during pregnancy, how to prepare for labor and delivery, and how to nurture our children. Surprisingly few books help us understand and cope with the workplace once we have children.

Being a working mother raises a host of issues on many different fronts: home, work, play. In *Everything a Working Mother Needs to Know . . .* * we focus primarily on how to deal with the "working" part of being a working mother: Will your experience change when you are no longer just a *woman* in the workplace but also a *mother* in the workplace? How are you treated at work? How do you treat your work? How much maternity leave should you ask for? What kind of child care should you seek? How can we all make the workplace better for working mothers? When work-related issues such as child care spill over onto the home front, we discuss these issues as well.

We start the book by discussing in Chapter 1 the way mothers are perceived at work, because these perceptions color our experiences at every stage: from being pregnant at work to being back on the job after one or more maternity leaves. Images of working mothers as not committed to their careers, or better

---

*Throughout this book, we use the term "work" as a shorthand for "work that you get paid to do" in order to be consistent with current terminology. We recognize that this terminology unfortunately results in devaluing if not ignoring the work that mothers do at home—the work of caring for children and maintaining a household. We have not as yet come up with a solution to this language problem. Suffice it to say that it is an indication of our society's conflicting views on the whole topic of motherhood— revered on the one hand, belittled on the other.

suited to being home, or grasping for more than they deserve, often form the basis for how their work is evaluated. Seeing through these images is the first step in taking control of your experience as a working mother.

With an understanding of the experiences of other working mothers, as well as the legal and financial realities of combining work and motherhood, you'll be better prepared for being a working mother. Knowing the facts and the array of available options will help you make more informed and, we hope, more satisfying choices as a mother in the workplace.

We talked with a number of women in a variety of careers—teachers, scientists, doctors, lawyers, managers, secretaries—to give you a sense of how it *feels* to be a working mother: the anxieties, the special rewards, the relationships with co-workers. We talked to Debbie Reed, a high school teacher, about the importance of her caregiver in her life. Susan Eilertsen, a principal in a public relations firm, told us about how she feels as the primary breadwinner in her family. We interviewed Tina Bailey, a chemistry professor who has adopted four children, now ages twenty-one to fourteen, about how attitudes toward adoption and working mothers have changed over the last twenty years. Elizabeth Cheng Krist described to us what happened when she and a colleague approached their boss about job-sharing a position as photography editor at a major business magazine. Diana Manning, a real estate executive, told us about the panic she sometimes feels over managing her children's schedule as well as her job. Their stories, and the many others in the book, will show you that successfully integrating work and family is partly a state of mind.

From Working Woman to Working Mother

As a professional working woman, chances are your work environment is male-dominated, or at least most of your supervisors are male. Many professions, such as law, medicine, and business, are still predominantly male. Even in traditionally female professions, such as teaching and nursing, the people in charge—school administrators and doctors—are often male. As a result, you are accustomed to and may have even adopted many of the behaviors and aspirations of your male colleagues. While you may be aware that being female sets you apart in certain ways, generally you do not consider yourself any different from the other people in the office, male or female.

Chances are also that you have decided to have a child only after working for some time. An increasing number of women are having their first child in their early thirties. If you are around thirty during your first pregnancy, you have spent five to ten years developing your career. You probably feel deeply committed to your work and see it as an important source of your identity and independence. Your work also affects your life outside work. Even if you met your husband before you began your career, it's likely that your work (as well as his) has shaped your relationship. As a vice president in banking says, "My husband fell in love with me when I was working; I don't know how he would think of me if I didn't work." In other words, work is central to your life and to your self-esteem.

Once you become a mother, things change—at work, at home, and within yourself. Not only do you have more to do, but you realize a complicated transformation taking place, rooted in societal as well as very personal notions of success.

Many women feel alone in their new struggle, as if they were the first ever to balance work and family. Part of their isolation comes from a lack of programs and policies that address mothers in the workplace. Yet, the better informed working mothers are, the better they can answer their own questions. To this end, we explore topics ranging from your legal rights when pregnant, to various maternity leave options, to the factors to consider in designing an alternative work schedule.

We address ourselves primarily to women because research and our experience have shown that balancing work and family falls primarily on the mother. Women more than men feel torn between the demands of work and family. Women bear the family responsibilities disproportionately, even if they are working outside the home. While we must acknowledge this disparity, we do not condone it. The status quo should be changed, and remedying this inequity will begin, in large part, with working mothers. As working mothers shoulder the burden of the status quo, they see most clearly its limitations and the possibilities of a new reality.

While society—and many women—view work and family as completely separate, the reality is quite different. Work and family are interconnected. Every working mother spends every day balancing the responsibilities, joys, and accomplishments of work *and* family. Yet, no one can give you a formula for success. Each working mother must find her own set of solutions; these solutions (and indeed definitions of the "problem" and "success") change over time. This book will help you discover your own answers. While it cannot (nor should it) replace conversations with other working mothers, it fills in the gaps in those conversations, and offers a starting point for women who do not yet have other working mothers they can call.

The Superwoman Myth

Working mothers must often fight to prove that they belong in the workplace and are entitled to the same employment opportunities as men. The number of working mothers continues to grow, but the workplace is moving glacially to accommodate them. All too often working mothers are confronted with resentment rather than reinforcement. The laws protecting pregnant workers and working parents are weak at best, and the vast majority of employers offer pathetic maternity leave and child care policies.

Employers may assume that they don't need to support working mothers because they get help from their husbands; this is a fantasy. Research has shown that husbands of working mothers do not share equally the responsibilities of child rearing. Equally troubling is that working mothers also do the lion's share of household tasks. Working mothers shoulder almost all the responsibility for laundry, cooking, cleaning, and other household chores. A 1987 Boston University survey concluded that men with working wives spend almost exactly the same amount of time on household chores as men whose wives do not work outside the home (about twelve hours per week[1]).

In other words, husbands act as if they have traditional wives at home even if they don't. Clearly, many husbands and employers are engaged in upholding the same fantasy: It's called "Superwoman." Superwoman can work full-time, care for the children, cook all the meals, do all the cleaning and laundry, and still have a smile on her face at the end of the day. She does not exist.

The Superwoman myth benefits everyone but working mothers, so we must ultimately be the ones to expose the myth, both at home and at work. Unfortunately, because we fear we will lose status and respect in the workplace when we become mothers, many of us try to hide—rather than expose—conflict between work and family. This creates a vicious cycle that Felice Schwartz, an expert on women's status in the workplace, calls the "conspiracy of silence."

Dana Friedman, a longtime proponent of work/family benefits, tells of a senior vice president at a Fortune 500 company who went to drop off her child at the baby-sitter's, only to find no one there. She managed to find another sitter for that day, but she was two hours late for work. What did she tell her boss? That she had a flat tire.

Why did she feel that having a flat tire would be a more acceptable excuse than a care-giver mix-up? Perhaps because *anyone,* including her boss, could have a flat tire; it's just "one of those things." Having a problem with a care-giver, however, sets her apart as a woman who has chosen to have a child. Her problem is perceived as an outgrowth of that personal choice; it's not yet accepted as one of those things that could happen to anyone. So she hid the truth to protect her image in the eyes of her boss.

Avoidance never leads to solutions; to break this vicious cycle working mothers must start raising the consciousness of the workplace. Breaking the silence is tricky (you may feel that your job is on the line, and it may well be) but in the long run we must either risk it or accept the Superwoman myth, with the exhaustion and guilt that go with it.

While tackling the workplace sounds like—and often is—a daunting proposition, we're in a better position to do so now than ever before. Our sheer numbers give us tremendous leverage. For many employers the choice is between providing benefits to working mothers or losing these employees, only to hire other young women who will soon present them with the same choices. The time will come soon when companies will need to have such policies in order to attract the most talented workers—male and female.

Change comes slowly. But remember that every time an employer and employee work out an arrangement that satisfies them both, progress is achieved, especially if the experience is shared with others in similar positions.

1

MOTHERS IN THE WORKPLACE

An Unusual Sight, a Beautiful Picture

Carol Barrett was director of planning for the City of Annapolis, Maryland, when she was pregnant with her second child and her son Craig was a toddler. She had to attend many evening meetings, so she had a complicated child care plan. Sometimes, however, her regular arrangements, and even her backup, fell through. One night she had no choice but to take Craig with her to a meeting of the zoning board. Her memory of that evening is still vivid ten years later:

> I left Craig in the back of the room properly armed with crayons and paper. Except he figured that the action was in the front of the room. So, all by himself, he came and sat at the table with the applicant and his attorney. You have to understand, this was a quasi-judicial setting, with the applicant and his lawyer sitting before the board.
>
> Everyone waited for me to do something. What was I going to do? I just kept on going. Like most circumstances when well-meaning people are confronted with something new for the first time, they take their cues from other people. I didn't act as if it were a terrible problem or a big deal. Although initially the attorneys moved their chairs over as if this kid were going to do a scene from *The Exorcist* and vomit green stuff all over them, it dawned on them after a couple of minutes that this was actually

1

no big deal. Then they slipped into what I think is a very human kind of situation. Between making their arguments they would look over at what Craig was doing and say, "Oh, that's really a beautiful picture."

Working mothers typically face surprise and discomfort at work when their motherhood role surfaces. Even if we are successful as *women* in the workplace, our concerns and issues as working *mothers* are often simply invisible. As we learn for ourselves what it's like to combine work and family, we must also educate our colleagues. This may sound easy, but it takes a tremendous amount of courage, persistence, and plain energy — qualities that often run low in the day-to-day routine of working mothers.

Although women have been in the workplace for decades now, the workplace still treats us somewhat like trespassers. Women still have to prove that they are as committed to their work as men are, and mothers have an especially high burden of proof.

Understanding the way mothers are perceived is essential to both your ability to educate your colleagues and your quest to combine work and family in a way that is satisfying to you.

Perception Problem 1: The Commitment Issue.

When women gain a family, they lose their commitment to work.

Most women notice immediately that once they are mothers they are taken less seriously as professionals. If you have experienced this problem, take comfort: You are not alone.

A female partner at a New York City law firm says, "Every single woman that I have spoken to without exception, partner or associate, has experienced rampant hostility and prejudice upon her return [from parental leave]. There is a sentiment that pregnancy and motherhood has softened her, that she is not going to work as hard. . . ."

Doubt about their performance and commitment is a real obstacle that many working mothers face upon return to work. Once a boss assumes that your commitment toward your job changes when you are a mother, that boss is likely to change his or her commitment toward you, which in turn changes your view of your job. Thus, for many working mothers, a manager's prejudgment becomes a self-fulfilling prophecy.

To break this cycle you have to begin by disconnecting "performance" from "commitment." Most women probably do their jobs just as well (if not better) after becoming mothers as before. Some working mothers find that the unique kind of interpersonal problem-solving that raising children involves has actually improved their job performance.

Shirley Strum Kenny, a college president and mother of five boys, has identified many areas in which having children has helped her perform at work: time management, negotiation skills, immunity to embarrassment, delegation of authority, and control of emotions. "I am almost always introduced [at speaking engagements] as having produced five books and five children. . . . Though I never admit it to those audiences, I know that I have learned far more from my children than I have from my books," she says. "By the time a book is published, the author has put everything she has into it and has learned everything she can from it. But you never stop putting all you have into your kids — and you never stop learning from them."

Ruth Messinger, a New York City politician for fifteen years, contends that motherhood is the best training for politics. As she sees it, politics is an exercise in compromise and negotiation, two skills honed every day as a mother.

TIME TO COMMIT

In addition to separating performance from commitment, it is important not to confuse either one with the number of hours you spend on the job. Virtually all the women we interviewed said that they did not feel that they performed less effectively at their jobs. Yet, most of them also said that they reduced their hours at work. Those who were, before the baby, willing to stay until seven or eight now routinely leave at five-thirty or six. Therein lie the seeds of the Commitment Issue. If your boss is using *time* as a measure of performance or commitment, then it's clear why your boss would think that your performance or commitment took a turn for the worse.

"Lots of industries still continue to perceive 'face time' as the indicator of good work," says Katharine B. Hazzard, work/

family program coordinator for John Hancock Financial Services. "The corporate culture has to change so that the quality of your work, and that you're there when you're supposed to be, mean more than whether you're in the office at six at night." As Susan Bacon Dynerman and Lynn O'Rourke Hayes, authors of *The Best Jobs in America for Working Parents*, describe it, "[Managers'] attitudes about 'power hours' and success may be the greatest single barrier to women's achieving equality in the workplace. If success means a seventy- or eighty-hour work week, it's difficult to imagine many parents who can sustain that level of commitment over the course of a career without an extraordinary support system at home."

Even if you were willing to put in power hours, you might still face questions about your commitment. Supervisors are looking for employees who are not only good at what they do but who are dedicated to the organization—who identify themselves strongly with their work and their workplace. They fear that any mother is going to put her kids first, before her work. It is a small step from that idea to thinking that no mother can be as committed to her job after she has children as she was before.

To stop your boss from taking this small step, there are several approaches you can follow. First, remind your boss periodically that your performance has not changed, and explain that you are just as dedicated to your work and your employer as you were before. After all, why else would you be willing to put up with the stress and general craziness of the balancing act?

Second, you need to be flexible enough so that your supervisor knows that if he or she *really* needs you to be there, you will not abandon him or her. While working her part-time schedule Anne once was involved in a contract dispute that heated up on a Friday afternoon. The client insisted that everyone meet over the weekend to discuss the situation so that it would be resolved by Monday. The partner in charge of the matter asked Anne if she would be available to attend a weekend meeting. Anne said yes without hesitating, knowing the gravity of the situation and the client's state of mind. She didn't think of the situation then as a test of her commitment. However, sometime after that incident, the partner told her that the partnership had been discussing the feasibility of part-time partners, and her flexibility in that instance had meant a great deal to him in his own thoughts about the issue.

As you spend less time in the office, your willingness to be flexible becomes more and more important. But be flexible wisely. The danger in being too adaptable is that your boss will begin to assume that you will always be there whenever he or she wants you. It is just as important to be firm about your limits. If you need to leave the office every day to pick up the kids from day care, don't let your supervisor get in the habit of scheduling meetings half an hour before you must leave. When you play into the notion that what matters is how much time you spend in the office you reinforce rather than alleviate the Commitment Issue.

While the Commitment Issue is created largely in the minds of others, you may find yourself wondering whether you are truly as committed to your work as you were before you had kids. We discuss these feelings at length in Chapter 7, but suffice to say now that work does not have to dominate your life in order for you to be a good, productive worker. On the contrary, we believe that having an identity outside of work actually makes us better workers.

Perception Problem 2: Woman as Nurturer, Man as Hunter. *Women are by nature more nurturing than men; men are biologically more suited to bringing home the bacon. Therefore, mothers are better than fathers at being responsible for family life.*

Most people assume that mothers are better suited to rearing their children than the children's fathers. The foundation for this belief is the undeniable biological fact that women bear children and men do not. For many, the idea of mother as nurturer is cemented the moment the baby is born and turns to her mother to be fed.

Whether or not scientific evidence exists for believing that mothers make better nurturers, social norms have so endorsed and fostered this idea that many of us believe it. As Faye Crosby, a psychology professor and an expert on gender issues, notes in her book *Juggling:* "A great number [of psychologists]—even of those who favor child care outside the home—still assume that there is only one kind of parenting: the kind called mothering." This is why, when the pros and cons of child care are discussed, the reference point is always the mother; the father's potential role in nurturing isn't even considered. For example, the National Institute of Child Health and Human Development, a federal agency, has sponsored one of the largest studies yet on the impact of child care. The study is designed to answer this question: Do working mothers imperil their children's inner security and future happiness?

What about the fathers? Does the government want to know the effect working fathers have on their children's inner security and future happiness? Dr. T. Berry Brazelton, a distinguished child development expert, answers with the observation, in *Working and Caring*, that public policy toward working mothers is shaped in large part by the belief that children should be cared for by their mothers.

NURTURERS AT WORK

This notion not only dominates legislatures and bureaucracies, it permeates the workplace as well. Most fathers will admit that having children does not change perceptibly the way they are treated or perceived in the workplace, even if their wives work. Everyone at *his* workplace assumes that *she* will take on the responsibilities of the children and the home, even if she too is in the office all day.

Supreme Court Justice Ruth Bader Ginsburg has told an anecdote that illustrates this perception problem. She had received a number of phone calls from her son's elementary school principal regarding her son's behavior. After numerous such interruptions, Justice Ginsburg reminded the principal that her son had *two* parents, and suggested that he call her husband the next time. The calls stopped. Apparently, the matter was not important enough to disturb the father at work.

We saw this attitude play out in our own office. We felt often that we were perceived as mothers trying to be lawyers, while a male colleague of ours who had a young child was perceived as a lawyer who also happened to be a father. The difference sounds subtle, but its effect is potent. Our availability to stay late was often questioned; his almost never was. This was true even though we can't recall a single instance when *any one of us* was unable to perform our assignments because of child care responsibilities.

The Woman as Nurturer attitude not only causes fathers and mothers to be viewed differently, it also weighs heavily on the mother. If women are presumed to be responsible for the well-being of the family (except perhaps financially), then anything that goes wrong in the family (and things always do) becomes her fault. Her work always will be seen as detracting from her obligations at home. That is a recipe for guilt, and it is a guilt that is borne by the mother, not the father. We should not have to bear that guilt.

NURTURERS AT HOME

Once you are a mother, you will frequently be asked how you find the time to work, be with the children, *and* do the grocery shopping, cooking, and cleaning. Underlying this concern is the assumption that all this is your responsibility.

We might debate forever whether men or women are better nurturers, but it's hard to make a rational argument that women are naturally better at grocery shopping or laundry. The way household chores and errands are divided is purely a matter of preconceived roles.

Susan Eilertsen, a partner in a public relations firm in Minneapolis who has two children, says, "I think this business about how a woman can go to work, do the grocery shopping, and pick up the cleaning by herself—and be good at it—is bullshit. We need a tremendous amount of support—practical support as well as emotional support. We need a person to clean the house, pick up the groceries, write the thank-you notes, and everything else that women who stayed home full-time have done all these years."

So, the next time your boss shakes his head in amazement over "how you do it all," remind him that you can't and don't do it alone; that you need (and hopefully have) a lot of help. If we fail to make this obvious, we must accept that working mothers will be considered to have two jobs, neither of which they can be expected to perform well. We must endure supervisors and colleagues who wonder *when* (not even *if*) we're going to collapse under the weight of it all. This constant doubt may eventually erode your own determination to combine work and family. All the more reason to expose the Woman as Nurturer assumption as a myth.

Many of the working mothers we spoke to acknowledged that, for everyone's peace of mind, *one* parent has to be ultimately responsible for the children, and that parent usually ends up being the mother. However, even if working mothers are willing to accept primary responsibility for child care, they shouldn't also assume responsibility for the myriad of time-consuming household chores and obligations. To shift some of this responsibility onto others — especially our husbands — we need to disconnect the link between household and child-rearing responsibilities in our own minds. We need to understand how much of the roles we play are based on preconceived notions. By doing so, we liberate ourselves from thinking that we can be good mothers only if we are also good housekeepers. We can make our husbands more accountable for the household — and distribute chores and tasks along lines other than gender.

Perception Problem 3: Having It All. *If working mothers think they can have it all, they can try. But they'd better not ask for any favors.*

Many people will say to working mothers, in effect, "I don't think you can have it all." The phrase "have it all" is code for "have your cake and eat it too." What these people really mean is that achievement in the workplace has always come at a price — usually a significant personal price; conversely, women who stayed home with their children were seen as having sacrificed a great deal of their own ambition for their families. Anyone who tries to construct a life that defies these experiences gets what she deserves.

At best, this attitude represents concern over how difficult it is to combine work and family; at worst, it represents hostility against women who are perceived as attacking the "traditional" order.

This resentment against working mothers takes many forms. For women in senior positions, for example, resentment against more junior women who are working mothers is likely to be displaced (and misplaced) resentment against a system that forced the senior women to choose having a career over having a family.

Working mothers also encounter resentment from men and women who had both a career and children when it was inconceivable even to ask that the workplace accommodate family needs and who may feel ambivalent about the choices they felt forced to make. As a male partner said to Anne when the firm was discussing the possibility of part-time partnership, he wished that he had had more time with his children when they were growing up; he didn't see why it should be any different for Anne now.

Colleagues and supervisors may also resent shouldering additional work during a co-worker's pregnancy-related absence. They may think that they will have to pull extra weight on a permanent basis.

Some people adopt a blame-the-mother attitude. They complain that having a child is an individual choice, so why should society—meaning employers or colleagues like them—bear the burden of supporting that choice? This argument sounds so logical, and cuts so deep, that at first it's hard to imagine the appropriate response. But the response is actually quite simple: Couples may choose to have children, but women do not *choose* to be the ones to bear the children. Nature takes care of that.

Beyond the physical reality, however, are the social realities we've discussed above: Women do not act in isolation when they assume the burdens of balancing work and family. Women have not chosen the social norms that give us primary responsibility for child care and household duties. In other words, these issues are as much about social conditioning as about personal choice. We all participate in weaving the social fabric; we should therefore all participate in patching the fabric when it develops holes— mismatches between old expectations and current realities.

What You Can Do

INCREASE VISIBILITY

To change the way working mothers in general, and you in particular, are viewed, first understand the perception problems. Then, point out the old beliefs when they surface and ask for the support and respect to which you are entitled. We've offered some counterarguments; it is up to you to make them heard. You can shatter the lens through which your boss and colleagues see you as a Superwoman who can handle everything by yourself. It's often scary to make your family obligations visible in the workplace, yet it is the *only* way that you will get the support you deserve.

When Anne was interviewing for jobs in New York City, she explained up front that she had a one-year-old daughter and a grandmother living with her. She knew that she couldn't handle a job where her employer expected her to stay until eight or nine o'clock at night on a regular basis. By being honest with interviewers, she hoped they would be honest with her. How naive she was! Rather than candor, Anne got blank stares: Interviewers forgot about her credentials (which presumably impressed them enough to ask her into the office in the first place) and saw looming before them the possibility that they would get fewer billable hours out of her than out of someone with no strings attached.

Even after Anne figured out what was going on, however, she decided not to change her approach. What was the point of pretending? Either she would be miserable (and end up quitting) or she wouldn't perform to expectations and end up being asked to leave. Eventually, she found a firm—the one where Anne and

---

> ### ♦ LET YOUR BOSS KNOW THAT . . .
>
> - ♦ No, you do not think about home all the time you are at work.
> - ♦ Yes, you are committed to doing your job well, including staying late when necessary, even though you have kids.
> - ♦ No, your brain does not stop functioning in the ninth month of pregnancy.

Carol met—that actually appreciated that she had a small child and was taking care of her grandmother.

Even in a firm that was relatively supportive of families, we still had to address colleagues' perceptions about our ability to work even though we had kids. Our "education" effort went on all the time and took a lot of energy. But, slowly, it also started to make a difference. A working mother who is still there thanks us for the support she gets at the office. If we hadn't engaged in this education process, it is unlikely change would have occurred at all.

Diana Manning, an industrial real estate developer in Los Angeles, stresses the importance of being candid about family issues. She has worked for her company since 1984, rising from an entry-level position to being the chief operating officer— managing both existing properties and the construction on new properties. Her family depends on her income (she makes twice her husband's salary) and Diana loves her job. But she has never shied away from mentioning family issues when they arise. As Diana says: "I feel that the only way to make any change is to be totally honest with your direct boss. Even in situations when I've compromised to appease my boss, when I've accommodated to his wishes against my own, I've told him that I'm not happy doing it. How else can you expect your boss to understand what working parents face? He's learning slowly, and with each new employee he's a little better."

"The fear that somehow you'll lose credibility with your boss for having to deal with these issues is bad. They have to see that these issues arise, and that you work through them," concludes Diana. "Change is starting to happen. What will encourage these changes to move in the right direction is honesty and openness on women's part, and a certain amount of courage and self-confidence. Show no fear! That's always been my motto."

ENLARGE THE VISION

Speaking out will eventually make the workplace more sensitive to your situation, but you'll be inclined to make the effort only if you understand your own priorities and goals. The mixed signals working mothers receive at work, in the news, and at home are confusing. Ultimately, you must step out of the crossfire and decide *for yourself* what you want out of your work and out of your family; in other words, what you want out of your life. Figure out *for yourself* what the "it" means in the phrase "having it all" so that other people's ingrained assumptions do not end up defining you.

"Living up to the expectations of a career can be as inhibiting as living up to a Donna Reed model," says Martha Stiven, a land-use consultant who works from her home near Portland, Oregon. "I feel that I *do* have it all, but it did take me years of talking to myself to realize what 'having it all' meant for me."

As Martha suggests, it is no easy task; nor is it one that is done only once in a lifetime. Trudi Ferguson and Joan Dunphy interviewed highly successful working mothers (including, among others, Justice Sandra Day O'Connor and former Vermont governor Madeleine Kunin) for their book *Answers to the Mommy Track*. Many of these mothers felt that "sometimes the best strategy is to define one's own path several times along the journey."

One way is to begin with defining what "success" means to you. Success does not need to include specific targets, such as achieving a certain position in your career or making a certain amount of money. It may simply be making progress in many areas of your life. We're not suggesting that, because you have children, you are no longer entitled to reach for your career goals. But you should sort out the emotional and practical reasons for seeking (or not seeking) a particular goal and decide whether they have changed simply by virtue of your having children.

We see defining "success" as coming to terms with both your ambition and your ideas of motherhood. This requires a fundamental sense of self-worth and conviction, in part because we are used to having our roles defined for us. Even as we have entered the "men's world" we have tried to fit ourselves into their image. In doing so, many of us have adopted their ideas of success. But these ideas may not work for many of us (nor in the long run, for many men as well).

It is time to enlarge our vision to include new models of success, especially those that seek to integrate meaningful contributions at work with stable, strong families at home.

It's Not Just Your Problem: Spreading the Work of Working Mothers

---

♦ SHEER NUMBERS: YOU ARE NOT ALONE

Women are in the work force in record numbers, and many are or will become mothers. While women used to "drop out" of the labor market to raise children, that stereotype is increasingly inaccurate. In recent years, 56 percent of women with children under six were working, and a full 50 percent of women with children one year and younger were working—double the number of new mothers who were working in 1970.[1] As of 1989, close to 60 percent of children (of all ages) had mothers who worked outside the home; by 2000, this number will increase to 75 percent.[2] Mothers with preschool children make up the fastest-growing segment of the labor force. Working women of childbearing years made up 80 percent of all working women in 1991,[3] and the vast majority (we've seen figures range from 75 to 93 percent) will become pregnant at some point during their work life. Most will return to work before their child's first birthday.[4]

The two-earner couple is now the norm. Single-parent households, usually run by the mother who *must* work, are also increasing. The "Norman Rockwell" family picture—the father who earns the family income and the mother who tends the house and children—is no longer the only model.

Many of us have the idea that families are independent units responsible for their own well-being. If families request support or assistance from society, we tend to view them as weak or inadequate. Tied to this is the assumption that work and family are separate spheres that have no business meddling with each other. This helps explain why so many people feel that it is somehow inappropriate for parents to expect the workplace to accommodate their family obligations, and why so many hesitate to make these demands of their employers.

However much we want to cling to this pioneer fantasy of the family, it produces more harm than good. Mothers are in the work force to stay; that is the reality. This means that society cannot count on mothers, alone and unaided, to maintain the family. At the same time, traditional support systems like the extended family are disappearing. We must build something in their place, such as work/family policies and good quality child care.

BENEFITS OF MOTHERS WORKING . . . FOR CHILDREN AND FATHERS, TOO

But society should make these changes willingly, not simply to avoid dire consequences. Working mothers aren't a social liability; the changes they are bringing—however slowly—are positive ones. To begin with, working is important to many women's self-esteem.

Working benefits women; it also appears to benefit their children. While many people want to think that children are damaged if they are cared for by someone other than their mothers, the evidence does not support that view. According to psychologist Faye Crosby, the studies show that no one form of child care (including care by a mother in the home) is always better for children than any other. Rather, children will thrive as long as their care-giver provides love, stimulation, and safety.

Indeed, children can actually gain by having working mothers. They develop intimate relationships with, and adapt to the styles of, several adults, which can foster independence and flexibility. In addition, working mothers (and working fathers who are more involved at home) provide their children with more relevant and, we believe, better role models. When children see women and men in a variety of roles, they are more likely to soften in their minds the sex-role stereotypes that they absorb from fairy tales, television, and other sources. As Dr. Brazelton says in *Working and Caring*, "The conscious sharing of roles [between father and mother] in families today will pay off for children in the future. Boys will 'know' and not question their cooperative roles in the next generation. Girls will 'know' that men can be, and will be, nurturant and supportive. Children have a richer experience in working families that are successful in sharing their many roles."

Not only do children benefit from their fathers' involvement in family life, but many fathers who have redefined their role in the family also feel rewarded. A male attorney in our office who has primary responsibility for his son when his wife takes research trips believes his relationship with his son has been immeasurably enhanced. In spite of the inevitable hassles, he is glad he is so involved in his son's life. The dual-earner family structure, it seems, has the potential to nourish families that are more diverse, more fulfilled, and more resilient.

CHANGING THE RULES

Given the obstacles at work and at home, many working mothers feel the cards are stacked against them, and that the rules of the game must change. On the home front, this means that fathers must become more involved. Being a parent — regardless of gender — must come to mean being intimately involved in the running of the household and the rearing of the children. This new role for fathers will do more than ease the strain on working mothers. As more and more fathers assume this new role, they too will bring change to the workplace. Indeed, working mothers may find their greatest leverage lies in the changes that are occurring in the role of father.

In the workplace, the balancing task must be spread more evenly among parents and the rest of society. Programs and policies must be established that ease and support the balance rather than frustrate it. Recently enacted family leave legislation is a start. Equally, if not more, important is the pressure that employers are already starting to feel from the demographics of the labor force. Employers faced with a labor pool that is half female will have no choice but to implement "family-friendly" programs at work. They can't advertise positions as available to men only. Besides being illegal, it cuts down the labor pool, and invariably decreases the talent available to them.

But beyond promoting family-friendly programs at work, society must resolve its ambivalence toward working mothers. We are here to stay, and we have a lot of talent to offer society. Although newspaper articles may give you the impression that women drop out of the work force like flies when they have children, the facts do not support that impression.[5] And society has a lot to gain by helping working mothers fulfill their talent and achieve the recognition they deserve for the integral, vibrant part they play.

2

PREGNANT AND WORKING

In July 1986, Carol was seven months' pregnant with her first child. She was preparing for a jury trial where she and a partner were representing a pregnant woman whose home had been contaminated by pesticides. One particularly warm and humid day, all the attorneys in the case were waiting in the stuffy courtroom for the judge to appear. When the judge did arrive, all the attorneys, including Carol, stood, as required by courtroom etiquette, and continued to stand while the judge conferred with his clerk. After several minutes, the opposing attorney placed his hand on Carol's shoulder, pressing her to sit. He whispered, "I'm not going to let you stand *in your condition.*" At first, Carol sat down obediently in response to this gesture of paternalistic protection. Then, realizing that she could decide for herself whether she needed to sit, she stood up again.

You can choose the image you want to project during your pregnancy—and affect how people treat you as a pregnant professional. You can, literally, stand up for your right to be treated with the proper balance of respect and concern.

In the absence of significant medical difficulties, the majority of women work throughout their entire pregnancy.[1] Both of us did. Books on pregnancy advise that you can work until your due date provided you don't have a medically complicated or high-risk pregnancy, and even the official guidelines of the American College of Obstetricians and Gynecologists say that there is "no reason a woman cannot continue to work until the onset of labor."

Yet, by and large the workplace still treats pregnancy as an oddity. A woman in her eighth month walking down the street with her colleagues in business suits still looks as if she doesn't belong. We were pregnant with our second children at roughly the same time. Even though the office had experienced Carol's first pregnancy, you would have thought by the comments made on an almost daily basis that our colleagues were seeing pregnant professionals for the first time. (To be fair, we did make a peculiar sight standing in the hall talking to each other — over our expanding bellies.)

Being pregnant and working is the first stage of being a working mother. The following "anatomy of a pregnancy" in the workplace prepares you for the issues you will face.

Deciding When to Announce

WAIT AND DELIBERATE

You have just discovered that you are pregnant. Your excitement, hopes, and fears have probably made it impossible for you not to share the news with your family and your closest friends. You may feel that you are bursting with this new information (even before you are bursting the buttons on your skirt), but resist the temptation to tell everyone as soon as you walk through the office door.

Although pregnancy no longer means an automatic pink slip, you should still consider carefully the timing of the announcement. It is the first act you perform as a working mother, and it will shape the image others have of you as a pregnant worker, and later as a working mother. Approach the announcement (as well as the decisions regarding how you and your employer will handle the various aspects of your pregnancy) in the same way you approach doing your job: carefully, gathering as much information as possible, and considering all the relevant factors. Think about the workplace "culture," the needs and personalities of your superiors, and your own needs and desires.

We have found that during the first three months, the best policy is to *act normal,* even though you may feel that your body (and your life) are undergoing wild, complete, and irrevocable changes. Many women wait to announce their pregnancy *to anyone* until after the first three months because of the high incidence of miscarriage during that time. Carol waited through her first trimester to announce her first pregnancy at work because she had had an earlier miscarriage. This is probably a wise policy, at least as far as co-workers and employers go. Telling people your pregnancy has ended can be both painful for you and awkward for them.

During those months, you can continue to wear your regular work clothes. Toward the end you may have to forego wearing the belt that goes with the outfit, but from our experiences, nobody notices—so don't worry.

Of course, just because you still look the same doesn't mean that you're not feeling different. Even if you're feeling great, you will start treating your body with special care. As a good obstetrics patient you will begin taking prenatal vitamins and drinking quarts of milk long before that little fetus is developing any bones or teeth. This can be awkward at work, since you probably aren't in the habit of ordering a glass of milk with your tuna fish sandwich. Knowing that the people she ate lunch with felt free to comment on each other's meals, Carol was prepared, the first time she ordered milk, to answer the question, *"Milk?* I haven't drunk milk since I was eleven years old. Why would you order *milk?"* "Well," she would say, with perfect casualness, "I'm taking seriously all the warnings about calcium deficiency. I don't want to have fragile bones when I'm older."

THE PHYSICAL FRONT: KEEPING UP APPEARANCES

Fatigue may be the most significant physical effect of pregnancy during the first three months. You may find yourself craving caffeine. The prevailing research now seems to have concluded that there is no significant risk from drinking tea or coffee in moderation, so don't assume you can't have any. Talk with your doctor for his or her advice.

Some women constantly have mild nausea throughout the first trimester. If so, try snacking surreptitiously on nuts and raisins and crackers you keep stashed in your desk. If you have severe morning (or midday or afternoon) sickness, it may be harder to keep your pregnancy a secret. If you need to go to the bathroom often, try to tie the trip to a visit to the supply closet for more paper clips or pads or to a trip to someone else's office.

Women who have physical complications may be required to stay home or in the hospital for stretches at a time. Your employer should treat this as a disability and give you the same paid sick leave or disability leave to which you would be entitled for any other illness or disability. How you handle your work, however, will depend on how long you will need to be out and how much you can accomplish on the phone and from a bed.

While we know that pregnancy affects your body but not your mind, it is important not to feed the negative images people have about pregnant women by complaining publicly about how tired you are or how much your back hurts or how swollen your ankles are. We understand all too well the need to complain to someone; after all, we had each other. But we caution you to pick your audience carefully. For your boss and your clients, you are better off giving the impression that you feel as strong as a horse, even if in fact you feel sick as a dog.

Share your aches and pains with your friends instead. Ellen Bonkoski, a chemist, was lucky to have three or four women friends in her lab who were pregnant when she was. "They tell me I used to doze off in the afternoon, and they would cover for me," says Ellen. That's the kind of support we all should have.

IT'S TIME

Most women decide to announce their pregnancy during the second trimester, as it becomes increasingly difficult to button their skirts. Waiting until then lets you get used to being pregnant and working, so that you are more comfortable projecting a positive image once you announce. Second, it adds credibility to your position that you intend to return to work. After all, if you announce during your fourth month, you are already almost halfway into your pregnancy—and you're still working! By waiting, you send a signal that the pregnancy has not consumed your being or made you lose interest in work.

Some women delay their announcement as long as they can

(into their second trimester) because they fear their supervisors and colleagues will view their pregnancy as compromising their performance. This fear is not fantasy; reports continue to indicate that some supervisors believe that "a once-assertive woman executive will ease up on the job [once she is pregnant]."[2]

Sheila Nielsen, a prosecutor in the U.S. Attorney's office at the time of her first pregnancy, says, "I thought I was going to show really early, and I kept thinking I was going to have to tell people soon. But I didn't start showing until my sixth month, and I waited until then to announce. I waited because I was afraid that I would get fewer assignments of a challenging nature once my office knew I was pregnant. I wasn't feeling particularly tired or upset or anything and I wanted to keep working the same way. If anything, I felt exhilarated and very peppy."

Sometimes, as in Sheila's case, the fears are groundless. She ended up trying cases well into her seventh month, and only then started to wind down. Mary Ellen Schoonmaker, a journalist, went out on field assignments until the end of her pregnancy. But, she cautions, her experience may not be standard. Several years after the birth of her first child, in researching an article on the treatment of pregnant journalists, she heard otherwise.

"Some women were forced to take desk jobs when they really didn't want to because they felt fine," she says. "For some, desk jobs were equivalent to a demotion—if, for example, they had been reporters and were asked to compile the wedding announcements for the style section. Some women were told they couldn't go out in the field because it would tarnish the paper's image."

The exact timing of the announcement during your second trimester may be tied to a particular project you are working on or the compensation cycle in your company. Many women wait to announce (if they can) until after an important deal has closed or a project has been completed. Women who are in the middle of salary negotiations and who sense that their employer sees pregnancy as weakening a woman's leverage may want to wait to announce until after the negotiations are over. On the other hand, postponing your announcement until right after you have received a good assignment or promotion can make others feel abused.

Susan Hession managed a small store in a national women's clothing chain when she became pregnant. At the time, she knew that she was being considered for a promotion to manage a larger store that was forty-five minutes closer to her home. "I decided that [although] it wouldn't be fair if I didn't get promoted because of the baby, . . . it would be a burden on me if I didn't tell [my boss]." So she told her immediate supervisor, the district manager, who was grateful for the information, but advised her to wait to tell the regional manager. Susan got her promotion, and the regional manager did not reproach her when he later learned of the pregnancy.

Just as you should not announce too early, you should not wait too long. If people are routinely guessing that you are pregnant, you've waited too long. You don't want people guessing since this interferes with your effort to control the flow of information.

While you should definitely consider your employer's perceptions of pregnant women, you should also consider whether your employer will feel betrayed or resentful if you wait too long. Being pregnant can, all too easily, engender resentment—in colleagues as well as your boss. Be careful not to let that potential develop into a reality. If you wait until the end of your second trimester to announce, others may feel pressured into making plans for your absence without adequate time to prepare. This situation can create a bumpy transition and consequent resentment, which is not the feeling you want to leave in the memories of your boss and colleagues.

In addition, you should consider how comfortable your manager is with change—even if it's just a temporary two- or three-month absence. Janet Grau, a city planner in Milwaukee, told her boss within her first month (even though she had a high-risk pregnancy) because "he is the sort of person who needs to plan everything way in advance."

ANNOUNCING AN ADOPTION

If you're adopting a child, deciding when to tell colleagues that you plan to have a baby can be trickier. Whether you are adopting privately or using an agency, you may wait much longer than nine months before you actually hold the baby in your arms, and you may not be certain it will happen until the moment before. On the other hand, you never know when that moment will come. "The difference between pregnancy and adoption is that you have to drop everything at a moment's notice," says Tina Bailey, a professor of chemistry at California Polytechnic State University, who adopted her four children. "We were called and told to come in the next day and get Karl."

The uncertainty and length of the waiting period can create a lot of anxiety for you, which you may not want to share with everyone in your workplace. "You can't say that you will be going on maternity leave in about six months," says a New York attorney who has adopted two children, "because it could be two months or two years before you find a birth mother or the agency finds a baby for you."

One advantage of adoption, as compared to pregnancy, is that you *can* keep your plans quiet: Your body will not betray the news. You will, however, want to give your employer some notice before you rush out of the office to start a new life with your baby. The attorney resolved this dilemma by telling the partner to whom she was primarily responsible about her plans to adopt once she and her husband had set the wheels in motion. She explained the process to the partner, so that he understood that she could not give him a precise schedule. She told him that she would prefer if no one else knew about the situation, and because of their long-standing, close relationship, she knew that he would respect her privacy. When the birth mother's due date drew near, the attorney started winding down at work, just as she would have if it had been her own pregnancy. In this way, she was able to maintain her privacy without leaving her employer completely unprepared for her absence.

If you do find yourself in the situation where the baby arrives without notice, you may have to make yourself available during your maternity leave to tie up loose ends and help with assignment of your work to others. Assuming you are willing to make such an arrangement, it is a good idea to reassure your employer, to ease any anxiety he or she may feel about the uncertainty of the situation.

Whom Are You Going to Tell First?

♦ IT'S YOUR NEWS

Guard your news carefully. Make sure that *you* are the first to tell your boss, and when you do, that you choose a moment that will maximize your boss's time and patience to listen.

Once you've planned the timing of your announcement, the next step is deciding whom you are going to tell first. The boss who must ultimately approve of your leave must be informed, but he or she does not have to be the first or the only person to whom you announce. For example, K.K. Gerhart-Fritz, assistant director of planning for a small midwestern city, decided to tell her secretary before she told her boss. K.K. works in an office with six other professionals and one secretary. Her boss is a woman who has never had children. The secretary they share, on the other hand, has a daughter K.K.'s age and was used to being the "surrogate mom" to people in the office. Since the secretary also knew the boss's schedule and gauged her moods, K.K. decided to tell the secretary first so that the secretary could advise her both on *how* and *when* to approach her boss. Confiding in her secretary gave K.K. the reassurance she needed.

CONTROL THE NEWS

K.K.'s strategy worked in large part because her secretary is a person who can keep a secret. If you do not tell your supervisor first, you need to be sure that he or she does not hear it from somebody else. Control the flow of information by telling only those you know you can trust.

The need for discretion is brought home by the following story: A woman who had planned on announcing her pregnancy after her first trimester nonetheless submitted insurance claim forms for her pregnancy test to her personnel department. Even though company policy was to keep such forms confidential, the personnel director evidently could not contain herself. Shortly thereafter, the pregnant woman found herself accosted in the halls by people who had heard the news, before she had let her boss know that she was pregnant. She then rushed to tell him, without being as prepared as she had hoped to be, just to be sure he did not find out from someone else.

If insurance forms always pass through your company's personnel or administrative office, the best way to avoid such a situation is to delay submitting your claims for reimbursement, if you can, until after you have made the announcement in your own way, at your own chosen time.

IDENTIFY THE RECEPTIVE BOSS

In many cases you will have a choice of supervisors to whom you can announce; choosing is particularly important if your employer does not have a written or standard maternity leave policy. Since the announcement sets the stage for asking for what you want, and for persuading your employer that your plans do not spell catastrophe for the company, you should identify the people with appropriate authority who are most likely to be receptive to these ideas.

Don't assume that your female supervisors are naturally more sympathetic than your male supervisors. Studies have shown that, rather than gender, one of the key variables in determining a sympathetic supervisor is whether he or she has been through a similar experience: i.e., has been pregnant—or is married and has a wife who is a working mother. A 1990 survey done for *Working Mother* magazine found that supervisors whose spouses are employed "are twice as likely to be very accommodating of employees' family needs compared to supervisors in single-income marriages."

When Carol announced to the partners in the firm, it was the female (but single) partner who immediately questioned her commitment to returning to work, not the male partner who was also father of three.

When Sheila Nielsen sat down with her supervisor at the U.S. Attorney's office to discuss how much leave she wanted, she told him that she wanted to come back to work on a reduced-hours basis, indefinitely. The supervisor had a wife who worked part-time, so he understood the issues. His response to Sheila's request: "I don't see any reason why you can't do that; that sounds fine."

However, when Sheila returned from her leave six months later, her old supervisor had been replaced with one who was single and childless. His greeting to her on her first day back was: "So, when are you going to start working full-time?" He was unwilling to honor her deal with the previous supervisor, and Sheila ultimately left the U.S. Attorney's office.

Unfortunately, however, living through the same experience does not guarantee that a supervisor will be supportive. In addition, some people say one thing ("Families are great—I'm so happy for you") and feel another ("She can try to have it all— but I know it's impossible because my wife gave up trying"). You need to understand as well as possible what is important to your supervisors, how they really feel about working women and working mothers, and how easily they can empathize with someone else's dilemmas.

Setting the Stage

Once you've decided whom you are going to tell, you need to set the stage for the announcement. Doing so can be simply a matter of making an appointment to talk with the supervisor you have chosen, and then checking on his or her mood that day. These steps, again, give you more control over the situation—and therefore the outcome.

Anne did not take these steps when she announced her second pregnancy, with unfortunate consequences. She decided to announce the pregnancy to the partner in her office who seemed the most family-oriented. He had young children and was always talking about them. In addition, this partner had worked closely with Carol throughout her pregnancy and her return to work part-time. Anne figured he made the perfect candidate, because he had both the commitment to family and the experience with pregnant associates.

One morning shortly after her first trimester, Anne walked into this partner's office and closed the door. She told him that she had exciting news—she was pregnant. An awkward silence followed. Anne kept waiting to hear some form of congratulation. But instead, the partner asked her tersely: "What are your plans?" She was so completely taken aback that she muttered something about a few months' maternity leave and then returning part-time. The partner responded that he was "not sure the firm could accommodate the request." Anne fled from his office and burst into tears.

In retrospect, Anne understands that the partner's reaction had more to do with his mood that day than anything else. Knowing the partner to be moody, Anne should have checked with his secretary about his frame of mind and made certain his schedule could accommodate a fairly leisurely discussion of this important and sensitive issue. While this same partner ultimately supported the firm's decision to allow a four-month leave (with one month's pay) and a reduced-hours schedule upon her return, the fact that things started so badly tainted Anne's feelings about the firm and changed her relationship with him.

The Range of Reactions

Having decided on a time and a person, there remains only one thing to do: announce! Then wait for the response. From our conversations with pregnant professionals, most often your announcement will be greeted with a mixture of congratulations and concern. Here is the range of responses that you may encounter:

"That's wonderful! Here are our policies on maternity leave and alternative work schedules, in case you decide that those options are appropriate for you."

Rejoice!

"That's great! What are you going to do?"

Here, you may have to resist the urge toward sarcasm, as in "we've decided to have the baby . . ." and make a general statement that you plan to return to work promptly after your maternity leave. Although roughly 85 percent of mothers return to work after their maternity leaves,[3] many managers still expect women to quit work once they have children.[4] You should dispel these doubts by firmly and clearly communicating your intention to return.

"My boss's boss at the time that I got pregnant was a man who was very pessimistic about my return to work," says Paula Scott,* a market research manager at a large food and beverage

---
*Not her real name.

company. "He was so certain that I would not return that he issued an organizational chart that was sent to fifty people several weeks before I was going on maternity leave, and he didn't even put me on the chart. It was as if I had stopped working for the company. I went and talked to him about it, and while he told me I was being overly sensitive, he did revise the chart."

Similarly, when Carol told one of the partners about her pregnancy, the partner said, "What are you going to do? Will you come back to work?" Carol was taken aback. What had she done, she wondered, that would make this partner think that Carol would—or could—completely abandon her career? The answer was that she had gotten pregnant. Some people think that women cannot combine career and family, so that wanting one means you do not truly want the other.

Hold the Details

Even if you have already decided what you want in terms of maternity leave and a work schedule on return (subjects we take up in great detail in the next chapter), you should delay discussing them. Unless your employer pushes you for details, you are better off waiting until the news sinks in. Waiting to discuss the details may avoid the pressure to take positions that you may or may not really believe.

"If [my supervisor] had asked me about my plans [in the initial conversation], I was prepared to say that I was definitely planning to come back to work full-time," says Paula Scott. "Actually, even though I had every intention of going back to work, I knew in my heart that what I really wanted to do was come back part-time. But people had advised me to say that I wanted to return full-time so that I would keep my full benefits and so that they would not give my job to somebody else. I was worried, based on others' experience, that if I told them that I was thinking of coming back part-time, they would slate me for a job that I may or may not want."

Luckily for Paula, her supervisor did not press her into a position and was willing to let her decide for herself what she wanted. He even told her that he understood that many women don't know what they really want until after they have had their child. The more unsure you feel about what you want, the less you should commit to when you first announce. However, do not be surprised if you have to initiate the follow-up conversation, and don't wait until the eleventh hour to do so. Otherwise you risk possible resentment and the confusion that comes with last-minute planning.

"Congratulations! How do you feel? Any morning sickness? I remember when my wife was pregnant with Billy . . ."

This response is probably a natural expression of concern for your well-being. It may also be your introduction to the intense level of interest in your body shape and bodily functions that pregnancy seems to elicit in colleagues (and even strangers). As your stomach expands, your body will become public property; hands will extend to feel your stomach without anyone asking if that's all right with you. This can get to be too much for even the most good-natured among us, although there is little you can do. We did hear of one woman who, after a man she didn't know rubbed her belly, asked him, "And what private part of *yours* can *I* touch?" He got the message loud and clear!

Others will try to take care of you. Anyone who has ever been pregnant or married to someone who is pregnant thinks that he or she knows exactly what you are going through — and will tell you about it. Even those who have not been through the experience will be curious about it and will not be shy to ask how you are feeling.

Your Body Public

"My pregnancy was the 'project' for city hall," K.K. Gerhart-Fritz remembers. "Everyone inquired how I was feeling and remarked on how my stomach was growing. They wanted to make sure I was going to my exercise classes and eating well. It was as if I suddenly had a hundred mother hens inspecting everything about me."

In extreme cases, some may try to "protect" you. Like the opposing attorney who insisted that Carol sit down before the judge was seated in a pretrial conference, they may treat you as if you are suddenly unable to do things for yourself. On the other hand, Carol also remembers a lawyer and his client who smoked cigars throughout a two-hour meeting in a windowless conference room, even though she was pregnant. While these two situations may seem worlds apart, they both forced Carol and everyone else in the room to focus on her pregnancy, distracting attention from the actual work at hand.

When you receive attention to your physical state, there are several possible subtexts to the story that you should consider. If you are lucky, a high level of care and concern indicates that your boss, while maintaining complete confidence in you, also holds motherhood in awe. This kind of boss should be receptive to helping you through work/family conflicts that arise.

Unfortunately, the more likely subtext to repeated questions about your well-being is that your boss thinks either that you will be incapable of maintaining your career while raising children, or that you should be home tending the children, or both. These bosses tend to make no effort to accommodate your new needs as a mother, because at heart they believe that mothers (or at least good mothers) do not belong in the workplace. If that describes your situation, then you have a problem to which, frankly, we have no solution, except to position yourself so that this person is not the only one who's in charge of your career progression.

"Oh! what are we going to do without you?"

Carol's announcement received a more drastic version of this response from one partner: "That's terrible!" he exclaimed. "I mean, it's wonderful for you, but it's terrible for the firm!" This kind of a response is uncomfortably, and perhaps intentionally, ambiguous. On the one hand, your employer may be complimenting your indispensability to the organization; on the other hand, he may be blaming you for the (perceived) burden you will be placing on the company. The best reaction is to assure your employer that you are committed to the job, are planning to return to work, and will make all the arrangements necessary to cover the gap while you are on maternity leave.

Hoping for Honesty

Whatever your boss actually says, be glad if your employer reacts honestly about how he or she feels. We heard many times that employers feel constrained to keep their responses to a minimum for fear of saying something that could create legal liability. This hesitation is compounded by ignorance about what the legal boundaries really are. If you sense this kind of anxiety, you can help ease it by reassuring your boss that while you are excited about the baby, you are also committed to your job, and will have your job fully in mind as you consider what kind of maternity leave to take.

Consider Your Colleagues and Clients

Besides your boss's reaction, you will have to consider the responses of your colleagues. While telling your colleagues will seem less traumatic than telling your supervisor, they may have different, similarly troubling, concerns. Some people may immediately be susceptible to the "having it all" myth and begin resenting you before you even have it all. Some people will worry about having to carry your work while you are "infirm" or away on leave. Others may feel jealous of your pregnancy because they too are trying to get pregnant. Still others may see you as vulnerable in the work hierarchy and begin jockeying for advantage. Of course, some colleagues may actually be happy for you and be willing to be supportive and helpful.

If you begin to sense that negative reactions are developing, reassure your colleagues that your pregnancy and motherhood will not affect them significantly or permanently. Again, it's important to be careful about whom you complain to; you want to give the impression that you can carry your weight (no pun intended) and are committed to keeping your job. If you sense that a colleague may become jealous, you may want to acknowledge her feelings by taking the time to tell her personally about your pregnancy (instead of relying on the grapevine). You will then need to decide whether to make her feel a part of your experience or keep your distance while being cordial.

Your "external bosses"—clients, customers, patients, etc.— may be among the people most likely to start looking at you differently when they know you are pregnant, questioning your ability to perform. We found that, while our clients were often the most obvious in their feelings, they were also the most easily appeased. All we had to do was continue to perform at the same level, and they soon treated the pregnancy as a nonissue.

The Last Stage

WINDING DOWN

As your due date looms closer, you should begin to wind down. Your body may signal that it's time: Whatever physical stamina and even exhilaration you had been feeling usually starts to give way to constant exhaustion. Even if you feel fine up until the day you deliver, you should stop taking new assignments in the last month before your due date.

Make plans (with your supervisor as well as your colleagues) about how your existing work will be covered while you are away. If you know that your leave will be as short as a month or six weeks, this exercise is similar to planning for a vacation. If, however, you are planning a longer leave, you will need to make detailed provisions.

Sometimes a company will bring in a temporary replacement from the outside while an employee is on parental leave. More often, matters or projects are transferred to various people within the organization. In any event, you will want to identify them and bring them up to speed on their assignments. Introduce them to the other people involved in the matter, whether they be outside clients or consultants or internal personnel involved in other aspects of the project. One successful approach can be to let your substitute begin working with you as backup before you leave, if your firm or company can afford the doubling up of staff.

Reassure your clients or customers or patients that their work will continue to be done, and that your colleagues are prepared to handle it. We recommend introducing the client or customer or patient, at least on the telephone, to those who will be covering for you. Some clients may need extra attention, either because they are especially dependent on you or especially important to you. In these cases (which you must try to keep to a minimum) you might give them your home phone number.

SETTING THE LIMITS

Set clear boundaries before you leave about when your employer or colleagues can call you at home—and stick to them. They can always be relaxed as you become more comfortable with your

---

♦ IT'S YOUR TIME

Maternity leave is your time with the baby. Don't promise to do more work than you can deliver. Delivering the baby is delivering enough.

---

new role. Silence on the matter is likely to be read as an invitation to call, because managers and others who have never been on maternity leave tend to mistake your leave for vacation time. After all, you're not working, right?

Sharon Cohen, a vice president of a large sportswear manufacturing company, admits that she "always thought of her employees' maternity leaves as vacations" until she herself went on leave. Now she knows better.

In the last few weeks at the office it is tempting to be generous—"If you have any questions, just call me at home." If you are having your first child, you may be particularly susceptible to this temptation because you yourself may not fully appreciate the amount of work involved in caring for an infant, and the fatigue that is sure to accompany it.

Martha Stiven learned this the hard way. She delivered her first child at the same time that the housing rehabilitation program she had started was getting off the ground. "I had hired a building inspector to work on the program. I told him he could call me at home during my leave, because my whole premise was that this baby is not going to slow me down," Martha explains. "But when the inspector called me at home constantly, he drove me nuts, and I had to put an end to the calls."

By the time Martha had her second child four years later, she knew that tending a newborn doesn't allow time for much of anything else. Breast-feeding alone is a full-time job. Then there are the diapers, the laundry, the cooking; in short, the stuff of everyday life. All of which you are doing on a night's sleep that consists of two hours or so at a stretch, with a twenty- to thirty-minute interruption in between for feeding (if you're lucky and the baby doesn't want to cry or play after being fed).

SEPARATION ANXIETY

In the final weeks before your leave you may also experience some separation anxiety. You will be stepping into a new and unknown world, and it is natural to feel some uncertainty and nervousness; your job may even seem more enticing to you because you know you will be away from it. One way to ease these feelings is to invite work into your home. Resist the temptation.

Better to take a firm position and then relax it if (by some miracle) your baby sleeps through the night and doesn't cry during the day. Women we know who have taken leaves on the long side (three months or more) told their office that they would take calls after a certain point—after the first month, for example. This approach protects the time you need to adjust to being a mother while calming the anxieties of those who cannot imagine the office without you. It shows that you are willing to be flexible in responding to your job, but that you are also firm about your own needs as a new mother. Another way to gain flexibility is to set up a system so that you can work from home. We do not advise *promising* anyone that you will produce anything specific during your leave. Rather, if you have the systems you need to work from home (computer or fax or modem, or some combination thereof), then you can decide to do so once you are home. Having these systems also makes it easier to return to work gradually at the end of your leave.

Try as we might to wrap things up before the baby comes, some of us end up back in the office to do just that, especially if the baby comes early. Susan Eilertsen's second child was born three weeks early, just before she could finish a major public relations campaign for an important client. Susan was back in the office the day after she delivered (with her mother and the baby in tow). Even though Susan couldn't sit down and was still bleeding heavily, she managed to finish the campaign and garner a favorable story in the *New York Times* for her client. While her partners acknowledged and appreciated this herculean effort, there is never really any way to compensate for the emotional disruption this kind of situation causes. You simply live with it and move on.

Even if you don't deliver early, there are circumstances

where you cannot avoid staying involved at work, as when you have just started a job, or when you are the head of a department and need to be visible in certain situations. When Carol Barrett had her second child, she had recently started as director of planning for the City of Annapolis, Maryland, so she was both new and the chief. She decided to attend staff meetings periodically. If you find yourself in this situation, pick certain key meetings—staff meetings or public hearings or the like—to attend, and make very clear to your colleagues and supervisors that you will attend these meetings and no more (barring true emergencies).

Your maternity leave is a very special time. As we discuss in greater detail in Chapter 4, it is an intense period—as you adjust to being a mother and enjoy the miracle of your newborn. No matter what you think you can handle before you go on leave, chances are you will regret any significant compromise of your time at home. So, if you feel pressure to take on commitments to work during your leave, resist it. Give yourself the time you deserve. By doing so, you are actually setting a good precedent for when you return to work.

3

MATERNITY LEAVE AND OTHER BENEFITS

In Chapter 2 we described what it's like to be pregnant and working. In this chapter we focus on how to think about maternity leave and other benefits so that you can structure a leave that is acceptable to your employer and satisfying to you. Your choice regarding maternity leave is, to most employers, a signal of your commitment to work. At the same time, your maternity leave is *your* time in a unique, special way—it's when your body is recovering from dramatic changes and when your entire being first learns what it's like to be a mother. The art of structuring a leave is finding the right combination of competing needs and expectations—taking into account your legal rights.

Your Legal Rights as a Pregnant Worker

FEDERAL LAW

There are two federal laws directly addressing issues of pregnancy and maternity: the recently enacted (and hard fought) Family and Medical Leave Act and the Pregnancy Discrimination Act of 1978. The Family and Medical Leave Act establishes a basic "safety net" for staff in companies of fifty or more employees working within a seventy-five mile radius, by guaranteeing that they can return to the same or equivalent job if they take up to twelve weeks off in any one year, either: for the birth or adoption of a child; or to care for a child or other family member.

♦ FEDERAL PROTECTION
_____

The Family and Medical Leave Act requires employers with more than fifty employees to provide women and men with twelve weeks' unpaid leave on the birth or adoption of a child.

The Pregnancy Discrimination Act requires employers with more than fifteen employees to treat pregnant workers the same as disabled ones: If they provide benefits such as paid leave or job security to employees with broken legs or heart attacks, they must provide similar benefits to pregnant women.

Male as well as female employees are entitled to such leave. Your employer must maintain your health insurance coverage on the same terms during the leave. You cannot lose seniority or other employment benefits as a result of taking the leave, but the employer is not required to allow your benefits to accrue further during the leave.

Under the new law, you need to give your employer thirty days' notice that you intend to take such a leave, if reasonably possible. If you are pregnant, therefore, you may have to decide well in advance the starting date of your leave. If you have a premature delivery, however, you cannot be held to this starting date. Similarly, if you are adopting a baby, you may not get much notice of the arrival, and Congress discussed this situation as an example of an exception to the notice requirement.

Notwithstanding the struggle it took to get this legislation passed (Congress passed versions of it twice, in 1990 and 1991, only to have it vetoed twice by President Bush), it has significant limitations. First, it guarantees unpaid, not paid, leave, and many people cannot afford to go without income for twelve weeks. Second, because it applies only to larger employers, the Family and Medical Leave Act does not protect about half of the workers in the United States.

There is also an important exception in the act: If you are among the highest-paid ten percent of employees within seventy-five miles of your workplace, your employer may deny you the same job upon your return if doing so would cause "substantial and grievous economic injury" to the business. (This is one of the many compromises Congress made in response to vocal business hostility to the bill, simply in order to get something passed.)

Be aware that your employer may require you to substitute categories of paid leave for part of the twelve-week unpaid period. In other words, your employer can decide not to allow you to use paid vacation and sick time on top of the unpaid leave available under the Family and Medical Leave Act. You may be limited to twelve weeks of total time off, even if you have accrued time that you would like to tack on to the guaranteed leave.

The Family and Medical Leave Act went into effect August 5, 1993, for nonunion workers (workers under a collective bargaining agreement have to wait until either the final date of the agreement or February 5, 1994, whichever is earlier). At this writing, the act has just gone into effect, so we cannot predict how employers will react to its requirements, or how the conflicts and murky interpretations inherent in any major federal law will be resolved.

The Pregnancy Discrimination Act, compared with the Family and Medical Leave Act, affects a far greater number of workers, because it applies to all private employers with fifteen or more employees, but it does not provide the same guarantees. The Pregnancy Discrimination Act prohibits the firing of a woman simply because she is pregnant, and requires employers to treat pregnancy as they would a temporary physical disability.

Unlike the Family and Medical Leave Act, the Pregnancy Discrimination Act does *not* require employers to guarantee a pregnant worker's position while she is out on pre- or postpregnancy leave, nor does it require them to provide such leave or even to provide pregnancy disability insurance. Rather, the Pregnancy Discrimination Act requires employers to guarantee job security to pregnant women *if* and *to the same extent* that they guarantee job security to people returning from other disability leaves. Similarly, the act requires employers to provide disability insurance for pregnancy *if* and *to the same extent* that they provide disability insurance for other conditions, such as heart attacks or broken legs. Usually, this means that a pregnant woman can get a leave for the period that a doctor will say she was "disabled"— or unable to work—due to the delivery of her child, usually four to six weeks after a vaginal delivery and six to eight weeks after delivery by cesarean section. In the jargon of the law, any portion of your leave that is medically necessary (for your body) is called disability leave; any leave beyond that is sometimes referred to separately as maternity leave or parental leave.

In addition to these basic provisions, courts interpreting the Pregnancy Discrimination Act have clarified various issues concerning pregnant workers' rights. For example, employers cannot discriminate against pregnant women in determining any benefits they offer their employees in addition to disability insurance, such as seniority, vacation time, and sick leave.

An employer cannot force an employee to take a leave of absence or eliminate her position because she is pregnant, even if the employer argues that the job endangers the health and safety of the fetus. The employer must allow the pregnant woman to continue to work. The question of whether an employer can reassign a pregnant worker is more complicated. In some cases courts have allowed employers to reassign a pregnant worker to a less strenuous job, especially if the worker's doctor agrees with the reassignment. However, a reassignment that is clearly a demotion is less likely to be upheld, unless there are strong medical or business reasons for the reassignment.

When you are interviewing for jobs, employers are prohibited from asking questions regarding your childbearing plans or how many children you have, unless they ask these questions of both male and female applicants.

STATE LAW

Some states have tried to fill in gaps in pregnant workers' rights. Twenty-three states have passed some form of protection for pregnant workers and working parents, and eight more states are considering legislation at the time of this writing. Some states' laws apply broadly and provide for generous protection; others are narrow and limited. For example, California's statute requires most employers to provide up to four months' unpaid pregnancy leave and to make reasonable efforts to ensure the same or equivalent job upon return. The statute was challenged by a California bank that had a pregnancy disability policy but reserved the right to terminate a woman on pregnancy leave if her position was eliminated. The case went all the way up to the United States Supreme Court, which ruled that California's law was consistent with the intent of the Pregnancy Discrimination Act because the state law "allows women, as well as men, to have families without losing their jobs."[1]

The Family and Medical Leave Act does not override stronger state laws; in each state, an employer is required to comply with whichever law (the federal Act or the applicable state law) provides more protection to the employee. A state-by-state summary of the laws governing parental leave is included in Appendix A.

THE LAW IS NOT THE LIMIT, SO LOOK BEYOND

Because of the Pregnancy Discrimination Act, most employers treat pregnancy the way they treat other medical disabilities. Unfortunately, this approach fails to consider the unique issues that arise from having an infant, even after you have recovered from the physical aspects of delivery. What if you have physically recovered, and therefore can return to work, but are not emotionally ready to do so? Most women have recovered from the physical trauma of delivery after six weeks, but it can take a lot longer to feel ready to go back to work. What if you have physically recovered, but your baby wakes up two or three (or more) times during the night? During the day you will be a walking zombie in no condition to confront work with your typical vigor. Your baby may have colic until she is three months old, meaning that, before then, you are conditioned to human interaction that consists mainly of howling, weeping, and whining (yours and the baby's). These forms of communication are rarely appropriate for business relations—another potential reason to delay a return to work. What if postpartum depression makes you feel unprepared to return to work?

Also remember that the Family and Medical Leave Act only guarantees job-protected leave if you work for a large company (over fifty employees) and that state laws that cover more employees are easy to skirt ("the company restructured during your leave") and are not vigorously enforced.[2] Therefore, as you think about your leave, don't limit yourself to the minimum to which you are entitled under the law. Think instead about what you would ideally want, and then figure out how far you can push your employer toward your ideal. Besides the length of your leave, think about whether and how you will maintain contact with work during your leave, as well as how to structure your return to work.

Plan to Negotiate

In developing your negotiating position, know what your rights are. If your employer's policies do not treat pregnancy as a disability, the policies probably do not conform to the Pregnancy Discrimination Act and applicable state law, and you should consider contacting the federal Equal Employment Opportunity Commission, or your state's equivalent, or an attorney, to explain what your rights are and how you might enforce them. There are a few women's legal advocacy groups that may be able to help you locate the appropriate agency or lawyer. These are listed in Appendix B.

You must also investigate what your employer's policies are and find out how people have been treated in the past. Look for written policies in employment manuals, if there are any. It also helps to know what the standard practice is in your profession or industry, as well as what is recommended by various sources such as professional organizations and child development experts. As you gather this information, keep talking to other working mothers about their experiences. Your decision will be a synthesis

---

♦ MATERNITY BENEFITS IN SMALL COMPANIES

A 1990 Bureau of Labor survey of companies with less than one hundred employees showed that only 50 percent of those employees (of 41 million surveyed) were covered by short-term disability coverage. Similarly, only 19 percent of all employees, and 29 percent of professional and administrative employees, received maternity leave, which was *unpaid*. On the other hand, small employers are more likely than large employers to offer flexibility to women when they return to work after childbirth.[3]

of this information with an internal evaluation of your own needs and constraints.

Because employers' policies on pregnancy rights and parental leave are as varied as employers themselves, it would be impossible for us to review each one. Many employers do provide programs that go beyond the minimum required by law; many do not. We will explain the issues you should consider when you are reviewing your employer's policies, as well as the arguments you can use for support if you need to negotiate your own arrangement in the absence of a written policy.

Thinking About the Leave You Need

When you present your leave proposal, you are taking the position (either overtly or implicitly) that you plan on returning to your job. For most women with careers, it is difficult to imagine not returning to work, and letting your employer know that may not seem like a radical proposition.

Once you have spent some time with your newborn baby, however, the decision may seem more complex. "Not working" is no longer just the *absence* of work but an alternative filled with its own challenges, joys, and frustrations. Of course, you will not engage in that part of the decision making until you are actually on leave; we have therefore chosen to discuss what it feels like to decide to go back to work in Chapter 4.

Ironically, however, the single most important factor in deciding what kind of maternity leave to ask for is predicting what you are going to want once you have the baby. Trying to figure out what your feelings will be after the baby is born may be harder than you think. If you have trouble imagining how much you will miss work or how much you will enjoy being at home, you are not alone. Some women, from the beginning, have a very clear sense of what they want; many others do not.

Nonetheless, you do have to make arrangements with your employer regarding your maternity leave before you go. So for now, the issues are the length of your leave and the transition back to work.

HOW LONG A LEAVE?

The Baby Factor

One of the big unknowns in this planning process is the kind of baby you have. Will the baby be healthy? Will he cry or gurgle all day? Will she sleep at night? Dr. T. Berry Brazelton has found that one of the most important variables in determining a comfortable length of leave for new mothers is how their infants behave.

Obviously, you won't know the answers to any of these questions until after the baby is born. (Unfortunately, the only predictable part of this whole experience is the sleep deprivation that you — and hopefully your husband — will suffer.) As a result, you may go through what Sheila Nielsen, a prosecutor at the U.S. Attorney's office, experienced: getting her leave extended because her baby had colic. Sheila originally asked to take three months off (unpaid) because that seemed to be what everyone else was doing, and because anything longer seemed to her like an interminable absence from work. But she had a difficult baby, and she ended up taking six months off.

"I thought I was going to be Supermom," she says. "I was not prepared for the feelings I would have about being a mom . . . I was so stupid about it. In the beginning, I felt pretty incompetent as a mother. I felt that I could handle litigation no sweat, but I couldn't deal with this squalling baby. That's why I decided to take another three months off. I decided I was going to figure out how to be a mom. I was not going to run away from this. It would have been so easy to run back to my work, which felt so fulfilling."

Carol's first baby also had colic for the first three and a half months; if she had not had six months off, she would have returned to work physically exhausted and unsure of herself as a mother. On the other hand, we also know women who cut their maternity leaves short because they had difficult babies and reacted by feeling frustrated and resentful.

Dr. Brazelton, in *Working and Caring*, gives an example of just the opposite situation: a woman whose baby was so cherubic that the woman got tremendous satisfaction from being home. In fact, she could not get herself to go back to work when her leave was over, and ended up reentering gradually. Anne too had a very calm first child who seemed happy no matter who took care of her. This made it easier, rather than harder, for Anne to go back to work when her short maternity leave was over.

Living with this uncertainty is no fun, we realize. But there is an equally important part of the future that you *can* think about before the baby is born: you. Try to imagine how you will react to the different scenarios described above. If your baby takes a lot of patience and energy to care for, will you want to spend more time at home (as Sheila did) or less? If your baby is easy to take care of from the start, will you have a harder time going back to work (as Dr. Brazelton's patient did) or easier?

We've heard many women say that they never dreamed they would feel the way they did about having children before they became parents. But, often, our feelings about ourselves and our roles as mothers before we actually have the baby aren't *contradicted* once we give birth; rather, they are much more intense than we imagined. Therefore, the exercise of imagining yourself a mother is not futile, and may at least give you some sense of control and comfort in a planning process that often feels completely outside your control.

What Else to Consider

Besides the arrival of your baby, think about the other changes maternity leave represents. We describe these in detail in the next chapter. For example, the tempo of your life changes dramatically when you go from being in the office every day to being at home with your baby every day. You may be used to a day that includes answering eleven phone calls, attending two meetings, and writing three reports; when you are at home with an infant you will feel you have accomplished quite a lot if you have a shower *and* a sit-down meal in the same day.

You also have to consider how you'll feel being away from work for an extended period. Many women we talked with said that the one thing they were most sure about before they delivered was that they wanted to go back to work and could not see themselves away from work for an extended period of time.

Given this uncertainty, try to build into your leave as much flexibility as possible. Do *not* ask for a short leave thinking that you can always extend it; err on the other side. It is generally easier for the employer, psychologically as well as practically, to welcome you back sooner rather than to have to do without you for longer than planned. Also, you are more likely to create an impression of eagerness to be on the job rather than reluctance to return. Another way to build in flexibility is to return to work gradually. You will probably feel more comfortable taking a shorter maternity leave if you know you can return gradually. In addition, this kind of arrangement reduces the anxiety you may feel about separating from your baby.

Consider Your Employer's Attitudes

Your employer's attitudes play a role in your decision even if you are told you can do whatever you like. As we have suggested, your employer will look at the way you handle your pregnancy and maternity leave as an indication of how you feel about your work.

According to Felice Schwartz, whose 1989 article about women in business ignited the "mommy track" debate, many professional women are afraid to take a long maternity leave for fear that it will be taken as proof of their diminished commitment to work. She cites a 1989 study of women attorneys in which a full "43 percent said that taking advantage of a normal maternity leave would hurt their careers."[4]

Carol Barrett, the city planner whose story started Chapter 1, agrees. "In my experience and that of other women I know, the people that take the maximum amount of maternity leave that their employer's policies allow find themselves discriminated against when they come back to the job," she says. "I really think so, particularly when it's more than three months. The perception of them as uncommitted gets cast in stone. Once you've made that level of commitment to some activity outside the office, even if you are still desperately committed to the job, the *perception* is that you're not. I think that women understand that this is not necessarily the case, but I'm not hopeful that we can educate a lot of men to that point of view."

Feed the Perceptions, Starve Yourself?

Your employer's perceptions are critical in deciding on how much time to take off. However, taking an extremely short leave (less than six weeks) is not, we believe, the solution to this perception problem and may ultimately fuel it. Here's why:

First, if these perceptions exist, they are not going to disappear simply because you return to work right after delivery. A sad story about a sales representative illustrates this point. She arranged to have a phone installed in her hospital room (we don't think it was the *delivery* room) so that customers could call her there. She then returned to work immediately, taking no maternity leave. Her concern was that taking time for herself and her baby would reflect a diminished commitment to her career. Despite these superhuman efforts, a few weeks later (after she had closed "the biggest deal of her career"), her boss was disappointed. During the time just before and after her daughter's birth, he claimed, her performance had "suffered."[5] That particular supervisor was so attached to his view that dedication to career is incompatible with motherhood that he was willing to ignore contrary facts. He is not unique.

"It's just not worth it to cheat yourself of maternity leave just to appease the feelings of these men," says Mary Ellen Schoonmaker, a journalist and mother of three. "Men reach positions of authority all the time, and they just delegate their work. Why can't women do the same thing?"

Indeed, pretending that becoming a parent is not the most monumental transformation of your life is pandering to people who think that women who have children should not have careers. By making all the accommodations yourself, you allow the workplace to get away without making any. You are establishing a dangerous precedent, so that whenever work/family conflicts occur, you boss will expect you to absorb and resolve all the conflict yourself. Ultimately, the destructive buildup of frustration and resentment will not only make you unhappy, but may backfire on your career as well.

If you return before your body is ready, chances are you will be physically exhausted and unable to perform in the same way you had before, further fueling any negative stereotypes your employer may harbor about working mothers. Assuming you take at least four weeks off to recover from the physical trauma of delivery (something that is very real even though the pregnancy books often downplay it), your stamina after the first month will depend on how well your baby sleeps and how well you function on six hours of interrupted sleep a night. If this scenario conjures up memories of all-nighters in college, remember that we are not talking about one night every six months, but night after night of little sleep with frequent interruptions. (And you probably don't feel like an eighteen-year-old anymore, either.)

In interviews conducted by Catalyst, a research organization, executive-level mothers who felt pressured to return to work sooner than they were physically or emotionally ready "felt overextended and unable to manage either work or family responsibilities."[6] On the other hand, if you give yourself the time you need to recover from the delivery, become accustomed to your new sleep schedule, and adjust to being a mother, you will have done what you can to return to work with the same concentration and attention that you gave to it before your maternity leave.

THE TRANSITION BACK

The transition back to work is almost as important as the length of leave. Both of us went from being on maternity leave one day to being back at work on our regular schedule the next. While many women make this leap in a single bound, some insist on a more gradual reentry (whether they are going back full-time or part-time). "If somebody came back after having been out six weeks or whatever with a heart condition, you wouldn't expect them to suddenly jump back into the work," argues Mary Ellen Schoonmaker. "You'd tell them to take it easy and ease back into it. If pregnancy is going to be treated as a disability, it should come with the same expectations." Fran Rodgers, the president of Work/Family Directions, a firm that consults with companies on work and family issues, has led focus groups at major corporations on maternity leave benefits. Based on this work, Ms. Rodgers says that "most women want a three- to six-month leave, plus the option of a gradual or part-time return."[7]

City planner Janet Grau was perfectly comfortable knowing that she was going back to work full-time and that her maternity leave was going to be eight weeks. But she did not feel comfortable about leaving her two-month-old son with a baby-sitter all day long. So she devised this transition schedule: half days, five days a week, for two weeks, then half days, two days a week, for four weeks. During that six-week period, her son, Peter, went from being two months old to being almost four months old, and

Janet went from being anxious to having great confidence in the baby-sitter and being comfortable leaving Peter.

Sharon Cohen, a vice president at a major sportswear manufacturing company, went back to work full-time after only a four-week maternity leave. Given her short leave, she decided to return gradually, and worked from 11 A.M. to 3 P.M. for five weeks.

For some, a gradual transition factors into the very decision to return to work. Paula Scott, a market research manager at a large food and beverage company, took a four-and-one-half-month maternity leave. While on leave she asked to return on a part-time schedule. Although she asked for three days a week, her supervisor strongly recommended that she work four days.

"I did not flatly reject his proposal, but I did tell him that I was uncomfortable with it and was not ready to come back four days at that time," she says. "So he came up with the scenario that I come back three days for two months, and then I would increase to four days. This was a reasonable compromise, so I agreed. I prepared myself mentally for going back to work during the weeks before, when the baby-sitter was coming two days a week. It helped a lot that I was only going three days a week." A gradual transition made it possible for Paula to accept a part-time schedule different from her original plan.

Negotiating Your Leave

REVIEW EXISTING POLICY

You should always review your employer's policy before announcing your pregnancy, so that you know what your employer is willing to do for its pregnant workers. If the policy is written, you will probably find it in a manual with other personnel policies, so you don't have to worry about giving away the news by asking.

If the policy is more or less in keeping with your desires, do not push it too far. If you do, your employer may then feel that you should be eternally grateful to him for that extra week, or your colleagues may feel that you got (but didn't deserve) special treatment. Consider these feelings when deciding what to ask for, because they will affect the reception you receive when you return to work. (These attitudes may be unavoidable in work-places without any policies, making it your task to minimize their effects.)

WHEN THERE IS NO FORMAL POLICY

If your employer does not have a formal policy, but rather treats the issues of pregnancy and parental leave on an ad hoc basis, the employer probably has not woken up to the realities of today's and tomorrow's labor pool. It may be your burden to educate your employer about these realities and about the value of good maternity and other "family-friendly" policies. The best argument is that consistent, good pregnancy and parental leave policies make good business sense: they reduce turnover and absenteeism and improve morale and productivity.

A 1990 survey performed for *Working Mother* magazine found that women who work for bosses who are flexible in accommodating the pregnancy and family needs of their workers are seven times less likely to want to quit, and nearly four times more likely to say that they love their jobs, than women who work for inflexible bosses. Likewise, the majority of employers with formal parental leave plans reported to the U.S. Chamber of Commerce that the plans help in recruiting employees and retaining them.[8]

In case your boss responds better to numbers than to words, you can remind him or her of the cost of employee turnover. Permanently replacing a professional-level employee can cost (in direct and indirect costs) about 1.5 times the employee's annual salary; replacing a secretarial-level employee can cost about three quarters of that person's annual salary.[9]

Some employers worry about the precedent created by taking any action, saying, "If I do this for you, I will have to do it for everyone." This attitude can make it very difficult for you, because its effect is to pit you against your co-workers.

Ad hoc approaches result in uneven treatment that can poison the work environment by creating resentment and competition between working mothers and other employees, and even among working mothers in the same office. An employee who is considered "special" or "irreplaceable" may be able to negotiate "special" treatment; the others are left feeling less valued, and with fewer benefits.

♦ THE BENEFITS OF PROVIDING
BENEFITS

A 1987 survey of over two thousand working women in their third
trimester of pregnancy disclosed the following:

♦ Pregnant women in workplaces that are highly accommodating to
pregnant workers take fewer sick days than women who work for
employers who do not accommodate pregnancy.
♦ Pregnant women in more accommodating workplaces are less
likely to feel sick on the job and are therefore more productive.
♦ Women working in highly accommodating environments work
later into their pregnancies than women whose workplaces are not
accommodating.[10]

On the other side, special treatment sets the valued employee
apart from her co-workers (depriving her of the support of their
solidarity) and sends the message that the benefit could be taken
away if she does not continue to be so highly regarded. She
should, the message continues, feel indebted to the company for
having treated her well. It is just this type of treatment that makes
working mothers feel that they must make all the accommodations themselves.

Although employers may regard an ad hoc approach as a
way to preserve flexibility and reward star employees, it is not a
good business practice. Any time benefits are distributed un-
evenly and unpredictably, some employees can claim that there
has been unfairness and perhaps improper discrimination. A
written policy that lays out the criteria for various benefits, if it is
carefully followed, can help to protect an employer from baseless
claims of discrimination.

Small businesses were among the most vociferous opponents
of the family and medical leave legislation during the Reagan and
Bush administrations, and their lobbyists made sure that smaller
employers were excluded from the Family and Medical Leave
Act. Having worked in a small law firm, we know that there is a
lot less "slack" in a small business, so that when one person is
out for an extended period of time, it can pose real burdens on
the others. Our firm was also very concerned about the cost of

both paying us while we were on leave and losing our productivity during that period.

While these are real issues for small firms or companies, other realities outweigh them. For one, small businesses employ a disproportionate number of women—usually women in their childbearing years. They will feel the pressure to provide maternity benefits from the numbers alone. Adding to that pressure is the cost of recruitment and training. If it takes up to six months to train a new person (not including the time and expense of searching for and recruiting that person), then it makes economic sense to give a trained employee three months off for maternity leave. Doing so also increases loyalty and morale—and helps attract highly qualified people to your company.

CONSIDER THE WORK SETTING

For some women, maternity leave options may depend on their work setting. If you're working toward a Ph.D. and teaching, and you deliver in the middle of a semester, chances are you are going to have to go back to work—at least back to your classes—fairly quickly. Women doctors who start a family while still in residency training programs feel tremendous pressure to minimize their leaves.

Susan Mirkinson, an internist in private practice, points out that if a resident goes on maternity leave, there is usually no system of "replacements" worked out, so the patients are cared for by other residents, who are already tremendously overworked. "In residency, nobody cuts you any slack," echoes Patricia Morales Wright, an orthopedic surgeon. To minimize the likely resentment, most residents take very short leaves. However, once doctors are in private practice, they probably have greater flexibility in designing their leaves than women in corporate environments.

NEGOTIATING BENEFITS OTHER THAN LEAVE TIME

We believe strongly that women should be able to stay home after the birth of a child beyond the physical disability period if they want to, but we also know this may have little or no value if it is not accompanied by wages. Most employers who offer maternity leave offer *unpaid* leave. We understand that many employers (particularly small businesses) do not want to pay employees who are on leave. However, there are other ways to finance the expense of wage replacement during maternity leave. The Yale Bush Center Advisory Committee on Infant Care (among other respected organizations) has recommended a financing system where employees and employers would contribute toward a fund to cover both short-term disability and longer-term parental leave.

Even if your employer does not want to give you a lot of time, consider bringing other benefits to the bargaining table. Check whether your employer will pay for your medical insurance coverage while you're on leave. (The Family and Medical Leave Act requires larger employers to do so.) This benefit costs your employer less than it would cost you, if you had to buy an individual health insurance policy. At the very least, try to convince your employer to keep you on the company's plan — and share the cost.

Another benefit could be helping to pay for any equipment you use to work at home so that you can extend the time of your leave. You — and your employer — should not view this investment as only a three- or four-month proposition. More and more people are working from home for some part of the week. Even if you do so only when your child is sick or the baby-sitter doesn't show up or the child care provider is on vacation, these days add up. Office equipment at home can keep you productive when your routine is interrupted.

If you are charting new ground, it is helpful to know what comparable organizations are doing. Your employer will see that such benefits are not unheard of and are, indeed, accepted. You can also compare your situation with various kinds of employees and organizations that already have benefits to see whether the profiles are similar; this exercise helps you assess the likelihood of getting what you request and frame arguments in support of your position.

PUT IT IN WRITING

Whether you negotiate your leave, or you negotiate a variation on your employer's policies, put your agreement in writing. It doesn't have to be an imposing, formal document. Write an informal memo about what you're proposing regarding the length of leave and plans for your transition back to work, as well as how you think your work should be handled during your absence. Go over the memo with your boss and get his or her approval. This way you will both understand the terms of your agreement—and take it seriously.

Leave for Fathers

One final note: Don't forget paternity leave! While fewer companies offer paternity than maternity leave, this discrepancy—to the extent the maternity leave goes beyond the period of physical disability after delivery—is illegal. Courts have upheld fathers' rights to the same parental leave (but *not* disability leave) available to mothers.[11] Therefore, if a company offers women disability leave only, it does not have to offer men paternity leave. But the Family and Medical Leave Act requires larger employers to provide job-guaranteed unpaid leave to fathers as well as mothers.

Even when parental leave is offered, how often fathers use this benefit is another matter. Many men feel even greater pressure than women not to let parenthood (or anything else) appear to diminish their career commitment. Most men conclude that taking paternity leave would hurt their professional image. Most corporate cultures do little to assuage that fear.

"Very few fathers take the personal leave that is available to them when they have children," says Katharine B. Hazzard, work/family program coordinator for John Hancock Financial Services. "Rather, they save vacation time for the birth of a baby. I think that's a cultural thing. You've earned your vacation time, and nobody thinks twice about it when you take it."

But beyond the legalities, paternity leave benefits both you and your husband. Assuming you can afford it, urge your husband to take leave. It gives him time to adjust to being a parent. You and your husband will begin parenting on an equal footing. You can take the leaves simultaneously, which allows you to share this time as a new family; or, he could take his leave *after* your leave ends, which allows you to delay making arrangements for nonparental care, and lets him experience parenting on his own. This is the start of the making of a "working father," a process we explain in greater detail throughout the rest of the book.

Equally as important is the signal that taking paternity leave sends to others in the workplace. As we've said, many men fear taking a leave for the same reason women worry about it—they believe they will send a negative signal about their commitment. This attitude will change when men actually take paternity leave in significant numbers. In October 1991, one of the senior managers at Apple Computer took a paternity leave to stay home with his two older kids and a newborn. He told *M* magazine, "For people to see a director do this sort of thing dispels some of the myth about the fanaticism of commitment that you have to have. In a volatile organization like ours where there have been layoffs in the not-too-distant past, there's got to be concern about job security. This says taking a leave doesn't compromise your commitment to the organization."

The point is, if everybody's doing it, people will have a much harder time holding on to their assumptions about work and family. Each paternity leave taken brings us that much closer to the time when child-rearing will be a "parental" issue, rather than simply a "woman's" issue.

4

AT HOME WITH
THE BABY

Oh, the joy of it! Oh, the anguish of it! If you thought being pregnant was hard, just wait until you get home with the baby, where you quickly realize how simple and fleeting pregnancy is compared to motherhood. We spend so much energy concentrating on doing our jobs and having a wholesome pregnancy that most of us never truly imagine life with a newborn. The emotional immensity of bringing your child home can catch you by surprise. Carol's husband captured this sense of unpreparedness when, as they were leaving the hospital with their first child, he turned to Carol and asked: "Are they really going to let us just walk out with this baby? Aren't they going to give us a test? Don't you have to have some kind of a license to be a parent?"

Adjusting to motherhood is as challenging (if not more so) as anything you have ever done before—including that emergency surgery you recently performed, or that Supreme Court brief you just filed, or that advertising campaign you sold to a new client. Your maternity leave is your adjustment time—don't cheat yourself out of it. So many things are happening at once. First, there are the bodily changes: the postpartum pain, the weight that you thought would drop off when the baby dropped out—but didn't. There's your psyche: the roller-coaster hormone levels, the disorientation, the scariness mixed in with the thrill of holding your child. Then there is what is happening to your marriage: the arguments over who is going to get up in the middle of the night with the baby; the ease with which your husband's life appears to go back to normal, while yours seems changed forever.

Every mother goes through some (if not all) of these adjustments after the birth of a child. For working mothers, the time at home also raises other issues: how to be at home when you're used to being at work; how to deal with work while you're at home; how it will feel to go back to work; and how to do it if you are still breast-feeding, to name a few.

No amount of reading or research can prepare you for both the overwhelming sense of responsibility (with the physical drain that goes along with it) and the emotional power that comes with having a baby. We cannot pretend to tell you what being a mother will mean to you, but we can share with you maternity leave stories from other working mothers.

The Initial Adjustment

TIME? WHAT TIME?

The intense emotional and physical experience of delivery is over, and you are now at home with your newborn. Your life feels so different now that you have a hard time believing you ever held a responsible job in the real world. You used to be able to take a shower, have breakfast, get dressed, and get to work — all within the first two hours or so of the morning. Now, you wander around in your nightgown, changing diapers, feeding and burping the baby, and praying that he doesn't start crying for a reason that you can't imagine. Remember that infamous TV episode of "Murphy Brown" showing her at home with her newborn: The professional superstar just couldn't seem to find the time to take a shower? As comical as it appeared on TV, it's true.

"There would be days when I wouldn't have a shower," remembers K.K. Gerhart-Fritz. "I never had time to do anything," says Leslye Katz, chief financial officer at a division of The Dun & Bradstreet Corporation in New York. "Gary [her husband] would come home and there would be nothing remotely like dinner ready. If I was dressed it was an accomplishment." Echoes Janet Grau: "All I remember of maternity leave is being so busy that I hardly had any time to go to the bathroom. I had lots of projects and reading that I had wanted to do during my leave, and I didn't do any of it."

Even though you don't have time to do anything, time seems to stand still. You no longer have the external signposts that mark the progress of each day. Days blur into each other, and you can't remember what you did the day before.

Patricia Morales Wright, a surgeon in rural Nevada, describes her feelings: "I don't think of myself as a Type A personality, but I guess I am. I never could decide whether it was postpartum depression, or just me, or a combination, but I would feel guilty because I wasn't accomplishing anything short of feeding and taking care of the kid. I had never realized that I go through the day and think at the end: I saw this many patients, I performed this many operations, I got this done, etc. Then, there I was on maternity leave and all I could point to at the end of the day was that I had fed the baby so many times, changed diapers so many times, and given him a bath. That was it. I felt really guilty about that."

If you are breast-feeding, your time will be chopped up into short intervals. The nurses in the hospital will tell you to feed every two hours, making it sound as if you will have two hours in between feedings. They forget to explain that they start the clock running from the *beginning* of a feeding, not the end. If feeding takes forty-five minutes to an hour (which is fairly typical, at least at first), then you end up with only an hour left before you have to start feeding again. There is usually no way to finish each chore or activity on your list when you only have an hour at a time.

Breast-feeding is also tiring, partly because of the calories you are burning, and partly because middle-of-the-night feedings take so long. For some, it's downright exhausting. "Nursing Tim, who was a big baby, was like nursing an elephant," says Mary Ellen Schoonmaker. "I was nursing constantly and I never had the time to eat to make up for it. I couldn't do anything—I was comatose most of the time."

Think of feeding the baby (whether breast-feeding or bottle-feeding) as a full-time job—it is—and adjust your "to do" list accordingly. Because Anne didn't understand how time-consuming breast-feeding was, she thought she would have time during the day to shop, return baby presents, and read the files on the cases she had brought home, as well as take a shower, make the beds, change diapers, do the laundry, give the baby a bath, and cook dinner. The second time around, she knew better. She didn't expect to accomplish a single errand or do any office work during the first weeks after Matthew was born. She streamlined the dinner menu (steamed carrots turned into raw carrots) and ordered dinner in a lot.

CONTROL? WHAT CONTROL?

Being a mother involves a lot more uncertainty and lack of control than being a professional. "One of the things I found very hard was to go from the exalted position of prosecutor to being an inept mother," says Sheila Nielsen. At work, you planned your goals and tasks and accomplished them. At home with the baby, things don't quite work that way. Anne would start each day of her first maternity leave with a list of tasks to accomplish. Around the middle of the afternoon, her husband would call from work and ask what she had done so far. She would feel foolish telling him that all she had done was take a shower and get dressed. Where had that efficient, competent lawyer gone? She almost didn't recognize herself.

The first step in coping with this lack of control is to let go of your expectations. Accept that you won't accomplish everything you planned. If your expectations are too high, adjust them! If you can't read the paper every day, try listening to the radio while you're feeding the baby. If you can't find the time to cook dinner, order a pizza. Anne's Lamaze teacher didn't know what a gift she was bestowing when she announced in class one night that pizza was nutritionally correct food for pregnant and nursing mothers! When you're home with a new baby, shortcuts are *not* a cop-out. Don't feel incompetent if you can't get as much done on five or six hours of interrupted sleep as you once did on seven or eight uninterrupted hours.

Letting go of expectations is good training for the rest of motherhood. "It's hard enough to adjust [to the lack of control] in the beginning," says Sharon Cohen, a vice president and single mother. "But then you realize that everything keeps changing, so you never regain control. I was just learning to take care of the belly-button stump, when it fell off. I had just learned to make formula really efficiently, when Sarah stopped using it. I had always been totally into making lists, keeping Filo-faxes, etc. But I've moved the other way now that I have Sarah. I've learned to let go of that. If I forget something, it's all right. If there is no soda water in the refrigerator, that's O.K. I also don't stand on ceremony anymore. If people come over, they bring a pizza. Good-bye, osso buco!"

THE VANISHING SENSE OF ACCOMPLISHMENT

Even if you conquer the yearning for control, you may find yourself longing for the sense of accomplishment that your career represents. Carol remembers giving herself credit for every little ounce that Sarah gained. It was as if they were partners in a very important project: Sarah's growth and flourishing. Carol needed that credit because she had no external feedback on how she was doing. No teachers or bosses praised or criticized her, no briefs or memos served as tangible evidence of her accomplishments. Instead, she was trying to be a "good mother" without knowing what that really meant. Added to that anxiety was Sarah's colic, which developed when she was about two weeks old. She would begin to fuss at about four-thirty in the afternoon, escalating into inconsolable screaming. Finally, at about one-thirty in the morning, Sarah would have exhausted herself and fallen asleep, and Carol would stumble to bed herself. There's nothing like being unable to console a shrieking baby for undermining one's self-confidence.

Elizabeth Cheng Krist, a photography editor at a major business magazine, says, "After about the first week [at home], the reality of it sort of hit me, and I thought, 'Oh, my God, I'm going to be home alone with this creature.' I began to panic. I felt I was doing nothing but repetitive tasks—changing diapers, doing the laundry, washing dishes, feeding the baby. There was no sense of accomplishment, because you have to do everything over again. It's so different from being at work. My first impulse was to call my boss. I told her I didn't think I was going to be able to take being at home, and even asked her to send me some work to do at home. People would tell me, 'You're raising a daughter and that's important,' but it felt so long-term. I wasn't used to working in that sort of time frame."

If you feel this "panic," don't be alarmed. Your old self— that independent, ambitious working woman—has not disappeared; it only feels that way because your new role, your new identity, is so overwhelming. Indeed, the emotional work you undertake during your maternity leave is to integrate these two identities. Even though Elizabeth went so far as to ask for work, she quickly realized that was not a good idea, and her boss was sensitive enough not to push it.

THE SHRINKING CIRCLE OF SOCIAL CONTACT

Once at home, your world suddenly contracts: It is no longer full of other people, meetings, social engagements, and adult conversation. Instead, you can spend much of your day alone with your tiny baby. In the moments that the baby is sleeping, you reach for the phone, only to realize that most of your friends are at work and can't talk to you, and that you don't know what you would say to them even if they *did* have the time (unless they really want to know how many hours the baby slept last night). Going out—even if it's just to the corner grocery store—becomes a major excursion. You begin to wonder whether you will forget how to have an intelligent conversation with an adult. Sheila Nielsen says, "It felt awfully lonely. I was shocked by the isolation. It comes like a cold shower. I felt so cut off and so separated from my office and my world."

Most women we talked with experienced this loneliness, and its intensity was related, in part, to how their husbands adjusted to fatherhood, including how much time their husbands spent at home.

WATCHING YOUR HUSBAND GO BACK TO WORK

It's hard to watch your husband go back to work. His life seems to return to normal within days (or perhaps weeks) of your baby's birth, while your life continues to feel like an emotional and physical tempest. The women whose husbands were home with them during their leaves did not experience the same degree of loneliness as did women whose husbands quickly returned to work. Patricia Morales Wright's husband is a rancher, so he was around the whole time she was on leave from her medical practice. They went on long walks together with the baby, and he was always there to talk to if Pat started feeling depressed. While Patricia experienced identity confusion during her leave, she did not feel lonely.

Unlike Patricia's husband, most husbands go back to work after a short stay at home. Our husbands both returned to work a week after our first children were born, and even sooner after our second. While our husbands had a steady stream of social contact during the day, we had only them to talk to—at the end of the day. Carol began to suspect that, after her husband's long day at the office, where he spoke to dozens of people about their problems, he did not have the energy to provide her with the full quota of stimulation she had missed during the day. Not only that, she was slightly embarrassed to realize that the most interesting thing she could share with him on some days was that Sam had breast-fed for ninety minutes without letup, or had developed a weird rash that disappeared before she could call the pediatrician.

NEW FRIENDS IN NEW MOTHERS

Talking with other new mothers is an excellent way to break the bubble of postpartum isolation. For Carol, finding other new mothers to meet and talk with became crucial to her adjustment to motherhood (many of these other mothers were themselves on maternity leave from work). She didn't have to be embarrassed about an obsession with weight gain (the baby's) or weight loss (hers). All the other mothers were as intensely interested in these matters as she was—and even had informed opinions about presidential politics and other worldly issues. The best part was that she didn't have to worry about still feeling fat from the pregnancy and wearing stained sweat clothes: Her general dishevelment was shared by all the other mothers.

You might want to have a mother's group lined up before you have the baby, but in any case, church or community center bulletin boards, your pediatrician's office, or friends may help you find one. Elizabeth Cheng Krist's postnatal exercise class grew into a play group of mothers and infants. (Given that the infants could not yet play, the "play group" was really a support group for the mothers.) Many of the above organizations organize such groups, as may your hospital or Lamaze instructor. If you don't feel like getting involved with an official "group," simply sitting in the playground is a very effective way to meet new mothers.

◆ SEARCH OUT OTHER NEW MOTHERS:

- ◆ for support
- ◆ for company
- ◆ to share information

Find them at:

- ◆ Lamaze class
- ◆ the pediatrician's office
- ◆ the playground
- ◆ anywhere else you take your baby

CUTTING THE WORK CORD

It's much easier to settle into motherhood if you don't think about work. That's why we recommend that you do not promise to work from home, especially for the first month of your leave, unless you absolutely cannot get around a particular project or other work commitment. Rather than trying to integrate your new role as a mother with your old role as a worker from the beginning, spend that time concentrating on being a mother.

Cutting the work cord can be hard for some women, yet the rewards run deep. Ann Huang, a geneticist who spent thirteen years working eighty to one hundred hours a week on her doctorate, redirected all that energy on her son when he was first born. "When Adam was born, and they gave him to me, he was so real, so vulnerable, and so dependent on me. I was Mommy with a capital M. I was responsible for his life, for his existence," she says. "From the very beginning, he touched in me something that no one else had ever been able to do. My husband thought I would go insane sitting at home, away from people. Instead, it was one of the happiest times in my life. It was just him and me. I never found him boring. I was fascinated watching him learn about his world."

Not all of us make the switch from professional to mother so quickly, but rest assured, you will adjust. As restless as she felt at first, Elizabeth Cheng Krist ended up enjoying her "magical time" at home so much that she extended her leave by several months.

REMEMBER YOURSELF

While it's fine to forget about work, don't forget about yourself. Your needs don't disappear when your baby arrives. Try to listen to your needs, whatever they are. Sheila Nielsen decided that she needed time to take walks by herself during the day: She hired a baby-sitter so she could walk once or twice a week. Go to a postpartum exercise class, even if it means that your husband won't have a home-cooked meal that night. Move getting your hair cut to the top of your list of things to accomplish instead of leaving it at the bottom.

Taking these little steps is an important way to wrestle with the guilt that many of us feel when we focus on ourselves instead of the baby or the marriage. Once you see that taking time for yourself is good for everyone *because* it is good for you, you have begun to deal with the guilt. Caring for yourself will also teach those around you—especially your husband—to adjust to some new realities. The sooner he embarks on this learning curve the better.

Transformation of a Marriage

What you and your husband talk about at the end of the day is not the only thing that changes in your marriage once the baby comes. For most two-career couples, maternity leave represents the first time that the wife is home all day while the husband is at work. Whatever arrangements you and your husband used to have for sharing the household responsibilities no longer apply. Instead, new patterns for allocating responsibility begin to form immediately.

WOMAN AS NURTURER COMES HOME

Having just brought the baby home, you and your husband are simultaneously exhilarated and exhausted. The baby is asleep, but she wakes up and starts crying. Your husband picks her up and hands her to you, saying (in a mildly panicked tone): "Here, honey, the baby wants (or needs) you." In that brief moment, you and your husband have traversed a whole world. In your old world, you and your husband probably operated on a fairly even playing field, both in the workplace and at home. In this new world, the even playing field collapses. Women become "natural nurturers" who know instantly and instinctively how to handle infants (and, by extension, how to raise warm and wonderful children).

Of course, this world does not really exist. The reality is that *both* men and women *learn*, by experience primarily, how to be parents. But, as Dr. T. Berry Brazelton observes in his book *Working and Caring*, "the learning process, which all new parents must go through, is particularly uncomfortable for men. The myth that women tend to know instinctively what to do in a child's crisis is deep-seated." Men who turn to this myth for comfort will inevitably fall farther and farther behind on the learning curve, giving the mother a greater and greater well of experience from which to draw. The more involved the mother, the less involved the father thinks he has to be. "This unconscious 'measuring-up,' comparing themselves against the 'all-knowing female,' is a way men have to keep themselves subordinate in the nurturing role," explains Dr. Brazelton. "In the process, they are likely to abdicate the real responsibility they need to feel to achieve a comfortable and sure relationship with a child."

Men are not the only ones who subscribe to this myth: women do too. New mothers want to feel (through a combination of social and biological forces) that they should know instinctively how to care for their babies. Take breast-feeding for example. The images of breast-feeding that we see when we're pregnant are soft, sweet, romantic pictures of a mother with her baby cuddling up to her breast, skin touching skin. Then the baby comes, and our breasts swell to the point of pain, our nipples ache and crack as we try to learn how to get the baby to attach properly, and the baby keeps getting tangled up in that clumsy breast-feeding bra you are told to wear twenty-four hours a day. So much for knowing "instinctively" how to breast-feed.

Even if we realize that instincts do not a parent make, many times we fail to show this to our spouses because we still cling to the traditional notions of the mother role. Men don't have built-in educational opportunities such as breast-feeding; in many cases, we must teach them that parenting is a learned skill, not an innate talent. This way, husbands cannot abdicate their parenting roles.

DANGER: PRECONCEIVED ROLES

Joan Feigenbaum's husband, Jeff, has been very involved in the child rearing from the beginning. For the most part, he participates equally not only in the physical aspects of care—bathing, changing diapers, etc.—but in the intangible aspects—making sure there are diapers and formula in the house. But when Jeff starts slipping into traditional patterns of behavior, Joan has to catch him. For example, the first time they took the baby, Sam, out for a drive, Jeff assumed that Joan would sit in the backseat with Sam to calm him down if he got cranky. "The only thing I can do that you can't do is feed him, and I'm not going to take him out of the car seat for that," Joan immediately replied. "So you're just as capable of figuring out how to soothe him as I am."

Jeff was assuming that Joan was going to take charge, even though she didn't know anything more about the situation than he did. Joan made it clear to Jeff that nothing about the mother or father roles should be assumed; they will define each role together.

Child rearing is not the only area of responsibility where roles are assumed: Housework is another. Before children, the majority of two-career couples share household chores and duties fairly evenly. However, this division of labor falls apart once they have children.

◆ CAUTION: CHANGE AHEAD

A 1991 survey of data on sixty thousand employees at fifteen major corporations concluded: "[M]en and women tend to share responsibilities during the early years, . . . but once children come into the picture, the situation quickly changes," according to Charles Rodgers of the research arm of Work/Family Directions, which conducted the survey. "The average working mother spends 44 hours at work and 31 hours on family responsibilities per week. This compares to 47 hours her spouse spends on the job and 15 he devotes to child care and household tasks."

Child rearing and household duties tend to become mixed up in the minds of new parents (and other people as well): This is part of what we call the Nurturer Problem in Chapter 1. You can tell this is happening, for example, when your husband decides after the baby is born that he is no longer capable of doing the grocery shopping because you are the only one who knows what to buy. In other words, when he passed the screaming baby to you, he also passed responsibility for the home and everything else associated with your personal life.

LOOK OUT: SHIFTING RESPONSIBILITIES

Anne experienced a change in her husband's role once Sarah was born. When Anne and her husband, Don, were in law school together, they each did some of the cooking, cleaning, grocery shopping, and laundry (not equally well, of course). After law school, the routine basically continued—until Sarah was born. Then, since Anne was home (for five weeks) she took responsibility for everything, and Don did only what he was asked to do. This dynamic meant not only that Anne was doing more of the housework, but also that Don started to perceive her as somehow *generating* the work. Now, a chore existed not because *it had to be done* but because Anne *wanted it done*. This subtle shift was really a change in roles rather than a reflection of a changed reality— and it occurred without either Anne or Don being truly aware of it.

Carol experienced the same shift of responsibility in her marriage more gradually. Before they had children Carol and her husband, Rob, traded off cooking, dish washing, and laundry. (Neither one ever did much cleaning, although Carol would succumb to the need to clean sooner than Rob.) After Sarah was born, Carol had a long maternity leave, during which she did all the cooking, shopping for groceries and baby supplies, and other chores except cleaning, for which they hired a biweekly housekeeper. They found they both preferred Carol's cooking, so when she returned to work, Carol continued to do the cooking. Rob would give Sarah a bath and wash the dishes. By the time Sam was born, and they had a house instead of an apartment, Carol had taken over almost all the domestic responsibilities, except for the traditionally "masculine" chores such as mowing the lawn and writing the checks.

It took both of us a long time to figure out what was

happening in our marriages, and we have spent a great deal of energy trying to undo the patterns established during our maternity leaves. The best advice is to catch the shift in responsibilities early, and to resist, as Joan Feigenbaum did, the impulse to assume roles.

Soul-Searching

TO GO BACK TO WORK . . .

After you have settled into a routine and you begin to feel comfortable with being a mother, you will begin to think about going back to work. This can be a time of intense soul-searching for some mothers, when they question their commitment to their jobs and career choice, their ideas of motherhood, and the patterns in their marriage.

For some mothers the choice is clear: They need to work either for financial or psychological reasons—or both. Even though Anne would have liked a longer maternity leave when her first daughter was born, she never doubted that she would go back to work. Similarly, Joan Feigenbaum never questioned that she would go back to work once her son was born. Joan has a Ph.D. in mathematics and is a theoretical researcher at Bell Laboratories in New Jersey. She recuperated from her delivery quickly and had her child care in place from the beginning of her leave. For her, being at work was more comfortable and less physically demanding than being at home. She went back to work after four weeks (even though she could have taken longer) and has never looked back.

Even though Susan Mirkinson, a doctor, had a cesarean section, she was back at work six weeks later. "I was ready to go back," she says. "You have to understand: I like my job. I *really* like my job."

. . . OR NOT TO

Other working mothers think that they won't want an outside job when they have children, only to discover that this choice is not right for them. Tina Bailey, a professor of chemistry at California Polytechnic State University, is such a mother. She and her husband have four adopted children ranging in age from roughly twenty-one to fourteen. When they adopted their first child, Tina was teaching high school chemistry. "Truthfully, what I originally intended is that I would stop working for ten to fifteen years, and then go back to work," she says. "But I noticed that after six months I missed my students and my work. There's a big difference between reading about what's going on in chemistry at home and actually doing it. I missed the contact; I needed that side of my life. So, I put that part back in [by getting a job as a part-time lecturer]."

Tina continues: "After five years, I felt that the part-time lectureship was not satisfying enough, that I needed more work. I needed to satisfy my own intellectual needs. I've always loved being a mother; I wouldn't have adopted four kids if I didn't. But there was a piece of me missing when I didn't work. It's not that I don't think that being a full-time mother is a job. Hey, that's more than a full-time job. It just wasn't the job that made me happy. It has to be what makes you happy."

We couldn't have put it better ourselves: The choice to work is a personal one; whatever you choose is right if it is right for you.

Carol's decisions about returning to work evolved while she was home on maternity leave. Before Sarah was born she had assumed she would go back to work. After Sarah was born, although she knew she wanted to return to work, she couldn't picture returning to the same pounding schedule. She concluded that a part-time schedule was the only alternative. She wasn't sure how the firm would react, and she had to consider what her choices would be if the firm refused. That led to more soul-searching. How she approached her bosses to negotiate a part-time arrangement, and what she negotiated, is covered in Chapter 7.

Susan Eilertsen knew she was going back to work full-time after her second child was born: She is the wage earner in her family. Because her earning potential is greater than her husband's (he is an artist), they decided that he would stay home with the kids and Susan would be financially responsible for the family. Asked whether her husband worked on his art at home, she laughed and replied, "No, he doesn't have time. He's with the kids full-time."

Susan's public relations business is growing and prospering.

"I am very happy and proud of my business and how well it is doing, especially given the economic climate. But I also feel like my life is riddled with conflict all the time," she says. "I am struggling with the grief of leaving my kids every day, and yet I want my kids to go to college and have nice things and good opportunities."

Although this tension never disappears, it softens as you grow into the role of working mother and as you watch your children develop and thrive. When her daughter, Sarah, was eight months old and not quite crawling, Carol used to think that maybe the baby would be developing more quickly if only Carol were home full-time, encouraging her. Later, she would listen with a tinge of anxiety to the mothers who would exclaim how glad they were to pick up their children at school at 3 P.M., because *that's* when children want to discuss the events of the day. What would she miss, she thought, if she didn't get home until 6 or 7 P.M.?

As it turned out, both of Carol's children learned to crawl, walk, talk, and everything else, at their own pace (and maybe with less neurosis than if Carol had been fussing over them full-time). And even though she doesn't pick them up at school every day, together they always manage to find a quiet moment to talk about the school gerbil who died in Sam's classroom or the book Sarah is reading to her teacher. As with everything, you adapt to the internal struggle until you find a place that is comfortable for you.

Getting Ready to Go Back

EASE INTO IT

Once you know you're going back to work, the major task of integrating the two parts of your life begins. It helps to do this gradually, instead of showing up at work one morning after six weeks or six months of zero contact. Ease into it by having lunch with your colleagues, or joining them for a lecture, conference, or retreat, before you actually start working. By returning to your work environment without any pressure to perform you give yourself a chance to rediscover all the things you enjoy about working and a chance to remember what it's like to be a working person. Just wearing stockings will start to bring back the professional in you who receded into the background during your leave.

Besides visiting the office yourself, you will probably feel an urge to bring the baby in. Even if this idea does not occur to you, the same people who treated your pregnancy as an "office project" will undoubtedly want to see the result of their (!) efforts. While the idea is great, actually getting the baby to the office can be a comical—and exhausting—experience.

"I brought my first baby down for everyone to see when she was about three months old," recalls Sheila Nielsen. "Everyone in the office was all excited. In fact, I did it because I was pressured into it. She behaved horribly. I spent the whole time trying to calm her as she screamed in the corner office."

Carol also remembers how difficult it was to bring her daughter, Sarah, into the office. It was bad enough dragging the diaper bag through the subway and midtown Manhattan. But she also felt so unprofessional. Here she was in the office with the baby crying and spitting up on her. It didn't hit her until then that bringing her baby in would result in her colleagues seeing her in a completely different light.

Yet, while you may be uncomfortable going to the office as the mother of an infant instead of as a professional, you will benefit from making the baby "real" to your colleagues and supervisors. They may want (at some level) to maintain strict boundaries between your personal and professional spheres, but your life will never be that neatly compartmentalized. The sooner you begin to dispel that notion, the better. Letting your co-workers get to know your baby makes it easier for them to relate to the work/family conflicts that will invariably arise when you go back to work. In its own way, this gives your colleagues some stake in your child, which, while not as strong as the stake they may have felt in your pregnancy, does factor in their willingness to accommodate your family's needs and responsibilities.

TO WEAN OR NOT TO WEAN?

If you are breast-feeding, just about the time you are feeling comfortable with it, you will probably have to think about weaning. Giving up breast-feeding can be painful. Ann Huang is not alone in saying, "Breast-feeding was such an incredible, satisfying feeling. When I stopped breast-feeding, I cried."

Breast-feeding at work has its own problems, however. Carol Barrett, then director of planning for the city of Annapolis, decided to come in for staff meetings periodically during her second maternity leave. Because she was breast-feeding, she brought her infant son, Andrew, with her, and breast-fed in the office.

"My breast-feeding at work engendered tremendous hostility, particularly from older women who felt that a baby in an office was completely inappropriate," Barrett says. "Someone even wrote to the mayor of Annapolis accusing me of being bare-breasted and nursing my baby in a public reception area." The letter was so vitriolic that Barrett framed and hung it in her office. But the experience was bad enough that bringing Andrew to work with her during her leave is the only thing she regrets doing as a working mother.

Many women decide to wean their babies before going back to work. Susan Eilertsen took six weeks maternity leave when her second child was born. Rather than wean her baby so soon, she had originally intended for her husband, who stays home with their two children, to bring the baby to the office for feeding. But during her leave, Susan realized that this plan was unworkable. So she weaned Nicholas at five weeks. Susan says, "I think working mothers have been sold a bill of goods about breast-feeding. How women go to jobs and nurse is totally beyond me. There is a lot of propaganda that I am very unhappy about because it makes working mothers feel guilty if they do not breast-feed. But I do feel very very sad to this day at how early I had to wean him." Susan's message is clear: Working mothers often measure themselves against standards created in a different context. We must learn to listen to ourselves, rather than to these external pressures, when deciding how to combine our roles as mothers and professionals. And we must learn to accept the trade-offs that our decisions involve.

Rather than bring the baby to work to breast-feed, some mothers are able to go to their babies—by visiting the on-site or neighboring day-care center during the workday. This may sound ideal, but it can actually be quite stressful. You cannot always coordinate your work rhythm with your milk flow: Your breasts may feel full just as an important customer calls long distance.

Introducing the Bottle

To give yourself flexibility, teach your baby to take a bottle as early as the first few weeks after birth. Not only does this free up some time for you, it also gives your baby the chance to be fed by someone other than her mother, most notably her father. Feeding the baby gives fathers the chance to bond just as it does for mothers. Teaching your baby to take a bottle early also makes weaning, whenever it occurs, much easier. After all, even if you pump at work, you will have to feed your milk to your baby in a bottle.

Mothers who do not want to wean completely before going back to work can breast-feed in the morning and at night. Anne settled on this approach after her attempt to pump at work ended in disaster. Your breasts may be sore for a few days during the transition (but no more sore than when pumping or weaning), and your milk flow quickly regulates itself to the two feedings. By breast-feeding at home you extend this special time without creating a lot of stress at work.

Dr. T. Berry Brazelton encourages this approach, observing that "the closeness that comes with successful breast-feeding is a mother's major reward. And, for a working mother away part of the day, the opportunity to enhance this closeness by nursing the baby at the end of the working day is a real plus."

Of course, many women decide not to breast-feed at all, especially if their leaves are relatively brief. They feel that the benefits of perhaps a few weeks of mother's milk are not worth the stress of weaning and confinement at home during this brief time away from work (not to mention the pain and discomfort that some women experience).

Pumping at Work

Some women pump at work to avoid eliminating breast milk from their baby's diet. Pumping sounds a lot easier than it is: whether you succeed depends partly on your personality, on your workplace environment, and on the predictability of your job. Anne tried pumping at work but gave up after a week of agony.

No matter how secure the lock on her office door was, she just couldn't get herself to relax enough for the milk to flow. She would spend her whole lunch hour painfully extracting a few ounces.

If your work requires you to travel, expect to experience additional conflict and stress. We did hear one—true—story of a woman prosecutor who, when required to travel soon after she returned to work from the birth of her first child, managed to breast-feed by mail—by pumping her milk and Federal Expressing it home. Our advice: Don't count on it. Pumping in the office is hard enough; we can't imagine doing it in a strange place far from home, let alone being organized enough to bring all the equipment with you and ensure that the milk stays fresh throughout its journey.

If you plan to pump at work, you will have to rethink your wardrobe. Suzanne Jacobson, a senior staff member at Jewish Federation in Houston and mother of three children, tells a funny story about her first day back at work. She was all set to pump, having practiced at home and set up a comfortable space for herself in the office, when she realized that she was wearing a dress that zipped up the back. She literally had to undress to pump! Other working mothers who pump advise keeping a spare blouse (or a jacket that can cover up a stained blouse) in the office in case of leaks.

INTRODUCING THE CARE-GIVER

As the day they return to work draws near, many mothers panic at the thought of leaving their children in someone else's care. Some also feel resentment and jealousy toward the care-giver they have hired—precisely because she represents the care and nurturing that they want to give their children. The more comfortable you are with your care-giver, the more comfortable you will feel going back to work. If possible, you should let your child develop a relationship with his care-giver, by having her work in your home, or taking your child to her home or to the day care center for a few days a week before you start work.

Paula Scott's experience illustrates the advantages—for you and your child—of beginning your child care before you return to work. She started preparing to go back more than a month before the scheduled date by hiring a baby-sitter who came one day a week, then two days a week, until Paula went back to work. "The first day back I called home once," she says. "Jackie [the baby-sitter] was very calm and told me what they had done. I anticipated that it would be a lot worse than it was. I thought I wouldn't be able to concentrate on work, that I would be thinking of him all the time. But I got involved in my work, and it took very little time to get back into the swing of things. The fact that I had this woman coming for six weeks already helped a lot. She knew the routine, Danny knew her, and I had already had experience leaving Danny with her."

The child care provider that Joan Feigenbaum, the mathematician, uses is her father: He comes to her apartment every day to take care of his grandson. Joan acknowledges that she was content going back to work early because she felt so comfortable with her care-giver. Elizabeth Cheng Krist started taking her daughter to the day care center two or three weeks before going back to work, giving mother and child time to adjust.

Like many people, Anne did not have family to help her when her first child was born. Anne and her husband decided to hire a baby-sitter who started working for them the day Sarah came home from the hospital. Five weeks later the baby-sitter was already an established member of the family, and Anne felt comfortable leaving the house for the office.

WHAT TO WEAR?

We all think that we will recognize our bodies once the baby is born; most of us are seriously disappointed. However, since you spend the majority of your maternity leave in casual clothes (anything with an elastic waist will do), you don't realize just how much your body has changed until you go to put on a blouse and skirt—only to find that you can't close either. Don't wait until the night before your first workday to look in your closet. You might have to borrow clothes from a friend or shop for a few "transition" outfits to tide you over until your body fits your old clothes again.

THE LAST FEW DAYS

As the actual "due back" date approaches, you may experience an emotional whirlwind: joy, anguish, trepidation, excitement, all swirl around you. These emotions coalesce around certain focal points, such as breast-feeding and getting used to your child care provider, as well as pervade every corner of your being. During the last week of her leave, Anne remembers trying to picture herself back at the office—and drawing a blank. Being at home with her newborn was such a different world that she simply could not imagine herself back at work. She didn't dread returning; she loved her job and was very comfortable with her baby-sitter. It was more that her life felt so new and still somewhat strange, that she wasn't sure the old routine would fit. Ellen Bonkoski, a chemist at Beckman Laboratories in the Los Angeles area and mother of four, remembers finally feeling relaxed at home only to begin feeling tense and anxious as the time to go back to work drew closer.

It's common, in the last days of maternity leave, to feel like you're on the edge of a precipice looking out into dense fog. Be patient; the fog does clear. Which is not to say, by any means, that there is a map at the other end that will tell you exactly how to balance work and family. Carol Barrett, now director of waste services for the city of Austin, Texas, says, "I think that this idea of working and having kids can be made to satisfy everybody's needs, but that it requires the same kind of leap of faith that getting married does. It is not ever going to be possible to map your way from A to Z. You really have to take an approach that says: I can figure out what the right thing is to do tomorrow, or the week after, or the week after that, and then events will just have to take care of themselves."

Especially during the transitions, don't worry if you haven't figured out how you're going to handle everything that will happen until you retire. As Carol Barrett suggests, take things one step at a time, one day at a time, and eventually, you will get the hang of it.

5

THE CHILD CARE DECISION

Deciding the kind of child care you want and then finding it are essential steps in combining work and family. Because we feel that child care is an issue that you shouldn't have to deal with alone, the next chapter discusses various child care programs that can be instituted by employers to help their employees with the work/family balance.

You must have child care in place when you return to work. Don't even think about bringing the baby to work, even on a temporary basis. We've seen what happens. Even when your job seems conducive to having an infant around (you go to meetings rarely, never have to answer the phone, dress casually, and work with understanding colleagues), you'll almost certainly feel the strain quickly. It's hard to concentrate on work when you are anxious about whether the baby will cry. Ultimately, you will feel less successful at motherhood *and* your job. Bringing the baby to work is possible only if you work for yourself, and even that lasts only a few months, until the baby is crawling around, tugging at everything in sight.

Feeling good about your child care arrangement is an essential part of preparing yourself *emotionally* to go back to work. Much of that emotional whirlwind is anxiety over leaving your baby with someone else. The better you feel about this other person, your child care provider, the easier it will be to separate from your baby.

Feeling Uneasy: The Case of the Ketchup-Smothered Chicken

If you feel insecure or uneasy with your child care arrangement, work becomes unbearably stressful, if not impossible. Study after study has shown that child care concerns are the primary source of conflict in the lives of working parents. On the other hand, when companies implement child care programs, they see marked improvement in their employees' abilities to concentrate and produce.[1] Anne remembers vividly the time when she was concerned about the kind of care a new in-home care-giver was providing. Anne and her family had just moved to the suburbs, and Sarah had just started a nursery school program. Something about this new person made Anne a little uncomfortable, but she thought her unease was concern about how Sarah would handle all the changes. A few days into the arrangement, Anne got a call at work from her grandmother, who lived with Anne's family at the time. Her grandmother was concerned because the babysitter, contrary to express instructions, had let Sarah watch TV all morning and had dumped ketchup all over Sarah's chicken for lunch, presumably to make the meal more appetizing. While neither of these actions was life-threatening, or even harmful, Anne couldn't think about anything else but how things at home were not as they should be. She definitely didn't get much work done that afternoon—and finally gave up trying.

Feeling Guilty: The Case of the Perfectly Healthy Child

When child care problems arise, mothers and fathers seem to have markedly different emotional reactions. Few things seem to generate guilt in working mothers more quickly than being at work if they're worried about what is going on at home. It's common for mothers to be almost paralyzed at work if they are worrying about child care, whereas fathers (even fathers who are significantly involved in and responsible for their children's daily routines) seem to be able to go about their daily business, knowing that this too shall pass. "Even though I was the primary care-giver in our family when our children were young, my wife always *worried* about them more than I," says Dr. Elliott Rosen, a psychologist and family therapist.

Mary Ellen Schoonmaker, a journalist and mother of three, told us a story about her youngest son, Timmy, that perfectly illustrates this point. Mary Ellen and her husband, Mike Hoyt, shared a job for many years (spanning all three pregnancies) so they could both be home with their babies. They truly shared work and family obligations, and even now that they are working separate full-time jobs, Mike does half the cooking, housework, and child care. But one day, as Mary Ellen and her husband were about to drive to work together, Timmy began to shriek. He had recently been exposed to chicken pox, and they thought he might be getting sick. But Mary Ellen's husband was going to miss the bus if they didn't get moving, so they left.

"I was convinced that I was abandoning this kid who was about to die of some strange disease, and Mike kept saying there was nothing wrong with him," says Mary Ellen. "So I raced to work, my stomach in knots. As soon as I got to work, I called the baby-sitter. She told me Timmy was still crying and she was unnerved, which is unusual, because she's a very stoic person. So I race back home ten minutes after I've gotten to the office, comforting myself by thinking that Timmy is going to see that I haven't abandoned him. When I get home, I race up the stairs to his room where, the baby-sitter has told me, he is laying in bed. When I get into his room, he sees me, leaps off the bed, and starts dancing around the bedroom chanting, 'Mommy, Mommy, Mommy!'

"There was absolutely nothing wrong with that kid. Then, I called Mike to tell him not to worry, and he was calmly going about his work having completely forgotten about the whole incident."

While the facts may differ, the emotions of this scenario are replayed over and over in the lives of working parents. The reality at the moment is that mothers bear the brunt of these emotionally exhausting and disruptive moments. Most mothers still feel that child care is ultimately their responsibility. This urgent sense of responsibility is at the core of our ideas of motherhood. At the same time, in most cases we have no choice *but* to assume the ultimate responsibility, because fathers have yet to truly accept this responsibility as part of fatherhood. A true change in these ideas is bound to be gradual. All the more reason to commit yourself (and your husband) to finding good, stable child care.

Preparing Yourself to Search

It is never too soon to start looking for child care. Most women who take a two-month or longer maternity leave wait until after the baby is born to start. But don't wait until right before you go back to work to begin investigating what's available in your community.

Janet Grau waited until two weeks before the end of her leave, only to find that the day care center she liked the best had no available spaces. She then scrambled to find alternatives, finding a good family day care arrangement only after several weeks of anxiety, during which she had to go back to work.

One woman we read about started investigating child care in her Florida community during her *first trimester:* By the time she had to go back to work, she knew exactly what she was looking for—and had found it! It's good to do this kind of research ahead of time both because of the scarcity of high-quality child care and because you will have a lot more time and energy to devote to investigating your options *before* you have the baby than afterward. However, even if you've thought about your options ahead of time, you may not be ready to interview providers and make a decision until you start feeling comfortable in your new role as a mother and have some sense of what the job of child care provider means to you.

No matter when you start, don't be surprised if you feel incompetent and insecure during your search. You may feel that you're interviewing people for a job that you cannot even describe. As Janet Grau says: "As a first-time parent, I didn't know what to ask a potential provider. I didn't know how to conduct that kind of an interview." You may want to visit a day care center or talk with child care agencies before the baby arrives, just to *learn what to look for* in a provider. The conversations can be very helpful, even if you don't use those providers.

Even if you have experience hiring people at work, you may suddenly find yourself unsure of how to interview and evaluate potential child care providers. Sharon Cohen, vice president at a sportswear manufacturing company, says, "When I was twenty-five and hiring a secretary for the first time, I didn't know how to do it. Now I'm forty-five and have done it many times, so I do know. I think hiring someone has a lot to do with experience.

And experience at the office hiring and managing people doesn't transfer very well to hiring child care."

To ease lurking feelings of insecurity, remember that the most important part of the child care decision is finding the right person for you; everything else will work itself out if you have a good relationship with your child care provider. And one of the most important elements you bring to the process of finding child care is not experience but *instinct*. As much as you try to ask potential providers all the right questions and check all their references, in the end it comes down to a gut feeling about the person and whether her style and personality are compatible with yours. (Because the vast majority of child care providers, no matter the type of care, are female, we refer to them as women throughout the book.)

Feeling Confident: The (Many) Cases of Misguided Instinct

Your instinct is your best indicator of a good fit; still, there is nothing wrong with you if your instinct sometimes misguides you. One woman hired a European au pair who sounded great on the phone, had fantastic references, and made a lovely first impression. The au pair hadn't even worked a week before the mother began to have faint doubts about the au pair's competence and judgment. But the mother just couldn't acknowledge that her own judgment had been wrong until another mother called to report that the au pair had left the woman's three-year-old son alone in the pool. At that point, facing up to having made a mistake with the au pair was a lot easier than living with the fear that a catastrophe could occur at any moment.

Carol had a similar experience with the first care-giver she hired. The woman was young, energetic, and affectionate with the baby. She was also, it turned out, irresponsible. The day before she was to start work (two weeks before Carol was supposed to return to work) the care-giver called to say she had changed her mind: She could make more money as a practical nurse. Carol cried after she hung up the telephone. After meeting Carol's beautiful baby, how could this woman not want to take care of her? Carol wondered how she could have been such a poor judge of character. Then she panicked. How was she going to go back to work? After her hysteria diminished (somewhat), she called her office and said there had been a hitch in her child care arrangement, and that she might need an extra week or two to straighten it out. No problem, they said, letting Carol breathe enough of a sigh of relief to give her the energy to reembark on the child care search.

We've known women who quit their jobs because their child care arrangement fell apart or went sour. They lost all trust in child care providers and in their own ability to choose a good one. Even though it's easy (and maybe inevitable) to think that something is wrong with you if your child care arrangement doesn't work, it is *not* your fault. You have every right to make sure your child is cared for the way you think is best. So, if you have made a mistake, don't be afraid to acknowledge it: the sooner you do, the sooner you can make a better decision.

"It took me a while to realize that my first nanny wasn't terrific, because of my inexperience," says Sharon Cohen. "I was so grateful that she was showing up on time, that I had somebody. When I started to feel that she wasn't right, I felt like I couldn't trust my own feelings. When she left, I hired a fabulous person, and there were four others that I interviewed that seemed like they would be equally fabulous. It was only then that I realized what I had been putting up with."

Acknowledging a mistake gives you a much better sense of what you are looking for, which in turn helps you find the right person.

Good child care is, to be honest, hard to find. As your search goes on for days and then for weeks, you may get desperate. You may question whether your standards are realistic and begin to think that compromise is inevitable if you are to find any child care at all.

"[Parents share] a desire to get this [selection] over as quickly as possible in order to remove the confusion and uncertainty, a sense of competition with all the other parents who may be making different choices, and a nervousness about how their choice will affect their child," says Ellen Galinsky, copresident of the Families and Work Institute and a noted researcher in the field.[2]

Parents in this frame of mind can easily end up "settling" for a situation. A decision made in this manner usually doesn't last long; if it doesn't feel right from the beginning, it's probably not going to get any better.

Don't let panic take over; it will increase the chances that you will make a decision you'll regret later. Take the time to find a situation that truly feels comfortable to you. This search should begin with figuring out what you want from a child care arrangement. "Although you may have a tremendous need for child care, unless you are psychologically ready to begin [a child care relationship], your efforts may be wasted," says Sonja Flating, the author of *Child Care: A Parent's Guide.* Believe it or not, once you are ready to accept child care as part of your life, eventually you will find the right arrangement for you.

But how do you figure out what you want from a child care provider? Of course, we all want "quality" care. But the definition of quality care is as individual as parenting itself. We realize that the choice you make is very personal and based on many different factors, including availability, age of your child, location, hours, cost, and, perhaps most important, the things you decide your child needs. While nothing we write can substitute for introspection, experience, instinct, and luck, we can launch your search by describing different child care options, and discussing how to determine what's available in your community as well as what to look for in a child care provider.

Child Care Options

The child care field, like any other, has its own confusing jargon. Despite what may appear as a morass of options, there are really only three different types of child care arrangements: day care centers, family day care providers, and in-home child care. (There are also numerous arrangements for school-age children, such as after-school programs and the like. However, because we are addressing primarily mothers with young children, we do not go into the issue of how to handle caring for your child after school hours.)

DAY CARE CENTERS

Day care centers are organizations that provide child care services in an institutional setting, such as a church, synagogue, school, corporate office, or other such building. These centers usually care for a relatively large number of children. Centers take children ranging in age from a few months old to school age. All fifty states license day care centers and prescribe minimum quality standards, such as minimum staff-to-child ratios (which depend on the age of the children). Some states also require that a center's staff have a certain amount of training. The Children's Defense Fund maintains up-to-date information on state laws regulating day care centers; check Appendix B for its address and phone number.

Day care centers, like any other form of child care, have advantages and disadvantages. One of their main advantages is reliability: Most are open every day except government holidays, when you may not need them anyway. You don't have to worry about your provider getting sick or taking a vacation in the middle of a big project at work. Day care centers are also relatively easy to locate, because of their size and more formal setup, which can be a relief when you are trying to fill a significant need without knowing where to start. If the center is good, its staff will be experienced child care providers, which can be very reassuring to a new mother and father. Lastly, they give children the experience of playing and learning with other children, and are more likely to expose them to children of diverse ages and backgrounds.

On the other hand, size can also be a day care center's main shortcoming. In choosing a day care center, Dr. T. Berry Brazelton advises parents to avoid those that do not staff a baby room with at least one adult for every three or four infants. The National Association for the Education of Young Children recommends limits on total group size as well as adult/child ratios: for two-year-olds, no more than 12 children with an adult-child ratio of 1:4 to 1:6; for three- to five-year-olds, no more than 20 children to a group with a ratio of 1:8 to 1:10.

Being around lots of children also makes your child more likely to catch every bug going around, particularly those that are highly contagious, such as conjunctivitis ("pinkeye") and chicken pox. For this reason, you should make sure that your child's pediatrician knows that she is attending day care, and that either you or the center has a backup system for caring for your child when she gets sick.

In addition to size, the other main concern with day care centers is the quality of the staff and staff turnover. Check that the child care providers at any day care center you are considering are well trained and relatively well paid.

Although easier to find, many day care centers have long waiting lists and cannot guarantee you a place at a particular time. This makes planning for your return to work very difficult and, in some cases, can eliminate a day care center from consideration.

Lastly, day care centers tend to be inflexible about their hours. If the center closes at 6 P.M. every day, somebody has to be able to get to the center then to pick up your child. Closing time can become a significant source of stress every day if your job (and your husband's job) demand more flexibility.

FAMILY DAY CARE

Family day care (or family child care) is the care of a small group of children in the provider's home. All sorts of people are family day care providers. She may be your mother-in-law, a retired person, or a new mother herself.

Family day care sometimes can be found in unexpected places. K.K. Gerhart-Fritz and her husband take their two-year-old daughter, Kelley, to the home of a new mother who is married to someone in K.K.'s office. Originally, K.K. approached her about taking care of Kelley just for the time that Kelley's first family day care provider was out having her own baby. The new mother had never really considered taking care of other children beside her own, but Kelley has been there ever since.

Most states regulate the number of children (of different ages) that a family day care provider can care for, and specify minimum health and safety standards (although few states require any specific training). The Children's Defense Fund has information on family day care regulations.

Some states also require family day care providers to be registered or licensed. Getting a license usually involves not only an application, but also an inspection of the premises to ensure that minimum safety standards are met. However, these inspections do not occur regularly, and there is little, if any, follow-up if the premises need repair or remodeling to comply with fire and other codes. Therefore, the fact that a provider has a license does not guarantee that her premises are safe, and you should not use the license as a substitute for your own inspection. In addition, a license is no guarantee of character. Therefore, as important as the presence of a license in evaluating a provider is your sense of the provider's standards and judgment.

Family day care is one of the most common forms of child care in this country for young children. Its main advantages are its home setting, flexible hours (some providers will adapt to unusual work schedules), and small group size.[3] In addition, most family day care is less expensive than day care centers or live-in child care, and the chance of finding a provider near your work or home is higher than for day care centers (because there are fewer of the latter).

However, a family day care provider arrangement is inherently more unstable than a day care center, because it depends solely on the life circumstances of one provider. Mary Ellen Schoonmaker's oldest daughter, Emma, had been with a provider for six months when the woman announced, without any warning, that she was going back to office work. Similarly, the first family day care provider Carol Barrett and her husband hired had to go back into the work force suddenly after her husband left her. K.K. and her husband originally placed their daughter with a provider who was pregnant at the time—but didn't tell them. As you can imagine, that arrangement didn't last past the delivery date.

To minimize crises that arise when the provider is not able or willing to provide care, make sure that you understand in advance when the provider plans to go on vacation, and what— if any—backup system she has when she is sick. Most people are not as fortunate as Debbie Reed, a high school English teacher. When Debbie asked about sick days, her family care provider, a retired woman, told her, "Oh, honey, I never miss a day." Even the most reliable family day care providers, like anyone else, get sick and have family emergencies, and you need to plan for these possibilities, just as you would like your own employer to do for you.

IN-HOME CARE

This option involves hiring a person to come to your home every day and care for your children in your home. There are numerous permutations of this basic arrangement—with as many labels. For example, there are professionally trained nannies, untrained mother's helpers or housekeepers, au pairs, and, of course, baby-sitters. Whatever the in-home child care provider is called, if she (usually) sleeps over, she is referred to as a "live-in" and if she comes and goes every day, she is referred to as a "live-out." In-home providers run the gamut from young women from other countries (usually called "au pairs") to women with grown children. While some may have an educational background in child development, most bring experience rather than formal training to the job. (You can always supplement their training by, for example, signing them up for a first aid class.)

In-home child care is generally the most costly of the child care options: We've seen estimates as high as three or four times the cost of day care centers. However, this arrangement also provides the most flexibility. If your hours at work are long, inconsistent, or unpredictable, or if you travel frequently, you may have no choice but to hire someone to come to your home who will stay until you arrive. A live-in care-giver will give you the most flexibility; however there are trade-offs. First, you need to provide her with space, a commodity not always readily available.

As a vice president at a sportswear manufacturing company, Sharon Cohen travels quite a bit, but she does not have a live-in baby-sitter. "When you're forty-five and single, you don't live in a house with an au pair suite," she says. Even if you're married, you may not have room or you may not want to put up with the intrusion on your privacy that having a live-in entails.

You Are the Employer Now

While flexibility and one-on-one attention are the strengths of in-home care, there are several other factors to consider. First, as with family day care, your care-giver can get sick; you need a backup plan when this occurs. Second, you are your care-giver's employer, and must consider the accompanying responsibilities. You will have to pay federal and state unemployment tax, state-required workers compensation and disability insurance (if any), as well as your half of her federal Social Security and Medicare tax. (While you are not *required* to withhold income tax on household help, you must do so if your care-giver requests that you do.)

Paying these taxes involves a seemingly endless amount of paperwork. You need to receive an "employer identification number," which you do by filling out IRS form SS-4 and sending it (you can even fax it) to the IRS. The federal Social Security and Medicare tax-reporting form (Form 942) has to be filed quarterly with the IRS; the federal unemployment form (Form 940 or 940-EZ) is filed annually. You will also complete a federal wage and tax statement (the W-2 form) annually and give it to your care-giver and file a Transmittal Income and Tax Statement (the W-3 form) with the Social Security Administration. On top of the federal reporting requirements, you must comply with your state filing and withholding requirements. We recommend you read IRS booklet Number 926: *Employment Taxes for Household Employers* and check with a tax adviser about both the federal and state requirements.

In addition, you need to think about insuring your care-giver in case of accident or illness. Don't assume that your homeowner's insurance policy will cover injuries that occur at home. It probably won't, because your care-giver is an employee and not a guest. Therefore, we recommend that you buy worker's compensation insurance even if it is not required under state law.

Health insurance for an individual is much more expensive and harder to get. Your best bet may be to talk with the International Nanny Association (see Appendix B) about carriers that insure in-home care-givers.

If you have decided that you want a care-giver who drives, be sure to check her driver's license, and ask her to take a drive with you to assess her skills. If your care-giver is a foreign nanny with an international license, you cannot assume that she will be covered under your auto insurance policy. Though it is legal to drive in this country with an international license, insurance companies have the discretion to deny coverage. Therefore, check with your agent. Either way, it is probably safest to list the care-giver on your policy, so there is no doubt she is covered. However, there may be an additional premium for such coverage. If she is transporting your children in *her* car, check the seat belts and make sure she has insurance.

The reality of the child care labor market (at least in large urban areas) is that the majority of in-home care-givers, especially those who live-in, are not working in this country legally.

Under current immigration laws you can be fined (and, in the case of repeat offenses, jailed) for hiring someone who is not authorized to work. If your care-giver does not have a "green card," meaning work authorization, you may consider "sponsoring" her. The sponsorship program is designed to give green cards to workers in fields that the United States Department of Labor has deemed to have a labor shortage. Housekeeping (including child care) is one of these fields. Sponsorship is generally a long-term commitment, taking anywhere from five to fifteen years, depending on the country from which your care-giver comes.

Be aware that sponsorship does *not* give your housekeeper authority to work in this country under the immigration laws. This was one reason why Zoe Baird, President Clinton's first nominee for attorney general, got into trouble. Under the law you are supposed to wait until the sponsorship application is granted (i.e., five to fifteen years) before you hire the person. Obviously, this system is completely unworkable in practice. (Zoe Baird is not alone, by the way. Many parents have decided that the immigration law, which was designed primarily to punish businesses that exploit large numbers of illegal aliens, imposes impossible limitations on finding the best person to care for their children.) If you do not pay your share of taxes for the person you're sponsoring, you are violating the tax laws as well. Because sponsorship is a complicated legal process, we advise that either you or your care-giver hire a lawyer who specializes in immigration matters to advise you on your obligations.

Beside the insurance and tax issues that come with having an employee, you will also need more day-to-day involvement in your care-giver's job than if your child were in a more structured child care setting. You must set detailed guidelines while at the same time giving your care-giver ample room for independence.

When Anne's children were infants, she required her care-giver to give them a bath every day, but left it up to the provider to decide when to do so. Anne makes sure there is food in the house for lunch, but doesn't set any particular menu. Anne also does most of the scheduling of activities, but on days when none is scheduled, she leaves it to the provider to decide whether to play at home or at the park. While day care centers and family day care providers may require or encourage parental involvement, it is not the same as supervising (from work) what is going on at home. Whether this is an advantage or a disadvantage depends on your personality and your job.

USING A COMBINATION

We have treated the three basic forms of child care separately, though there are no bright lines between them. Some people use a combination. Carol Barrett and her husband sent their children to a family day care provider when they were babies. As the children got older, both went to a preschool program, but the family day care provider picked them up from preschool and brought them back to her house until Carol's husband came for them. Diana Manning's husband took care of their two children for almost two years while he was getting his master's degree. When he went back to work, they decided to send their children to preschool from 8 A.M. to 2 P.M. and hired college students to bring them home and care for them until Diana and her husband arrived. Just as you need to be flexible enough to recognize that your child care needs change as your children get older, so, too, can child care arrangements be designed to fit your changing needs.

Making the Decision

No one but you can make the right child care choice for your family, and you should ask yourself certain questions when making a decision. The first set of questions has two basic components: time and money.

TIME

Try to be *really* honest and realistic about your hours and work schedule when considering the options. Ann Muscari and Wenda W. Morrone, the authors of *Child Care That Works* warn, "The single greatest cause of failure with child care doesn't lie with the caregiver but with parents who try to get by with less care than they really need and then spend their days sliding for bases."

If emergency projects appear at 5 P.M. more than once or twice a year, don't talk yourself into thinking that you can get to a day care center or family day care provider by 5:30 or 6 P.M. every day.

Patricia Morales Wright is the only orthopedic surgeon in a hundred-mile area in rural Nevada; emergency surgeries at the end of the day are inevitable. When she went back to work after her first son, Tabor, was born, she started taking him to a baby-sitter. "She was wonderful," recalls Patricia, "but my life was incredibly hectic. The baby had to be out of there by six at the latest, so I would end up calling people to go get him." The Wrights soon changed their arrangement, and began using a live-in care-giver. In such a case, the emotional costs and stresses associated with getting to the provider in time just aren't worth the savings on child care costs, and you may well find yourself paying for it anyway in late fees or extra baby-sitting costs.

MONEY

Similarly, talking yourself into spending twice as much as you can really afford on child care doesn't work either. Child care is generally the third or fourth largest household expense. You and your husband have to budget for it just as you budget for other household expenses. The good news is that quality and cost are not always synonymous: An excellent family day care provider can be cheaper than a mediocre day care center, and there is a significant range in what in-home care-givers are paid, even within the same community.

Deciding what you can afford for child care involves certain assumptions that differ from other financial decisions. It is not simply a matter of comparing your salary to a child care provider's fees, although many working mothers start out looking at child care costs this way. When they do, they find that there is not much left of their salary after child care and job-related expenses are deducted.

We believe this is the wrong way to look at child care expenses. It reinforces the idea that the mother is solely responsible for child care, including its financing. Rather, child care expenses should be reviewed as a responsibility *shared* by *both* parents, just like the mortgage or utility bills.

In addition, comparing child care expenses to your paycheck is shortsighted, especially if you are a professional whose earning

---

◆ THE GAP WIDENS

The costs to women of dropping out of the work force, even for relatively short periods such as a year or two, are significant—you may never reach the salary level you would have attained if you had stayed in the work force.[4] This wage gap has a lot to do with most employers' feeling that a woman who has taken time off from her career to raise children cannot be committed to her work.

---

potential increases with experience. Child care is, in part, an investment in your future earning potential, and the costs of child care should be viewed with this long-term perspective.

Lastly, mothers who stay at home will need—and pay for—some of the same items that working mothers need and pay for. While an at-home mother may not need full-time child care, she will need occasional baby-sitting. According to a report in the *New York Times*, a 1989 study by the Bureau of Labor Statistics says that dual career families spend only 18 percent more for child care than families in which the wife doesn't work. In addition, expenses for clothes, transportation, lunch, and the like do not simply evaporate when you are no longer working. The numbers can be deceiving, so think through child care costs carefully before you make a permanent career decision based on them.

LOCATION

Besides time and money, consider a third factor: location, location, location (as they say in the real estate business). The added time it takes in the morning and at the end of the day getting children to and from child care is time that you have to carve out of something else: sleep in the morning or work in the evening. Even a little time (say, half an hour) can add a lot of stress. The closer you are to your child care, the more flexibility you have to respond to calls from the child care provider if your son is too sick to stay, or your daughter cut her lip and needs stitches. While these emergencies do not happen often, knowing that you can respond to them easily reduces your overall stress level.

It was this kind of reasoning that led Carol Barrett and her husband, when she worked in Washington, D.C. and he worked in Annapolis, Maryland, to decide *not* to live someplace in between. Rather, they decided to live where one parent (in this case Carol's husband) was near both his work and the kids' family day care provider.

Ellen Bonkoski, a chemist and mother of four school-age children who lives outside the Los Angeles area, agrees that location is key. "I look for things in proximity," she says. "My work is five miles from home. The family day care provider was near home. Now, the school is just down the street from work. Our doctor and dentist are within a few miles from work, so if emergencies come up, they are close." Of course, the quest for convenience should be — and will be — tempered by the quality of care that is available; no parent makes child care decisions based on convenience alone.

THE NATURE OF CARE

Figuring out what kind of care you want from your child care arrangement is harder than it sounds. Do you want a warm, nurturing person who will give your child a lot of love but may not get around to teaching him his shapes and colors? Or do you want someone who will organize his play with these lessons in mind? Do you want your child to interact with lots of other kids or have more individual adult attention? If you decide on in-home care, do you want someone who will do your laundry and make your bed as well as change diapers, or do you consider housework a separate responsibility?

♦ THE CHILD CARE DECISION

- ♦ What trade-offs are right for you?
- ♦ What are reasonable expectations?
- ♦ How will your needs change over time?

Don't think of your child care provider as your clone: She cannot and should not be just like you. On the other hand, you should seek to have as much consistency of care as possible, given that your care-giver is not you, and vice versa. What we mean by "consistency" is that her approach to raising children should be similar to yours, including how to discipline, give positive feedback, encourage independence, comfort and console, and learn from experience and play.

You may find yourself fantasizing about "the perfect care-giver" who will devote her attention completely and constantly to your child. But, let's face it, you probably don't spend every second paying attention to or entertaining your child when you are with him; you shouldn't expect (or necessarily want) someone else to do so either. When forming your expectations, try to put yourself in your child care provider's shoes to give yourself a sense of reasonable expectations.

Your child care needs and expectations will change as your children grow. For example, while your child is an infant you will probably look for a high degree of one-on-one attention, which is found most often in a family day care provider or in-home care arrangement. As your child grows into the toddler and preschool ages, you may look for more social contact and stimulation. You may consider a day care center at this point. Precisely because of the changing nature of the decision, you should approach it one stage at a time. You should think about your needs in roughly two-year intervals, even if any particular arrangement doesn't last that long—which is fairly likely, given the high turnover in the child care area.

The Search

Looking for child care is an exercise in resourcefulness and persistence. We have always started by checking the classified ads and asking everyone we know (and some we don't know) for tips or leads. You'd be surprised at how many people you can ask. Hang out at the playground and ask other parents. Ask co-workers, the librarian, the people at your local Y or community center. Go to preschools and day care centers and check out their bulletin boards. You can even ask the teachers there if they know of any providers. Churches and synagogues usually have bulletin boards where you can place a notice or where care-givers may advertise that they are available. Ask your pediatrician and her staff if they know of any child care opportunities.

ADS AND AGENCIES

Some day care centers and even family day care providers advertise in local newsletters or parents' magazines. For example, in our area there is a local family-oriented magazine that carries such ads. If you don't see any ads, call these publications directly and ask them if they know of good centers or referral services.

There are governmental and nonprofit agencies that help find child care. You can get a list of agencies in your area that help locate legally operating child care of all kinds from the National Association of Child Care Resource and Referral Agencies. If you decide on family day care, the National Association for Family Day Care publishes a directory and can help locate referral agencies in your area. If you decide on in-home care, the International Nanny Association publishes a national directory of in-home care-giver training and placement agencies, and the American Council of Nanny Schools keeps a register of graduates from nanny-training programs around the country. More information on these organizations is listed in Appendix B. In addition to these resources, you can check with the government agency in your state or county that is involved in licensing and regulating child care centers and family day care providers.

If you decide on in-home child care, you can advertise the position or use a placement agency. Advertising can mean anything from putting up notices on bulletin boards at your pediatrician's office or local preschool, to placing a help wanted ad in your local newspaper (many have a "domestic help" section in the want ads). If you live in a large metropolitan area, there are usually a couple of small newspapers that are "known" in the baby-sitter community. For example, when Carol decided to hire a live-out baby-sitter, she learned that the publication everyone advertised in was a small community newspaper called *The Irish Echo*. Even though it's a paper targeted to New York's Irish community, Carol received calls from potential care-givers whose nationalities spanned the globe.

Your advertisement needs to be specific enough to inform applicants of your minimum requirements but general enough so you can negotiate other items. You need to indicate the hours of the job and requirements such as driving or cooking or cleaning. You can leave salary vague (as in "competitive salary") because

---

◆ CLASSIFIED AD

Child Care Provider: Need loving, warm care-giver, reliable as a rock, to care for perfect child. Requirements: Be the ideal person for us. Salary: Only what we can afford, but you will have the reward of knowing that you are helping parents feel wonderful about going to work in the morning and excited about coming home. *Call immediately.*

---

there are significant discrepancies in what people expect to be paid. We have found it best to ask the applicant how much she wants and then negotiate from there.

You need to be prepared to handle the calls you get, especially if you live in a large urban area. The first day her ad ran in the local paper was a nightmare, explains Leslye Katz, chief financial officer at a division of The Dun & Bradstreet Corporation in New York. "I got all these calls and I didn't have a clue what I was doing," she says. "The phone kept ringing and I kept trying to ask intelligent questions to people who could barely speak English. By the time Gary [her husband] got home, I had had at least thirty calls. I handed him the phone and announced that I wasn't taking one more call."

Similarly, when Carol placed her first ad, she received over one hundred calls. To handle this volume, you absolutely will need an answering machine and a notebook or some other way to keep track of the calls.

If you do not have the time to wait for responses to an ad, you can use placement agencies. They will give you a list of prospective providers based on your job description and let you interview whomever you want. In addition, some agencies will replace a provider if she leaves abruptly or if you are unhappy with her. Most agencies claim to screen their providers' backgrounds, such as their health and criminal records. For their services, most agencies require you to pay a fee that is some multiple of the provider's weekly salary; a few require the child care provider to pay the fee.

While agencies can be extremely helpful, you should approach them with some degree of caution. Many of them are seat-of-the-pants operations that do not last more than a year or so. To protect yourself, use an agency that has been in business for a while. You may even want to ask the agency for references and talk with other people who have used the agency. Make sure you know precisely what the agency's fee covers, such as whether the agency will find you a new care-giver if the first one doesn't work out. Also, find out how the agency performs its screening and ask to see the files of any applicants the agency refers to you.

Au Pair Agencies

If you are looking for an "au pair" from Europe, there are certain agencies that match American families with young European women and men under the approval of the United States Information Agency. These agencies typically charge a flat fee for their services. The government gives these au pairs permission to work in this country as child care providers for a year and sets requirements governing their hours (forty-five hours a week), responsibilities (only child care duties—no general household duties and *definitely* no cleaning), vacation (two paid weeks during the year), and the like. (American au pairs obviously are not governed by the same restrictions.)

Au pairs are by far the cheapest form of in-home care: Due partly to government rules, they can only be paid a stipend of roughly $100 to $150 per week. On the other hand, because the au pairs come from Europe, you can interview them only by phone before you decide to hire them. Even if they turn out to be as lovely in person as on the phone, the one-year limitation is a significant drawback. While twelve months sounds like a long time, when you consider adjustment time at the beginning (a good month) and "winding down" or withdrawal time at the end (another month), you really only have him or her for ten good months. These months fly by, and the turnover can be difficult for both you and your kids.

Hiring Your Child Care

Sooner or later, you will actually have to choose a specific center or care-giver. First you will have to interview potential providers, which usually involves a two-step process: the first cut and the final decision. The initial conversation, which can be on the phone, should establish both that the situation and provider meet your minimum qualifications; the second stage is an in-person interview. What questions you ask depend on what kind of child care arrangement you decide on.

DAY CARE CENTERS

If you are investigating day care centers, make sure to talk with people on the staff as well as the director. Find out how long most staff members have worked at the center and what their qualifications are. Find out what its "sick child" policies are and how the center communicates with parents.

FAMILY DAY CARE

In the case of a family day care provider, the first conversation should cover how many children she cares for and their ages; what her hours are; how flexible she is; and other concerns such as whether she smokes or has pets. During the second interview you should get a good sense of how she structures the children's day, what her approach is to discipline, what backup she provides when she gets sick or goes on vacation, and how she involves and communicates with parents.

On-Site Visits

If you decide to bring your child to either a day care center or family day care provider, you *must* visit the sites to determine whether the facilities are maintained according to basic health and safety standards. Check to make sure the diaper-changing area is not next to the food-preparation area; that exits are clearly marked and unobstructed; that there are no exposed outlets or wires; that the outdoor area around the center or home is securely enclosed. While on your site visit, observe the staff or provider interacting with children, including how discipline is handled, conflicts among children resolved, and the like. A checklist to use when visiting a day care center or family day care provider is included in Appendix C.

IN-HOME PROVIDERS

If you are interviewing for an in-home position, get the basics during your first conversation: name, phone number, where they live (to gauge how easy it will be for them to get to your home), prior experience, work authorization, and references. You should also give them a good sense of the job. For example, do you expect your laundry done as well as the baby's? Do you want her to do any cleaning or other housework? Do you insist on homemade rather than store-bought baby food? Will you need her to work late on a frequent or occasional basis? Write down your impressions of your conversation, including the applicant's response to your job requirements. Try to get an idea of whether she is truly interested in the job.

In-Person Interviews

From these first conversations, decide whom you want to interview in person. Your questions during the interviews should explore the candidates' motivations for doing this kind of work, how long a commitment they are willing to make, what duties they have performed in the past, how they deal with discipline, what kind of food they like to prepare, and which activities they enjoy doing with children. During these interviews you can negotiate salary and specific job details.

Record your impressions from the interviews in your notebook. Keep your notebook, even after you hire someone: It is a treasure of information that can come in handy the next time you—or your friends—are looking for child care. When Anne first moved to New York and was looking for a live-out babysitter, she didn't have to place an ad: She used the short list of good applicants that Carol had developed!

You may find yourself selling the job and your kids to the potential provider rather than the other way around. Of course, you want to be friendly and make your child seem a pleasure to take care of. Resist the temptation, however, to adjust your criteria or job description for the person or center that seems wonderful but doesn't match your basic requirements. In all cases, avoid leading questions, such as, "You would never spank a child, would you?" Let the provider speak for herself—and listen carefully.

Backup Is Hard to Do

Only the most organized (and clairvoyant) among us actually think to have a backup plan for child care emergencies — before the emergency occurs. For the years when Anne's ailing grandmother lived with Anne's family, Anne had a de facto backup arrangement in the form of the person who took care of her grandmother. However, when her grandmother passed away and her care-giver moved on, Anne ended up relying on her friends in crises. While there's nothing like a child care emergency to create a feeling of community, you cannot assume your friends and neighbors will be available.

If you decide to use a family day care provider or day care center, it is not unreasonable to put the burden of organizing backup on them. In addition, as discussed in more detail in Chapter 6, child care reference and referral services offered by some employers can be used to help find last-minute child care when your own system falls through. If your company does not offer such a service, you can contact a local placement agency directly. If you have in-home care, you can also set up arrangements with other working mothers with in-home care to be each other's backup.

For most parents, though, backup consists of deciding which parent is going to stay home when the child is sick or the caregiver has her own family emergency. Working parents have come up with various ways of sharing the backup responsibility, from having the mom do it always (not such a great system) to splitting shifts. Our favorite is the system developed by Diana Manning and her husband, Brian. When one of their kids gets sick, Brian stays home the first day, and Diana makes sure everyone at her office knows that Brian is home tending their sick child. This lends instant credibility to the situation, because people assume that if her husband stayed home, the child must *really* be sick. When Diana says she has to stay home the second day, no one questions her.

Child Care Tax Credits

If you have child care expenses that you can document, then you may be able to take advantage of the federal child care tax credit.

As you might expect, the IRS has a complicated set of tests to determine if you qualify for the credit, but it boils down to this: If both you and your spouse work (or if you are single or divorced and work), and if your child lives with you, you will probably be able to claim the tax credit. To take advantage of the tax credit, you will have to provide your care-giver's Social Security number. If you are already receiving a child care tax benefit through your employer, you *may* not be eligible for the credit.

The maximum amount of the credit (which is taken off the top of any taxes you owe) is $2,400 for one child, or $4,800 total for two or more children. Calculating the precise amount of the credit that you can claim is too complicated to detail here, but the credit is substantial enough to be worth checking with your accountant or calling the IRS directly for more detailed information.

The Role of Child Care in Your Life

Many working mothers, especially those raised by stay-at-home moms, worry that child care will have long-term, harmful effects on their children. It's hard to envision your role as a mother when you are at work all day and someone else is at home with your child. For many mothers, this fear first takes the form of, "What if my baby thinks the care-giver is his mother instead of me?"

When Carol returned to work after her first maternity leave, one of her greatest concerns was that her six-month-old baby, spending four days a week with a baby-sitter, might be confused about who was her mother and who was the baby-sitter. We can say only that no one will ever replace you, and your child will always know the difference between you and his baby-sitter. It's natural to have insecurities, but you will just have to trust us and the thousands of other women who have gone back to work: Your child will never treat anyone but you as his mother.

A close friend adopted her second son as an infant. He spent a lot more time with his child care provider (a live-in baby-sitter) than with his adoptive mother, yet he always knew that she was his mother, gravitating to her when she was home. Looking back, his mother wonders how he knew, although ultimately it doesn't really matter. If the baby always knows, then you too should always be confident that you are the parent, and therefore the person in charge.

This is not to say that child care doesn't affect your role as a parent to your child. You will have to share your child with others; you will have to accept that he may at times feel more comfortable sharing certain things with his care-giver than with you. You and your care-giver may differ in where you draw the line: when to give in to a particular demand ("one more candy, *please*") and when to stand firm. At times, you will have to accept the care-giver's decision.

On the other hand, a care-giver can be a friend and a teacher. "Our family day care provider taught me about my kids and how to teach them things," says Ann Huang. As a new mother, Leslye Katz readily admits that she learned a lot from her care-giver: "I learned some coping skills from her, by seeing how smoothly she would handle situations that to me seemed like crises."

Debbie Reed, a high school English teacher, was a single mother when she moved to Nevada and had to search for affordable child care for her two toddlers. She found a family day care provider who cared for her daughters for six years and now takes care of a third daughter, Hannah, born to Debbie and her new husband three years ago. "She saved my life," says Debbie. "I couldn't have moved here and done what I did [including getting a master's degree while teaching full-time] without her."

You know that child care is working when, like Ann, Leslye, and Debbie, you feel that it is an integral and positive part of your family's life.

6

CHILD CARE BENEFITS: GETTING YOUR EMPLOYER TO CARE

Employers' responsibilities toward working mothers do not end when maternity leave starts; in fact, it's just the beginning. More far-reaching than maternity leave are issues of child care benefits and other family-related supports. Unfortunately, most companies have yet to appreciate fully the importance of child care benefits; more likely, they are still congratulating themselves over having adopted a maternity leave policy. Employers who do not provide child care programs endorse, at least implicitly, the Superwoman myth. These employers place the responsibility (and therefore the blame) for child care conflicts on you, instead of accepting a share of the responsibility by developing policies or programs to ease the burden.

Just as you may find yourself persuading your employer to adopt reasonable maternity leave policies, you may have to do the same for child care. In fact, your educational function is even more critical in the child care area, because, unlike pregnancy rights, for which there are federally mandated minimum requirements, there are no laws requiring employers to address their employees' child care needs.

Some governments have taken small steps in this area. The city of Los Angeles, for example, has created the position of "child care coordinator" and adopted a "child care policy" that, among other things, requires any vendor bidding on a city contract to state whether and what kind of child care policy it has, and gives vendors that have programs preference in certain circumstances. For the most part, however, government has done next to nothing to encourage, let alone ensure, quality child care.

In this chapter we arm you with the necessary information to show your employer the benefits of company child care policies, as well as information on the variety of child care benefits available and strategies on arguing your way to success.

The Cost of Avoidance . . .

Study after study has documented what any working mother can tell you: finding stable, high-quality child care is critical to combining work and family responsibilities. The spillover effect of child care on work is tremendous. For example:

> In eight company surveys [performed between 1985 and 1990], about half of the women and more than a third of the men contend that child care responsibilities affect work to some degree. . . . A survey of the Adolph Coors Company found more than one-third (36 percent) of employees reported a decline in productivity due to the child care problems of *co-workers*.[1]

Similarly, a survey of Honeywell Corp.'s workers performed in the early 1980s showed that

> Twenty-five percent of their working parents said child care problems caused stress at work and lowered their productivity. One-third had to make new child-care arrangements two or three times a year.[2]

A 1990 child care survey of twenty-three hundred employed mothers found that "15 percent reported some lost time from work, and 6 percent reported lost days from work *during the past month* because of child care breakdowns."[3] Conversely, one study has shown that good child care is the most significant factor in relieving the stress of balancing work and family, more than marital happiness or success at work.[4]

Employers are clearly affected by their employees' child care concerns, but most employers have barely begun to take steps

---

♦ WHO PAYS?

Employees' child care problems cost companies money. The Child Care Action Campaign, an advocacy group, estimates that child care "breakdowns" cost American companies three billion dollars per year.[5] According to a study by the Los Angeles Department of Water and Power, the agency paid out one million dollars in one year to people who were absent because of child care.[6]

---

toward easing the child care strain. A 1988 survey by the U.S. Department of Labor of over ten thousand companies found that 89 percent of U.S. companies do not provide direct child care assistance to employees (not including flexible schedules that help parents deal with child care problems).[7] Only "2 percent of governmental employees were offered child care assistance."[8] The good news is that more and more companies are becoming interested in child care.

. . . FROM HIGH TURNOVER

When child care problems and other conflicts between work and family become unbearable, some working mothers leave their jobs, leading to high turnover. A 1990 survey of working mothers found that roughly 25 percent of working mothers left their previous jobs for family reasons, including child care problems.[9] While many managers would like to believe that these women drop out because their interest in pursuing careers was only fleeting, the reality is quite different. A retention study for a major accounting firm showed that women do leave more frequently than men. However, "contrary to the prevailing belief, they do not leave to take care of their families. They leave to take other jobs they describe as more predictable. They take positions where they may work just as hard, but they can count on certain regular hours and are able to make arrangements for dependable child care."[10]

Carol made such a move: She left private practice and now teaches law. Even though she teaches full-time and her law firm job was nominally part-time, the latter demanded that Carol always be available to clients and partners in emergencies, which made her hours unpredictable and required enormous flexibility. The pressure to accommodate these demands generated stress; after a while, Carol decided that the satisfaction she was getting from her job was not worth the stress. Her current job is much more predictable and flexible and, therefore, more manageable.

Companies and firms experiencing attrition and absenteeism because of work/family conflict would do well to implement low-cost child care programs, especially considering the odds, given undeniable demographics, that the company which just lost an employee to work/family conflicts will face similar work/family issues with the next employee.

The benefits of these programs to working mothers are not simply logistical. Because they indicate a sensitivity to working mothers and an attempt to deal with their problems directly, they signal a supportive work environment. Support and understanding from management go a long way toward easing work/family conflict; to many women, a supportive supervisor is critical to feeling that they are successfully balancing work and family.

The Pay-Off . . .

. . . IN LOWER TURNOVER

Concerned employers have found that investing in child care pays off in reduced turnover and higher productivity. Natalie Scott is a spokesperson for America West Airlines' child care program, which consists primarily of sponsoring a mixture of day care and family child care slots for the children of its employees. She says the program has resulted in lower absenteeism and turnover. "The child care program also serves as a recruitment tool," she says. "A study of the program done in 1991 showed that roughly one in four employees with children were influenced in their decision to work for the company by its child care program."

Many companies, and particularly those that rely heavily on skilled workers, find that having child care benefits significantly affects retaining employees and attracts top candidates.

"Chemists are in high demand and more than fifty percent of our employees are women," says Carol Miller, head of human resources for Lancaster Laboratories in Pennsylvania. "Before we opened our child care center in 1986, less than fifty percent of women taking maternity leave returned to work; now ninety-four percent return."

...AND HIGHER MORALE

But women aren't the only ones attracted to Lancaster Laboratories because of its child care benefits. "Candidates that would never use these benefits, such as older men whose children are grown, tell us they chose to work at Lancaster because the benefits demonstrate the company's commitment to its employees," explains Miller.

America West Airlines also values its child care program's effect on employee morale. "The company feels the program is cost-effective because of its positive effect on morale," explains Ms. Scott. Evidence of its importance is the fact that it has been untouched by the company's considerable downsizing in the last few years.

Some experts in the work and family field even foresee the day (in our lifetime, no less) when job applicants will routinely ask about a company's child care programs and expect an affirmative answer.

Where Employers Can Help

Most employers, even if they want to address the child care issue, do not know where to begin. They must first be educated about the nature of the child care market and then guided through the various programs that address weaknesses or holes in the market.

Most people are vaguely aware that there is a shortage of high-quality child care. But why? One reason has to do with changes in family structure. Twenty years ago, relatives cared for over 60 percent of children whose mothers worked.[11] By 1988, that figure was down to 40 percent.[12] This trend is expected to continue, resulting in a situation in which, at the same time that the need for child care is increasing, the availability of informal, family-based care is decreasing. Structured child care programs will become as much a necessity in the lives of working parents as transportation and housing.

On the other hand, the child care labor pool is unstable.

First, child care providers are, in general, poorly paid, earning well below what janitors earn, and usually receive no health, unemployment, or disability benefits. The *New York Times* reported that people who take care of animals in a zoo typically are paid more than child care workers. As a result, there is tremendous turnover in child care workers: 40 to 50 percent each year is not uncommon.[13]

Second, there are no universally enforced standards, leading to huge variations in quality. This stems in large part from a general societal attitude that child care is something that "anyone can do." (The low status, low pay, and high turnover associated with child care providers are interrelated.)

Lastly, even though the pay to providers is low, child care is expensive for parents. Good child care is by nature a labor-intensive business: low child/provider ratios are critical to good care.[14]

Employers, therefore, can help most by increasing the supply of structured child care programs and helping to stabilize and improve the child care profession.

The Wide Range of Child Care Benefits

While the media have focused on day care centers as the corporate benefit of choice, there are actually many different child care programs a company can offer that involve varying amounts of initial investment and ongoing administrative supervision. The programs fall into three categories: direct child care; resource and referral services; and financial support for child care expenses. (Flexible work schedules are another kind of response to working parents' child care needs. We take up the issue of flexibility at length in Chapter 8.)

DIRECT CHILD CARE

On-Site Centers

The most obvious—or visible—form of direct child care is the on-site day care center. Few companies that offer child care programs provide them on-site or near-site, however, because of their significant initial and ongoing costs. For example, according to the Chicago *Tribune,* the cost estimate to establish an on-site center in 1988 was five to seven thousand dollars per child in the Chicago area. Beside cost, zoning can be a major issue, particularly in large metropolitan areas. Safety codes usually dictate that a child care facility be located on the first or second floor of a building, a space requirement that can be prohibitively expensive in big cities.[15]

Even so, more and more employers of all sizes are investing in this option. CMP Publications, a twenty-year-old company in New York, has between twelve and thirteen hundred employees. It had been operating an informal on-site after-school and vacation program for its employees' children, when it decided to do a more formal survey of its employees' child care needs. This led, in 1987, to the decision to construct an on-site day care center, which opened in 1988. CMP financed the center itself and charges a sliding-scale rate based on an employee's salary.

Dunning, Forman, Kirrane & Terry, a law firm of eight attorneys and fifteen support staff on Cape Cod, had provided day care stipends to its employees for some time. However, parents were having an increasingly hard time finding care. "It became evident that it was a lot of work just arranging to come to work," says Pamela Terry, one of the firm's partners. In 1987, the firm moved into a new building owned in part by some of the firm's partners. They decided to build a day care facility in the basement and first floor of the building for use by its occupants.

"Our employees come from all over the Cape," explains Terry. "We figured that it would be easier to have child care where everyone works." The firm subsidizes the center's fees, as well as the child care expenses of employees who choose not to use the center. "These child care benefits are a way of attracting people to the firm and keeping them here," says Terry. "There's a lot of competition for good people, and we have close to zero turnover."

John Hancock Financial Services (the parent corporation to the insurance company), a large international company with over fifty-five hundred employees at its headquarters in Boston, built an on-site center in Boston in 1990. The company decided to do so based on a survey of its employees' work and family issues.

"The center made good business sense in terms of attracting and then retaining people," says Katharine Hazzard, work/family program coordinator for Hancock. "If it hadn't made good business sense, who knows what would have happened, but it did and it was a good thing to do for our employees. In addition, several women have told me that they came back to work after maternity leave sooner than they would have otherwise because of the day care center. They felt comfortable coming back to work knowing that they could see their babies during the day."

Even when employers put up the capital for a center, they do not necessarily manage it. Many enter into arrangements with outside child care organizations—whether it be a nonprofit educational group or a for-profit consulting firm. Lancaster Laboratories and Dunning, Forman contract out their day care center operation. On the other hand, the people who work at CMP Publications' center are employees of the company who are entitled to the same benefits as other employees. As a result, there is very little turnover in the day care center staff.

Some companies that cannot afford (or do not want) to build an on-site center for their use alone have teamed up with other companies and labor organizations to finance these ventures. The Chinatown Day Care Center in New York City is financed by a consortium of union, city, and local business groups. The Children's Place outside of Boston is financed by a group of companies in the Prospect Hill Office Park. IBM, American Express, Allstate Insurance, Duke Power, and University Research Park, a developer, teamed up in Charlotte, North Carolina, to build a two-million-dollar, 194-child day care center.

Reserving Space

Companies also can "sponsor" existing centers or family child care providers. Under this arrangement, a company contracts with existing child care facilities, including family child care providers and day care centers, to reserve a certain number of slots for children of the company's employees. America West Airlines chose this approach because its employees have extremely varied schedules and live throughout the Phoenix metropolitan area. The company decided that a single on-site center would not work as well as having its employees choose from among numerous scattered facilities.

Increasing the Supply of Child Care

The American Business Collaboration for Quality Dependent Care, conceived by IBM and joined by over one hundred other companies, has established a twenty-five-million-dollar fund used to recruit, train, and license child care professionals, usually family day care providers, in the communities where these companies have employees. Similarly, a consortium of companies around Rochester, New York, organized to provide low-cost group health benefits for child care providers in the area. These efforts increase the supply of child care and stabilize the profession, thereby giving employees more and better child care options.

Helping with Child Care Emergencies

Rather than address the need for basic child care, some companies have chosen to target their assistance to child care emergencies — of which sick children ranks the most common by far — because they create so much stress for working parents. For example, Minnesota Mining and Manufacturing (3M) in St. Paul has an arrangement with a home-health agency that runs a program for sick children called TenderCare for Kids. A 3M employee can call TenderCare for Kids when his or her child is sick, and the service will send a health care worker to stay home with the sick child. 3M subsidizes some of the cost of this help. Both John Hancock and Lancaster Laboratories have added "mildly sick" rooms to their on-site day care centers. These facilities allow employees to go to work even when their children have a runny nose and cannot attend their regular child care.

Cravath, Swaine & Moore, a large law firm in New York City, has a fully staffed child care emergency center at the office (in operation since 1989) that allows employees to bring their children to work when their care-giver is sick or on vacation, or when day care centers are closed but the firm is not. Both Salomon Brothers and Goldman, Sachs & Company, two large investment banks on Wall Street, opened similar facilities in 1993.

Recognizing that sometimes parents simply have to stay home with their sick children, John Hancock allows its employees to use up to three of their allotted sick days each year as family illness days. "You can call in and say you are staying home because your daughter has chicken pox, even though you are feeling fine," explains Katharine Hazzard.

Some child care "crunches" are predictable: School is on vacation and you're not, for example. Some companies have established programs for their employees' children to keep them busy (and keep their parents at work) during those times. Besides the day care center, John Hancock runs a program called "Kids-to-go" that organizes field trips and other activities for employees' children during one-day school holidays and spring break. As a result of Hancock's various programs, Katharine Hazzard, herself a working mother, has to worry about child care only on days when school is closed because of snow.

If you are interested in getting your employer to consider one of these child care benefits, and want to find out what other companies are doing in your area, you can start by reading the most recent "100 Best Companies for Working Mothers," an annual report on family-friendly corporate programs published in *Working Mother* magazine. You can also contact the Child Care Action Campaign, whose address and phone number are included in Appendix B.

RESOURCE AND REFERRAL SERVICES

Resource and referral programs can take many forms, but their basic purpose is to help employees find good quality child care in their area—whether permanent or emergency backup care. In 1988, over eight hundred companies provided this type of service, which commonly involves an agreement between a company and an outside child care consulting firm that allows the company's employees to call the firm and get child care referrals.[16] Work/Family Directions, a consulting firm based in Boston, was one of the first to offer such a service nationwide, and IBM was one of its first clients. Since IBM has 220,000 employees in more than 400 locations in 50 states, the referral service made more sense than on-site day care.

Child Care Database lists licensed family day care providers and day care centers nationwide. You can search the database by ZIP code as well as by type of child care. The database is offered through the Human Resource Information Network, an on-line system that allows a user to access numerous other human resource and labor databases. Most of the network's subscribers are human resource professionals. Subscription to the Network costs roughly fifteen hundred dollars a year (plus the hourly rate) and is available from National Standards Association, 1200 Quince Orchard Boulevard, Gaithersburg, MD 20878; (800) 638-8094.

FINANCIAL SUPPORT

Financial support from your employer can come in the form of subsidies for child care expenses or benefits. Companies that sponsor slots in day care centers, for example, may also underwrite part of the cost. Some companies, such as Polaroid, offer child care vouchers.

In addition to direct financial support, employers can set up a dependent care assistance plan, under which the employee can elect to contribute up to five thousand dollars of compensation each year, which will not be subject to income tax. This money must be used on child care (or other dependent care) expenses. This plan comes with certain restrictions, and cannot be used simultaneously with the child care tax credit. The program does not cost employers anything (except to administer the program), so even small employers can afford it. According to the *Monthly Labor Review*, these plans or accounts are the most prevalent child care benefit.

EMPLOYEES NEED CARE TOO

Some employers have gone beyond helping working parents find child care to providing support in dealing with the personal issues related to combining work and family. They offer parenting workshops that deal with family issues such as guilt, discipline, and the transition between parental and provider child care, as well as work-related issues such as handling stress, time management at work, and making use of child care benefits such as the tax credit. These employers have come a long way toward recognizing that the bright line between work and family spheres is fading.

Talking Your Employer into Child Care

Employers must be alerted to child care problems, but we don't suggest that you blurt out your problems to the next supervisor who walks by. The more measured and informed your approach, the more likely your success.

Just as in asking for maternity leave, assess which supervisor has the greatest ability to empathize with work/family issues. If you are reluctant to talk with him or her, look for an existing forum—such as a task force on women or employee benefits—to approach management as a group. If there isn't a forum, consider creating one. Management is more likely to consider seriously the request of many people with a common problem.

This is the approach some women on Wall Street used. Female employees at Bankers Trust began meeting informally to discuss workplace issues, including work and family problems. As these informal gatherings attracted more and more women, a more formal organization, the Global Partnership Network for Women, was established. The network invites speakers to address a wide range of women's concerns, circulates a newsletter to roughly six hundred employees, and has written a position paper on how to foster leadership roles for women at Bankers Trust. The paper, presented to a management committee, has received a very positive response.

"The network has helped create a better working environment for women," says a female vice president at the bank, "by bringing more attention to certain issues, and by giving women a chance to talk to each other."

CREATING YOUR OWN SUPPORT BASE

If you have to create your own support base, make it as broad as possible. Remember to involve the fathers. "Be careful not to make child care simply a woman's issue, because it's not. It's a work force issue," advises Katharine Hazzard. "Fathers use these benefits as well as mothers. You lose potential leverage when you talk about these issues as affecting women only."

Get information from both mothers and fathers on their child care problems and gather specifics on time spent worrying about these problems at work, time taken off from work to care for sick children or deal with other child care emergencies, and what happens during holidays and summer break.

Be prepared to present a list of possible solutions. Prepare a list on what your company's competition is doing (unless, of course, they aren't doing anything). Talk with the people who run other corporations' child care programs. You can also talk with corporate child care consultants, but you may have to pay them for their advice. Consultants can help you design alternative solutions as well as present solutions in a palatable way to managers who may not have thought of these issues before.

Lastly, consider the timing of any presentation. Is your company about to post record losses, or is it in a fairly stable condition? Is the firm involved in a major campaign or new project, or is work proceeding at a regular pace? Clearly, it is better to present a child care benefits proposal to management when it is not under a great deal of stress.

Also, if you are spearheading such an effort, how you are perceived around the time of your proposal is important to its success. If you have just come back to work and are trying to dissipate your colleagues' "commitment doubts," wait until you have shown that you are indeed capable of doing the same work even though you are now a mother as well as a professional.

Convincing your company to care may seem like an overwhelming task, given the other demands on your time. But the investment will pay huge dividends—in both your life and the lives of your colleagues. Not only will you receive practical help dealing with a very real issue, but child care programs lead to changes in the way that working mothers are perceived. They help dissipate the Superwoman myth. And this is in everyone's interest.

7

GOING BACK TO WORK

The time has come. Your child care arrangements are in place. You have chosen your most attractive outfit. You've checked the train or bus schedule to make sure it hasn't changed since you had the baby. Now you're thinking, "What is work going to be like?"

Returning to work after a maternity leave is both terrifying and exhilarating. Your first days of balancing your job with the host of responsibilities, demands, and satisfactions that remain at home may seem overwhelming. On the other hand, after living in the irrational, unpredictable world of a newborn baby, it can be a relief to return to the familiar workday routines that you mastered successfully in the past.

The First Day

When you walk through the door you will be struck by how little the workplace has changed in your absence. *You've* undergone one of the most dramatic transformations a typical adult will ever experience: You've become a parent. At work, however, papers pile up and the telephone rings incessantly, just as before. The sameness can be almost eerie, as if you are a character in *Invasion of the Body Snatchers:* It's as if you are masquerading as the person you were before. Your face is the same, but the emotions behind it have been rearranged, because your life now has a whole new dimension.

Take time to adjust to your changed working persona. Unless your boss or clients have been chomping at the bit to throw assignments your way, ease back into a routine. Even if you have the same desk or work space, you will probably need to replenish the supply of pens or prescription pads. There will almost certainly be a stack of mail and periodicals to wade through. (You remember, the ones you were going to have plenty of time to peruse while you were on maternity leave . . .) If you're lucky, someone will take you out to lunch, at least on the first day, and you will have a chance to catch up on all the gossip. And, if your co-workers are at all civilized, they will tell you how slim you look and how beautiful your baby's pictures are.

This is not to say you won't feel anxious about leaving the baby. The amount of anxiety you have about leaving your baby on the first day will be directly related to your confidence in your child care. If you feel comfortable that your child is being well taken care of and has already adjusted to the new care-giver, then all you have to worry about is *your* adjustment, rather than the baby's.

No matter how comfortable you are with your care-giver, you will almost certainly feel some sadness, or at least nostalgia, at leaving the first stage of parenting behind. Many women share the same experience on the first day: They hug and kiss their babies, smile bravely, and go off to work, only to burst into tears as soon as they are out of the house. It helps to bring lots of baby pictures and look at them often. (Teddy bears and blankies are not recommended, however; your baby might need them.) Don't be afraid to call your care-giver several times during that first day; each call should increase your comfort by reassuring you that all is well with the baby.

Beyond the First Day

As you get back into the office routine, you will discover that doing the work itself is not as difficult as you had imagined. When she returned to work after six months away (the longest time away from school or work she had ever had) Carol was worried that she would have trouble picking up old projects. In fact, in a telling sign of the glacial pace of the legal process, most of her cases seemed to be at the same point as when she left, although other lawyers had been working diligently on them for six months. Susan Mirkinson, a doctor, found that for the first week or so she would have to take an extra split second to remember the entire list of medications appropriate for a particular ailment, but it all came back to her soon enough.

You too will find that, however long your leave, your professional knowledge has not leaked out of you with the breast milk. You may even get the chance to surprise those colleagues who think that caring for babies is a mindless activity and, therefore, anyone who cares for them is, herself, mindless. When Carol remembered an obscure fact from one of her cases shortly after her return to work, one lawyer remarked admiringly, "You haven't missed a beat!" Maybe he had assumed that six months with a newborn baby would turn her brain into scrambled eggs; she was pleased to torpedo that myth.

HOME THOUGHTS

Another stereotype is that working mothers are always thinking about their children while at work. Neither we, nor the women we spoke to, experienced this "one mind in two places" problem. Sure, we call our care-givers once or sometimes twice a day to check up on things or relay information. But don't most men talk to their wives (if not their children or their children's care-givers) at least that often? Just as talking to your wife doesn't mean that your mind is on your marriage all day long, talking to your kids or care-giver doesn't mean you can't concentrate on anything else.

For some women, going back to work is simple. "I have to admit, I went back to work and *I went to work.* I didn't call home every half hour, or anything like that," says K.K. Gerhart-Fritz. However, even if you can't imagine leaving your baby to go to work, once you're back at work, you'll feel much better about it.

"The transition back to work was actually a lot easier when I got really busy," says Elizabeth Cheng Krist, a photography editor. "I just didn't have time to think about Anna constantly."

TIME CHANGES

While your work habits do not change, you will almost certainly adjust your work hours. Professionals who don't have significant family responsibilities can allow their working hours to fill up their waking hours — if they wish. You can no longer afford such extravagance. Even if time was already your most valuable commodity before you had a child, it will be even more precious now. No matter what type of child care you have chosen, at a certain point of every day (or at least most days) you need to walk away from work, because there is a care-giver waiting to be relieved and a child waiting to be picked up, or fed his dinner, or just hugged.

Now you leave when you *must* leave, instead of when you feel like it. This has an impact not only on your schedule but on how you pace yourself during the day. You may feel more pressure about completing projects, because you don't have the built-in cushion of overtime. You will almost definitely become more efficient, realizing that you do not really need all the time you previously devoted to accomplishing particular tasks.

Before having her baby, Sharon Cohen never left the office before 7 P.M. Now she has a nanny who must leave at 6 P.M., so she walks out the door of her office at 5. "I'm leaving way before anyone at my level leaves. I take a lot of work home. I might do two hours of reading at home after the baby is asleep, and on weekends. . . . As a result, . . . I have become very efficient both in terms of time and in terms of focus."

"When I am at work, I am very focused," concurs Ann Huang. "I don't take long lunches. I don't take coffee breaks. I don't shop. And yet all I want to do at the end of the day is go home to my kids. So it's not hard for me to leave at 5 P.M."

You may find that "lunch" takes on a whole new meaning once you go back to work. "I make the most use of my lunch hour as I can possibly make," says K.K. "I don't have the flexibility any more to work late, so I work through lunch. And I've become more efficient at what I do."

GOING PUBLIC

From the beginning lies the question of how public you want to make your working mother status. You won't be able to (or want to) hide the fact. Yet, how much do you want to remind your fellow employees that you have a new role? On the one hand, you should feel justifiable pride in motherhood. You may even have a private sense that you should be recognized or applauded for taking on the task.

On the other hand, you need to be prepared for the negative reactions. As we discussed earlier, some people may resent you for wanting to "have it all." Other people, who have accepted the idea that becoming a mother automatically dilutes your commitment, may be looking for "objective" proof of this notion. Elizabeth Cheng Krist describes one new mother in her department at a major magazine: "People were just much more critical of her performance, sort of looking for mistakes, . . . worrying about whether she was really up to speed."

If you suspect that there are people in your workplace (particularly superiors) who harbor these attitudes, you should not flaunt your motherhood. You are better advised to search out one or two colleagues whom you know you can count on to understand your new joys and stresses.

Don't Hide the Pictures . . . or the Emergencies

This does not mean hiding the baby pictures in your bottom desk drawer. We firmly believe in displaying pictures of your beautiful children. But it may mean refraining from worrying aloud to your boss about your daughter's sore throat. His immediate thought might be "I wonder if she'll be running to the pediatrician when I need her to do that presentation," thus nurturing any doubts he may have about your commitment. Instead, tell a friend whose immediate thought, like yours, is likely to be, "I hope it's not strep."

Don't, however, hide child care emergencies or other significant work/family conflicts from your boss and colleagues. The only way to change the perception that working mothers cannot do it all is to educate your boss and colleagues about the true nature of these conflicts. They arise and are handled just as any other personal matter. Life goes on and your work gets done.

But Be Careful with Clients and Customers

Being forthright with your colleagues and your supervisor is important. How you deal with your clients, patients, or customers is more delicate. There is nothing wrong in telling your client that you have to leave for a meeting at 6—even when the meeting happens to be a Girl Scout event you are hosting. After all, you wouldn't necessarily tell a client the details about your next client meeting. There is no advantage to being specific about your obligations outside the office.

However, your clients or customers do need to know that you routinely leave at five-thirty now instead of six-thirty. If you are evasive they may end up feeling deceived or betrayed, which leads to confusion, anger, and resentment—not attributes conducive to a successful long-term relationship. A much better approach is to explain your schedule and the procedure for getting assistance or reaching you during your off hours. Eventually, your clients will learn that you can service their needs within your schedule.

SETTING LIMITS

Even if you become really good at handling work and family, you will probably still have to deal with your colleagues' assumption that, once you have a family, you will always put them first—i.e., before your work. Somehow, having children seems to remind people that you have a life outside of work.

♦ FIRST THINGS FIRST

"My personal life absolutely comes first, just as it does for everyone," counters Diana Manning, an industrial real estate developer in Los Angeles. "I don't care who you are, we each take care of ourselves first. People just somehow don't see the way they operate in that light; they only see it that way when you have kids."

Ironically, the best way to deal with this perception is to be straightforward about your priorities. "My husband and my family come first, and I have always let my employers know that," says Ellen Bonkoski, a chemist. "I do not expect to work overtime unless there is a real emergency, and I expect not to be called in on Saturdays. They're pretty understanding if you let them know up front."

For some women, the problem is not how others perceive them, but how they perceive themselves. If you are used to doing everything that anyone at work asks you to do, it's hard to set limits. "Medicine is a very insidious thing," says Patricia Morales Wright. "There's always someone who is hurt and needs you. At some point you have to say, I can't do this for everybody. I have finally decided that I can't make everything great for everybody. Since I've had the baby, I've become very good at setting limits."

Setting limits is *not* the same as lowering your standards; it's actually a way of making sure you do not burn out trying to do everything at work and at home. A firm statement from you setting the tolerable level of intrusion is likely to be respected — and necessary to preserve your sanity.

MANAGING THE MANAGERS

Shaping your image as a working mother has to be done with an understanding of your different relationships at work. You also will need to distinguish between minor and major emergencies and to develop your own criteria for determining what falls into which category. Minor emergencies should be dealt with matter-of-factly and should disrupt your work only minimally. By dealing with small matters efficiently you'll sow the seeds of good will and flexibility in your boss and colleagues — which you will need for the major emergencies that are bound to occur occasionally.

While you have a great deal of control over your image, ultimately your ability to successfully combine work and family will depend to a significant degree on something over which you have no control: the people you work with, particularly your boss and his or her management style. What we mean by "successfully combine" is feeling good about what you are doing, despite the stress, pressure, doubt, and guilt you may sometimes experience.

♦ NURTURING LOYALTY

"Mothers who work for flexible bosses are seven times less likely to want to quit, and nearly four times as likely to say they love their jobs than women who work for inflexible bosses," concludes a study for *Working Mother* magazine performed by the Families and Work Institute.[1]

If your boss is flexible and supportive, chances are you will feel good; if your boss is inflexible and uncaring, chances are you won't.

Flexibility

The key attribute of management flexibility, from a working mother's perspective, is giving employees responsibility for their own schedule (within certain parameters, of course). After eight years as a mother in the work force, including a final year on a part-time schedule, Martha Stiven quit and eventually set up her own consulting practice.

"My boss at the time kept a strict time clock. My hours were eight to five, and there was *no* flexibility," says Martha. "I couldn't come in early if I needed to leave early. If I had spent the evening at a City Council meeting making a presentation, I was still expected to show up at work at eight the next morning. [My boss's] attitude accelerated my dilemma about whether to continue working. If I had been working for somebody fabulous, maybe this all would have turned out differently."

In contrast, Mary Ellen Schoonmaker has stayed at her job in part because "my boss has been very understanding and flexible. He is not a real clock puncher, as long as you get your work done." Mary Ellen has had offers to do freelance work, which would give her more time with her children, a commodity she is eager for. "But there is something that keeps me from doing it. I like where I am and I like what I do," she says. "Even though it's stressful in terms of hours and responsibility, I really enjoy it." An inflexible boss would probably have pushed Mary Ellen in the other direction.

Attitude

Managers' attitudes can affect your own attitude. When Tina Bailey first applied for a tenure-track professorship in chemistry at California Polytechnic State University, the department head told her that he did not think she could do the job, because she was a working mother. The faculty appointed her to the position anyway, and three years later Tina won a "distinguished teacher" award. In contrast, "the department head at the time of my tenure decision was very supportive of me and was a central reason for my being able to maintain a positive self-image and keep going," she says. She is now a full professor and mother of four adopted children.

Ann Huang, a geneticist on the technical staff of a nonprofit research organization, had a similar experience. "The first boss I had in my present job felt that mothers should not work," she explains. "In the end, I confronted the company about the problem and said that I would leave unless they transferred me. The company ended up transferring me and removing him from a managerial position."

It is unlikely that you will change the personalities of managers, and only you know whether you are willing to risk your job by requesting a different supervisor. However, more and more companies are stressing the importance of flexibility in management training and are educating their managers on work and family issues. There is light at the end of the tunnel.

Soul-Searching Again

During your first few months back on the job, you will probably spend a lot of time thinking about what you want from your work as well as what is important to you in your home life. The fact is, you don't have time for everything. You need to decide what is most important to you and how best to preserve and nurture those priorities.

Defining your goals will help you structure your job and family to accommodate each other. Aside from the financial reward of working (which for most people is the most prominent if not the only objective), there are many other sources of professional satisfaction: social interaction, a sense of accomplishment, professional advancement and status, intellectual challenge, and the pure enjoyment of the work itself. Consider which qualities are central to your satisfaction.

Many women, for example, discover while on maternity leave that interaction with people in a professional setting is, by itself, a source of pleasure; discussing the latest technological breakthrough or political controversy is something they miss intensely. If that's your feeling, be sure that your schedule allows you to spend time with colleagues and clients, instead of being locked away in your office or lab reading, researching, and writing. You are certainly not one who will ask for a home-based office. If, on the other hand, you find that professional status is important to your identity, you will need the flexibility to attend professional conferences and meetings, many of which occur in the evening or require travel. These goals are not necessarily mutually exclusive, but you'll have to choose your priorities.

GOAL SETTING

Defining your goals will involve more than picking out which aspects of your job are most important to you; it will mean coming to terms with your professional aspirations and how they fit into your new life as a working mother. Being comfortable with your ambition is key to feeling good about your life as a working mother.

The following three women lead very different lives, yet they combine work and family in remarkably similar ways that do not have to do with schedules, status, or systems, but with understanding what they want out of their lives.

Patricia Morales Wright, an orthopedic surgeon in private practice in a small town in northeastern Nevada, has a three-year-old son. She has the training and experience to have pursued the "fast track" in medicine: practicing in a large urban medical center, teaching, and doing research. Instead, she chose to settle in her husband's rural community, raise a family, and join a local clinic.

"I have a good friend from medical school who chose to stay in academics," says Patricia Morales Wright. "She's on the cutting edge in her field; she publishes papers and speaks at conferences around the country. She also commutes an hour to and from work—and has two children. She's one of the friends who warned me about the guilt. But, if I am really honest with myself, I have to admit I don't feel guilty. I don't have a whole lot of guilt because I like what I do. It's me, and I think I'm a better person if I get to do it."

"I feel like I'm very successful," Patricia says. "What's successful to me is going grocery shopping and running into the little old lady whose hip I put in last year, and she is bebopping down the aisle. That's how I measure my success."

Ellen Bonkoski, a chemist for a multinational company

outside the Los Angeles area, has four school-age boys. "There are higher levels that I could try to reach," Ellen acknowledges. "But, to be happy, to like what I'm doing, and to have time with my family is more important to me than clawing my way up the corporate ladder. I enjoy what I'm doing and I want to keep working, but I'm perfectly happy where I'm at."

Ann Huang spent years working toward her Ph.D. in biochemical genetics: "I was *Doctor* Ann Huang, and that was my identity." However, when she started having children, she stopped measuring herself in terms of how many papers she had published. "I used to be very impatient. I had to have things yesterday," says Ann. "The children have taught me to be comfortable with not having everything at once. I have spent the last ten years focused on my children. My professional life has been on hold: I have not moved up the management or technical ladder. My options have been limited, but that choice has been totally my own. Now, I am very keen on resuming my career."

All these women work hard, but each has found her own balance between work and family.

FINDING *YOUR* BALANCE

You may not strike this balance perfectly at first; indeed, in the beginning you might feel that the right balance is unattainable. "After my first child, Emma, was born, I spent a lot of time worrying that I was missing something," recalls Mary Ellen Schoonmaker, a journalist and mother of three. "I thought my career was over." Nine years later, Mary Ellen doesn't feel that way anymore. In fact, she recently took herself off the list of finalists for a prestigious position on the editorial board of a major metropolitan newspaper because it would have meant longer hours and therefore less time with her family.

"I called the newspaper up and said I couldn't do it," says Mary Ellen. "It didn't make me feel bad to make that call at all. I didn't feel any regret. I realized at that point that I was happy with the compromises that I have made. I'm sure I could have gone further without kids, and I occasionally have regrets, but I don't think about it often."

Martha Stiven, a land-use consultant in Portland, Oregon, went through a similar soul-searching. "When my first child was born, I had a diehard attitude that having this baby wasn't going to slow me up," she explains. "Four years later, when I had my second child, my entire philosophy had changed. My sense of accomplishment had changed. Before I had children, a whole lot of my self-esteem was caught up in my career. After my children were born, over time I figured out that my business is not the end all to my life, my sense of worth, and my satisfaction. I think this is a difference between men and women, and I also think part of this is a function of age. Age is wonderful, I think."

IT IS YOUR DECISION

Some women make decisions that seem incomprehensible to those in the office whose core identity is located at work. When Leslye Katz, then a manager at The Dun & Bradstreet Corporation, first asked to go on a part-time schedule, her boss agreed but warned her that this change could slow her down and might even affect the endpoint of her career permanently. This did not affect Leslye's request. "I was absolutely willing to take this risk, because I have never really known what that endpoint would be for me, and I still don't know. I am not driven to become the chairman of the board of The Dun & Bradstreet Corporation. I am driven to see my children grow up."

Soul-searching about your career doesn't always mean that you slow your professional progress. You may see new opportunities or be galvanized to take advantage of opportunities you didn't take seriously before. You may realize that you don't go to work just for the paycheck, and that it's worth a little risk to propose a creative new project or ask for a deserved promotion. Because being with your children is so fulfilling, your job ought to be rewarding enough for you to want to make the effort to balance work and family.

The Pressure of Providing

As we become more and more financially responsible for our families, coming to terms with our ambition is compounded by the pressure of being in a provider role. Men have traditionally resolved the conflict between being a parent and provider by distancing themselves emotionally or psychologically from the family. But this approach doesn't work for most women (and for an increasing number of men), because they are less willing to define their parental role narrowly.

Dr. Elliott Rosen, a psychologist and family therapist who has worked with dozens of two-career couples, comments, "Most women do not find in money their primary source of identity or symbol of power. Women are much more driven by their children."

Susan Eilertsen, the financial provider in her family, says, "I don't know how fathers do it. I want to tell you: It breaks my heart every time I cannot go with my child to the pediatrician or cannot take my children to the playground."

STILL COMMITTED . . . TO NEW IDEAS OF SUCCESS

While our *ambition* may change as we settle into motherhood, this does *not* mean that we are less committed to working. "I am no less committed to my job than anyone else at the paper," says Mary Ellen Schoonmaker. "But I do have more demands on me outside the office than some others do." Our standards of performance do not change; rather, we are molding our idea of success in our own image.

Rather than try to fit ourselves into a single model of success, we should recognize that there are many definitions of success. The choice to stay home full-time should be as valued as the choice to work full-time; we should applaud those who reach professional heights as well as those who cut back their hours to spend time with their children. Doing so will broaden both the definitions of and the avenues to success and will make it an inclusionary goal rather than an exclusionary one.

SUCCESS AT HOME

Define, too, your version of an ideal home life. You want to be a good parent and spouse, and raise happy, healthy children, but the issue is how to define those goals in practical terms. You cannot answer the question in the abstract, and the answers change over time. The concerns break down into simple categories: your children, your husband, yourself, and your home.

These categories generate myriad questions about the details of your life. Do you still need to iron all your clothes, or would you rather spend that time reading a book? Do you want to give your kids their bath, or can you let your care-giver do it and use the time to play with them instead? Is it more important for you to cook for your family or to sit down with them for dinner? Do you want to have an evening alone with your husband during the week, or do you want to spend every night with your children? Is a clean, neat, well-organized home crucial to your sense of well-being?

Address these issues directly; assuming that they will take care of themselves will probably result in tension, dissatisfaction, and even a sense of failure.

Children's Changing Demands

At the same time that our identity is shifting, the needs of our children are also changing. When they are babies they need a loving person to cuddle them, change their diapers, and make their formula. Once you get the hang of these tasks, they (especially the cuddling) are relatively straightforward. The older your children get, the more complicated become their demands.

It started to get "hard" for Martha Stiven when her son started school and the forms started coming home. "There were forms for the PTA, forms for Cub Scouts, forms for sports with practice at four-thirty in the afternoon." Not to mention homework and special projects. Things become "harder" not only because there are more inflexible demands placed on the family's schedule, but also because these activities require a much higher level of involvement in children's lives.

At the same time that our children's lives offer us more and more opportunities for involvement, there are fewer and fewer external signals in their lives that having a working mother is acceptable. Day care centers and preschools seem to be more conscious of — and prepared for — working mothers than elementary schools. PTA meetings are almost always held during the day, for example.

Perhaps the most telling indicator of the lack of support is the paltry number of children's books that are either about working mothers or have them as characters within the story. We asked an excellent local children's bookstore to create a list of such books. They could find only a dozen, and we've added one or two more. The list appears in Appendix D.

Efficiency Comes Home

Your first impulse will be to become more efficient at home, just as you have become more efficient at work. You will need that efficiency: Your free time is precious. No longer will you be able to squander your time deciding at the last minute what to prepare for dinner or making two or three food-shopping trips per week. Gone are the days when you buy just one of something. You live by schedules and shop in quantities, in order to spend as little time as possible on errands.

Most people are familiar with shopping for groceries in quantity (which saves money as well as time), and with making twice as much soup or meat loaf, so that you can eat leftovers rather than cook every night. Carol saves time by buying her children's clothes almost exclusively from catalogs; she studies the many (many, many) catalogs that march into her mailbox like lemmings, makes her lists, and then orders by telephone at ten o'clock at night, when the stores are closed and she doesn't have the energy to do anything else anyway. The children love it too. Instead of being dragged to crowded stores, they discover their new clothes in boxes that come in the mail like holiday presents.

Anne buys other things in quantity, such as baby presents (once you have a baby, you'll realize everyone else is doing it!) and birthday gifts. Although your baby probably won't receive many birthday invitations, once she is three or four years old it seems as if there's a party every other week. Find an age-appropriate present and buy four or five; the birthday children are always happy and you don't spend every other Saturday morning at the toy store.

KEEPING TRACK

Lists and calendars will probably become central to your life. By the time your child is two or three years old, and begins to have his own social life, you may find you can't live without at least one calendar. Writing lists may become an addiction.

For those of you who, before having children, thought of yourselves as footloose and fancy-free, the required level of organization may be a rude shock. However, we strongly recommend keeping lists of *everything*, as well as a big calendar placed strategically in your home, so that you can't help but check it every morning. If you need an extra push, you can even make a game of checking the calendar: From the time her children were babies, Carol has always hung a huge wall calendar in her kitchen, with pictures of storybook or cartoon characters such as Babar or Snoopy, and talked to her children about them in the morning. Now that her daughter Sarah can read, she reads the day's listings to Carol, already understanding her mother's tendency toward absentmindedness.

FORGETTING

Much as we hate to admit it, no matter how many lists and calendars you have, eventually you'll leave something out, or you'll schedule two events for the same time. Keeping track of everything at home and at work can become simply too much. And because forgetting appointments or deadlines at work can jeopardize your job, family appointments and schedules end up bearing the brunt of this overload.

"Coordinating your family's activities is really, really hard. There is no margin for error," says Diana Manning. "There are times when you panic because you can't remember whether you told your husband when the kids are getting out of school, and you can't reach him because he's in some meeting. What am I going to do? Are my kids going to walk out of the classroom and find nobody there and cry because they think nobody loves them?"

A mother can begin to worry that her children will wonder about her competence. But every parent slips sometimes. And every generation of mothers worries about (and is blamed for) something.

No matter how much you organize, though, be prepared for weekends without the long stretches of leisure time you enjoyed before you had children. "I never relax," says Laura Conway, a legal secretary with two young sons. "I don't have time." When she's at home, she finds herself trying to do two things at once, such as cleaning the bathroom while the boys are taking a bath.

"The weekends get stressed because everything else gets put off until then," explains K.K. Gerhart-Fritz. When you add sports practice, birthday parties, and religious school to the weekends, they can become more work than work. "I look forward to going to work on Mondays to get some rest," says Ellen Bonkoski. "At least at work I know what's going to be happening, and I can schedule my time and my work load, whereas at home I'm just fighting fires. I'm in much more control of my life at work." You too may come to see work in this new, positive light!

Handing Over the Controls

No matter how efficient you are, you cannot do everything yourself; you'll have to set priorities. After you have decided what is important, then you must decide what is important to do *yourself*. For many women, this decision comes down to an issue of control. For example, your care-giver will be feeding the baby at least some meals. Does that mean that you will ask her (or allow her) to do all the preparation? Who will choose what foods the baby eats?

What about family dinners? "One of the things I have not been willing to do is to eat a lot of premade, prepackaged food," says K.K. "I insist on having a home-cooked meal, so that is our family time together. My toddler, Kelley, sits up on the counter and helps me or plays with her pots on the floor while I cook. She understands that is what we do when I come home." In return, K.K. has had to adjust her notions of cleanliness. "It's been hard for me to learn not to get stressed out about dirty dishes on the counter or the carpet that really needs to be vacuumed," she says.

Laura Conway works from Tuesday through Friday. "On Monday, I cook for Tuesday," she says. On the other days, her father cares for her children and prepares dinner, and the family eats a lot of spaghetti and pizza.

Sue Kaplan worked full-time directing a state commission in New York. She always had bought all her daughter's clothes—until one particularly busy month. Rachel needed new shoes and the weekend opportunities for shopping trips kept slipping by. At first, she did not ask her daughter's care-giver to take over the job. Choosing shoes and making sure they fit seemed like the quintessentially maternal task. Everybody sees your child's shoes, and if they don't fit properly or are the wrong color, the world may judge you a "bad" mother. Finally, she overcame these doubts and asked her baby-sitter to take Rachel shopping. As you might expect, the project was thoroughly successful.

If you do not have in-home child care, delegation may not be so easy. There are still ways to arrange for others to help you out (though they usually cost at least a little more than doing things yourself), such as buying take-out or prepared foods, taking clothes to a professional laundry, or hiring someone to clean the house or do the gardening. Some day care centers now offer auxiliary services such as children's haircuts.

You may be surprised at the liberation you feel by allowing someone else to do what you have always done for yourself. These small luxuries help even those families on a tight budget. You don't need to purchase these services every day or every week; every once in a while you can order Chinese food for dinner or have a cleaning service visit your house without feeling like a failure.

Educating Your Husband

Ultimately, setting priorities will mean giving up some control over the domestic sphere—and educating your husband to assume some responsibility at home for both the children and the housework. We use the word "educating" purposefully because you should not expect your husband to take on domestic responsibilities simply because you are ready to shed them. "Nobody changes to take on more responsibilities because he has a revelation in the middle of the night that it is the right thing to do,"

♦ WHEN DADDY STAYS HOME

"Being home with the kids irrevocably changed my husband's attitude about what is involved in taking care of them," says Diana Manning. "In retrospect, it was one of the single best things that we as parents ever did. Of course, he wasn't prepared for the demands. But is anybody? No. The first couple of months were tough for him, because he just wasn't experienced at taking care of them. I'd come home to disasters occasionally, but both he and the kids loved it."

says Dr. Elliott Rosen, a psychologist and family therapist. "We do it if we're forced to. So make your husband take the kid to the doctor," he suggests, instead of playing his favorite sport on the weekend.

Real-life experience dealing with balancing work and family is the best possible training. Diana Manning's husband took care of their two toddlers while he finished his master's degree. When he went back to work full-time, they began to alternate taking the children to school in the morning. Whoever is the "taker" oversees preparing lunches, hair brushing, dressing, and all the other morning preparations. The one who is "off duty" can get to work early (or, occasionally, lounge around and not rush). "We've had that schedule since 1985, and we've never broken that pattern," says Diana, with justifiable pride.

Not long ago, Carol found that she was waking up at 6 A.M. every morning to leave for work at 8:15, and still felt rushed and harassed. Why? Because she was making breakfast for herself and the children, packing a lunch for her daughter, and preparing a main course for dinner, to be heated up by the baby-sitter in the evening. She finally saw the absurdity of making three meals before eight o'clock in the morning and realized that something had to change. Because her baby-sitter couldn't cook, she felt she could not delegate the dinner preparation, and being a morning person, she would rather cook dinner in the morning than the night before. She fastened on the brown bag lunch and assigned the job to her husband, Rob. In the beginning, Rob simply made lunch and would announce to Carol when "they" had run out of lunch-making material. Now, Rob keeps track of whether there is enough yogurt and tuna for the week.

In "educating" your husband, it's important not to focus only on the obvious tasks, such as changing the diapers, taking the baby to the doctor, driving the toddler to a birthday party, or picking up the children from their care-giver. Don't forget all the other things you do to make sure that these tasks can be accomplished, such as: monitoring the diaper supply; keeping track of when the last checkup was; remembering about the birthday party and making sure to buy a present; and talking to the care-giver. Not one of these tasks *needs* a woman to perform the job: Don't assume that you are the only one who can be in charge.

In sum: delegate, delegate, delegate. And start delegating *early*. However, be aware that some tasks are easier to delegate than others. Organizing your children's lives is the most difficult task to share. First, it can't be divided up easily: You can't have your husband organize Mondays and Wednesdays, while you keep track of the other days. In addition, the doctor's receptionists and playmates' parents will not always treat the father as the final authority on scheduling even if he makes the original appointment: They may call you to reschedule. If this happens, you will have to remind them, gently but firmly, that scheduling is his turf. When this happens repeatedly, you may be inclined to give up—don't!

Where Do Working Parents Live?

You've probably gotten the hint that having a child changes your life. Your baby will also make her mark (or marks) on your home and may change your ideas about where you want to live. Your priorities now include having enough space for stuffed animals, playpens, and baby walkers and being close to parks and playgrounds. Your cozy old-fashioned apartment suddenly seems cramped and full of hazards such as chipped paint and unprotected windows. If you live in a city you probably used to enjoy its attractions: movies, restaurants, museums, and even occasionally the theater. Now that you have a baby, your taste for culture probably hasn't changed, but your ability to satisfy it will. You can no longer meet your spouse at your favorite Italian restaurant after working late or sneak off to the latest sneak preview on the spur of the moment. You must arrange for a baby-sitter, have enough ready cash to pay her (and in New York and Los Angeles, at least, the baby-sitter usually costs more than two movie tickets and the Chinese dinner combined), and worry about whether the baby will suffer such a severe case of separation anxiety that the baby-sitter will never work for you again. The attractions of the city have lost their sparkle.

Add to this your increased needs for greenery and financial and physical security, and you may find a little suburban bird singing in your ear. While the topic of life in the suburbs may seem a bit far afield for this book, we think it has an impact on how you combine work and family.

Suburbia can be great if you have someone at home all day to drive your children to preschool and play dates. That description may fit many men whose wives stay at home, but it fits far fewer working mothers. Day care centers in convenient locations can be much harder to find in the suburbs, especially in affluent or spread-out areas, and it may be more difficult to meet their drop-off and pickup schedules if you have a lengthy commute. You are therefore more likely to need an in-home care-giver and, at least after your baby is old enough to have a schedule of her own, one who drives. That arrangement is usually the most costly form of child care, as we discussed in Chapter 5.

You may also find that commuting any distance leaves you feeling more distant from your child and therefore less in control of his life. The logistics of taking him to the pediatrician for a quick throat culture or visiting the preschool become depressingly complicated. Flexibility is wiped out if you're at the mercy of train schedules or traffic patterns.

Finally, our own experience shows that working mothers are much less visible in the suburbs than in the city, especially in the affluent suburbs where many mothers do not work. We're out there, but it seems harder to get to know each other than in the city.

"Inside the city, my neighbors all worked," says Martha Stiven. "Then we moved to one of Portland's affluent suburbs. At first, I felt bias from the schoolteachers because I worked—and a lot of isolation because I was the only one going off to the office."

When Anne and her husband were looking at homes in the suburbs of New York City, she asked their real estate agent how many of the mothers worked. The agent said 20 to 30 percent, which sounded like a decent number. What it meant, however, was that, in any given class of twenty children, only four to six had mothers who worked. When their daughter Sarah started in the public school, she also started complaining about the fact that Anne worked, even though having a working mother had been part of Sarah's life since birth. Anne has had to repeatedly discuss this issue with Sarah, explaining to her that work is as important to Anne as school and her friends are to Sarah.

We do not mean to advise against moving to the suburbs. We do mean to say that, if you are considering such a move, fold into the calculation the fact that suburbia can place additional weight on the strong but already burdened shoulders of working moms.

The "Mother Side" of Being a Working Mother

When your time with your children is limited to a few hours each day during the week, and your weekends seem crammed with errands and emergencies, it is only natural to want the most out of every minute with your children. "Quality time" is a shorthand expression for this desire. Shorthand can be misleading, however: Many people automatically interpret "quality time" to mean stress-free time, when you can focus on your children to the exclusion of everything else, or time spent doing something "special" with children, such as taking them to puppet shows, movies, or other performances.

Once we have substituted the idea of spending time with our children with the idea that our time must be focused completely on them, or that we must share something extraordinary, we are headed for trouble. As soon as you sit down together to have "quality time," the phone will ring. The puppet show will be scheduled during the only time the pediatrician can see you. Because we have so little time to get just the basics done, when we pressure ourselves over "quality time," the most notable feeling we end up with is not happiness but stress. "Quality time" becomes just "another opportunity to fail," as Barbara Berg has pointed out in *The Crisis of the Working Mother*.

Rather than think of "quality time" in terms of what you *do* during your time together, think of it in terms of how you are *relating*. Are you and your child sharing something together? Are you talking about what happened that day or how pretty the spring flowers are? If you think of your time together this way, the pressure to achieve "quality time" diminishes, and you can find pleasure in doing even errands and chores.

"Time is just time. If you are going to the grocery store together, you are spending time together," says Janet Grau, a city planner in Milwaukee.

When Anne takes her four-year-old son, Matthew, to the grocery store, instead of engaging in a battle of wills over whether he will remain in the grocery cart, she gives him a job: He picks

---

♦ THE FANTASY OF QUALITY TIME
_____

If you fantasize about how much time mothers who stay home spend
with their children, reality may be reassuring: At least one study has
shown that *both* working mothers and at-home mothers spend about
three hours per week watching television with their children, two
hours per week on teaching and learning activities, and one hour per
week reading aloud to their children.[2]

---

out the fruits and vegetables. The extra time it takes to shop by
consensus is worth the pleasure they have in talking about the
colors, shapes, and sizes.

QUALITY THINGS VS. QUALITY TIME

It is also important to remember that quality *things* are no more
satisfying than quality *time.* You may be very tempted to reason
that, since you are spending less time with your children because
you are earning money, you ought to spend some of that money
on expensive toys and games. If you think about it, though, this
reasoning is circular: If the primary reason you are working is to
have the money to buy pricey items for your children in order to
compensate for the time you don't spend with them while you
are at work, why work? In any event, children don't buy it. They
are smart enough to realize that toys are not the same as time,
and the only result is a never-ending spiral of ever more expensive
gifts and toys.

ALWAYS A MOTHER TO THEM

We are all "full-time" moms, whether or not we have other jobs.
None of us takes time off from our responsibilities as parents for
the eight hours (or four or ten) that we devote to our responsibilities as professionals.

We want to know what is going on with our children when
they are in someone else's care, and if you set up a system for
keeping in touch with the care-giver, you will feel more comfortable about your role as a working parent. Some day care centers

have set up their own routines for keeping in touch: One of the care-givers fills out a list of what the child ate, how long she slept, and (if she is an infant) how many diapers were changed. If your child is in a center or family day care setting without such a system, you can do it informally, by setting aside a few minutes in the morning at drop-off or the afternoon at pickup time to chat with the care-giver. If you have in-home care you can have your baby-sitter write down some notes about the day's activities, naps, and meals. Also, take time at the end of day to talk with the baby-sitter about the day. When you ask about what your child did, you are not doubting the care-giver's capabilities but instead are reinforcing your partnership in caring for your children. A good care-giver will appreciate your involvement and interest. Asking questions will also keep the lines of communication open and encourage the care-giver to express her questions and concerns. You should seriously reconsider the competency of any care-giver who does not welcome your questions and participation.

Not Always a Bowl of Cherries

As you make decisions about child care, the direction of your career, and the organization of your home life, you'll grow into your role as a working mother. Complex new emotions will surface. You may have been a perfectionist at work or at home, and you will have to accept new limitations in both places. Again, this is not the same as lowering your standards but, rather, having less margin for error and training yourself to function within those margins. Recognize that it is your life, your career, and your family at stake, and so your decisions (and your comfort with those decisions) count.

One woman, returning to work after a three-month maternity leave, said, "Everyone has an opinion about working mothers." Unfortunately, everyone does. You have to let go of the idea that you can be everything for everyone, however, and decide what's best for you.

Invariably, at some point during our interviews with working mothers, each would apologize: "The way I [fill in the blank] isn't perfect, but it's the best I can do."

Working mothers seem to carry around a burden of guilt

because they aren't being "good enough" mothers to their children, and they aren't being "good enough" workers. It's as if we feel that we are asking too much of the workplace or our families to be allowed to continue our careers while we have children, as if it's a privilege we don't completely deserve. Every time something is missed or seems wrong, we tend to blame it on ourselves.

BEYOND GUILT

Guilt is not the only negative feeling. Frustration, resentment, and just plain exhaustion will rear their heads at times. While there are strategies to make your life easier, no one can make being a working mother *easy*.

A friend, Mariana Hogan, told us a story that crystallizes those feelings. She had taken her three-year-old daughter, Jessica, to preschool on the way to work, leaving her fifteen-month-old son, Christopher, at home with the baby-sitter. Not more than half an hour after she arrived at the office, the preschool teacher called to say that Jessica was sick with a fever and implied none too subtly that any good mother would have noticed the fever *before* school. Mariana then called the baby-sitter to have her pick up Jessica and take her to the pediatrician. The pediatrician telephoned a little while later to tell Mariana that not only did Jessica have a raging ear infection in both ears, but so did Christopher! Mariana couldn't even go home to be with her sick children because she had papers due in court and a class to teach.

Having spent so much time on the telephone talking with the school, the baby-sitter, and the pediatrician, she had little time left to polish the court papers or prepare for class. Somehow, she got through the day, went home, and snapped at her husband, Bob, over a trivial transgression—and then collapsed into tears. Through her sobs, she said to Bob, "I can't stand it. I'm a C+ mom, a C+ lawyer, a C+ teacher, and a C− wife." Bob replied coolly, "And you're an easy grader." (As far as we know, Bob felt no guilt whatsoever that he had not participated in the day's crises.)

Fortunately for both of them, Bob knew Mariana well enough to know that this comment was more likely to make her laugh than jump out a window. Every working mother has had more than a few days when it seemed it could go either way.

Even if you're working out of choice, there are many days when it seems that no sane person would make such a choice, when it seems all you are doing is satisfying other people's demands. Those days can't be prevented, but we do hope that at those times your husband, a co-worker, a friend, or your baby will manage to make you laugh.

You will have to work at maintaining your sanity. Diana Manning says, "At a certain point, there's nothing more that you can do to eliminate that stress. . . . We take time-outs: We unplug the phone, we don't pick up the mail, we pack up and disappear. A lot of our extra resources or fun money has gone into 'disappearing.' "

If the time is not right for "disappearing," remember (and remind each other whenever possible) that glitches are not the result of personal failure or inadequacy. Rather, they are, in large measure, a result of workplace *and* family structures and traditions that have not begun to adapt to our lives. These changes will take place only if we push for them. So whenever you start thinking that you're a failure, or that you can't do anything well, just remember that you are part of a transformation that can honestly be called a revolution—and be proud.

8

ALTERNATIVE WORK ARRANGEMENTS

Almost certainly, you'll fantasize about combining work and family in a stress-free, intellectually satisfying, financially rewarding way. You may wish you could work part-time or work at home on a regular basis.[1] What working parents crave most is flexibility, meaning less time at work or more control over when and where they work. Flexibility willingly granted and fairly structured may be the most significant work/family benefit that employers can offer.

More and more people (women, mostly) are working part-time.[2] However, before you go looking for an alternative arrangement to the traditional work schedule, you should understand that alternative arrangements will not bring work and family into perfect balance magically, because combining work and family is not simply a matter of logistics. As we have emphasized throughout this book, feeling good about what you are doing as a working mother results from a complex blend of emotions and influences that leads to very personal choices.

Is It Right for You?

SLOWING DOWN THE PACE OF YOUR LIFE

This is not to say that there aren't significant advantages to alternative arrangements. (For now, we are talking primarily about working part-time, since that is the type most working mothers seek. However, there are other alternative arrangements, such as telecommuting and job sharing. They offer similar advantages and disadvantages but to different degrees.) The most obvious benefits are more flexibility and more time with your children. You can actually step off the tightrope of working full-time—and not find yourself falling. You don't need to worry as much, for instance, about taking the kids to the doctor: You can schedule appointments during your time off. Because not every minute is spoken for, you can take a few hours off to attend the school play, and make up that time when you would otherwise have been off.

Leslye Katz, then a manager at The Dun & Bradstreet Corporation, went back to work full-time after her first child was born. Eight months later she asked to go part-time. "I felt really strongly that I wasn't getting the job done at work and that I was missing all kinds of fun things that were happening at home," she says. "Weekends and evenings were incredibly hectic. I felt this tremendous pressure on me that I wanted to get out from under." She is not the only working mother with these feelings.

Finding Time for Yourself

A less obvious benefit to reducing your work hours is that you can actually (gasp!) find time for yourself. When Anne went on her part-time schedule, the first thing she noticed was that she no longer spent her entire weekend on chores and errands. She did those during the week. On the weekends she started reading the Sunday paper again (her idea of a real treat) and planning family trips to the zoo or the circus. She even discovered she could play in the backyard with the kids without looking at her watch every two minutes, worrying how she was going to get everything done. The highly structured, almost programmed nature of her day loosened up, leaving more room for spontaneity.

For some mothers who would (and could) choose not to work if their only available option was working full-time, part-time arrangements have the important advantage of keeping them involved in their field or profession. This not only makes going back to a full-time job easier, it also stems the severe slide in pay faced by women who take time out of the work force.

SLOWING DOWN THE PACE OF YOUR CAREER PROGRESS

On the other hand, alternative arrangements come with certain costs. The most obvious ones are less money and almost invariably lower status and slower advancement at work. How much less money depends on how you structure your compensation, which we discuss in more detail below. How your status and advancement changes when your schedule does is much more complicated.

If working mothers generally are confronted with an assumption that they are less committed to their work than others, part-time working mothers face this attitude in spades.[3] These women are, after all, visibly trying to change the status quo. Cory Amron, as chair of the American Bar Association's Commission on Women in the Profession, has conducted many hearings and interviews on work/family issues. At one, a male attorney waxed eloquent on his firm's part-time policy, and seemed genuinely proud of it. However, when asked privately whether he had worked with any of the part-time attorneys, he responded that he hadn't—and wouldn't. When pressed to explain his position, he admitted that he would not consider working with them because he did not want to work with anyone who didn't work as hard as he did.

Misunderstanding and Resentment

Even if colleagues are willing to work with you they may misunderstand and resent your arrangement because they think that you are getting special treatment. After all, they reason, you don't have to work as hard as they do. One research scientist who worked four-hour days five days a week for several months after the birth of her second child, says, "Male employees at all levels—management through technicians—have insinuated to me that I have all the luck to be working half time and express incredulity when I remind them I'm only getting paid half salary." She complains, "It makes me angry that while I'm exhausting my savings and myself to keep things going smoothly at home and at work, my co-workers joke about me spending afternoons watching the soaps!"

Colleagues who have this attitude are probably the ones who mistake maternity leave for vacation. Unfortunately, resentment from co-workers can make it harder for you to get your job done during your scheduled work hours (as when colleagues schedule important meetings on your day off). This, in turn, can make you feel taken advantage of and isolated.

The Infamous "Mommy Track"

The phrase "mommy tracked" is often used to describe the loss of status and advancement that part-time professionals experience. The "mommy track" label resulted from an article in the *Harvard Business Review* arguing that employers should try to identify women who are "career primary" (i.e., have no intentions of having a family slow them down) and those who are "career-and-family" oriented. Employers, the *HBR* article suggested, should then allow women who are "career primary" to zoom to the top at the same speed that men do and give those who fit into the "career-and-family" category the flexibility to slow down for as long as they want so that they can spend more time with their families.

Even if you agree with the basic concept, the problem with this approach is that most employers are not going to investigate each woman's ambitions and desires; they are instead going to *assume* that, if you have children, you are not career primary. Before you know it, you're off the track altogether.

For some, being "mommy tracked" means receiving mediocre assignments that offer little potential for professional development or advancement. For others, it may mean being explicitly removed from the path that leads up. Tina Bailey, a professor of chemistry at California Polytechnic State University, went back to a full-time position after working part-time for five years, because part-time professors do not work with students in their major field. "I needed more recognition for and satisfaction from the work I was doing," says Tina.

Part-time Advancement

Even if there is no explicit policy regarding advancement for people working part-time, the overwhelming majority of employers assume that part-time workers will advance more slowly. The sometimes glacial pace of advancement for part-time professionals is evident in the *New York Times* article about a female attorney who in 1992 became the first part-time partner at a large law firm in New York City. While the firm's partnership track is typically eight years, this woman had practiced eight full-time years and *twelve* part-time years before she made partner.

"It is much harder to be promoted if you're working part-time," says Paula Scott, a marketing manager at a large food company. "It takes disproportionately longer. There is a woman who has been working part-time for four years and she has not been promoted in the last five years. Five years is a long time when the normal career path is a promotion every two years. And she got an award two years ago for being one of the most valuable employees to the company in our division."

Some decrease in the pace of your advancement is to be expected if you go part-time. A reasonable trade-off here is only fair. The question is, how do you figure out what is "fair" when you and your boss have different agendas? The high-profile case of Meredith Viera, the CBS correspondent for "60 Minutes" whose request to work part-time on the show was refused, illustrates this tension. The program's executive producer told her (and the press) that the show's structure and identity depends on full-time correspondents. Viera questioned whether changing the format to accommodate part-time professionals would have had the devastating impact that the producer predicted. In the end, CBS gave her another, part-time job. While Viera clearly lost status in the company, *USA Today* accused her (and other working mothers who are in broadcast journalism) of using work/family issues to become celebrities!

SPEEDING UP THE PACE OF YOUR WORK

While you will probably lose status by going to a part-time schedule, you will probably *not* lose any of the pressure or stress from work. In fact, you will probably feel increased pressure to perform, because your work load will not decrease in proportion to the decrease in the number of hours you are supposed to work. As a result, you learn to be superproductive. We both experienced this phenomenon when we worked part-time. You have probably heard part-time professionals complain that they are getting part-time pay for full-time work. In most cases this is not much of an exaggeration. So that, while you may no longer feel like your whole life is a tightrope with no margin for error, you may find the time you spend at work even more stressful than when you were working full-time.

♦ THE PART-TIME SQUEEZE

"I have a lot less time to schmooze now," says Elizabeth Cheng Krist, a photography editor who job shares. Paula Scott not only works four days a week, but works almost an hour less per day than she used to in order to accommodate her child care. "I need to be home by six to relieve the baby-sitter," she explains. "I used to take lunch, but now I very often work through lunch. So my day is really eight forty-five to five-thirty with a fifteen-minute break, where I grab a sandwich and something to drink. I definitely think that I am more productive now during the time at work. Having a baby makes you a better worker in many ways. I do less rework. I also take work home with me, especially miscellaneous reading. I really think it's a misperception to think that people who are in the office long hours are working harder than those who aren't. Lots of people work long hours, but they go to the gym or they take lunch during the day. Your output does show and should speak for itself—but it doesn't always."

If you are not able to have full-time child care, the stress intensifies. No one we know has ever been able to stick to their part-time schedule 100 percent of the time. If you have child care that is structured around your part-time schedule, you will inevitably find yourself panicked one day over what to do with the baby because your boss has just called an emergency meeting on your day off. Leslye Katz anticipated this issue when she went to a three-day-a-week schedule at Dun & Bradstreet. "In order to give D & B the flexibility I promised them, we had to retain our care-giver full-time," she says.

PART-TIMERS AND PROFITABILITY

Not only may you lose status, your position may become more vulnerable. In times of recession or downsizing, part-time workers are often the first let go. In part this occurs because companies believe they owe a greater loyalty to those who work full-time. However, part-time professionals are often seen as the least profitable sector of a company's work force. Here again, perception plays a key role in defining reality. Part-time professionals can be as profitable as full-time professionals (because of the increase in productivity that we referred to above, as well as cost savings in terms of space and support). Part-time workers also can provide an employer desirable flexibility in its work force, and are usually very loyal because they value so highly their part-time arrangements. However, while some companies actually *increased* part-time and flexible arrangements during the 1991–92 recession in an effort to "cushion the effects of the downturn" and retain good workers, according to the *Wall Street Journal,* many do not think positively of alternative arrangements.

Lastly, you may feel as if you're letting down your "sisters." When Carol first decided that she was unwilling to go back to work full-time (during her first maternity leave), she was afraid that she was somehow admitting that she couldn't be a real professional and a mother. She worried that asking for a part-time arrangement would reflect poorly on all women, or at least all women lawyers, and make it more difficult for women to get jobs at her firm. Fortunately, Carol talked with a close friend, an urban planner with a son a month older than Carol's daughter, who had already returned to work part-time. Carol's friend persuaded her that she had to do what was right for her and not think in such earth-shattering terms. Even if Carol was to consider the macro effect of her micro proposal, she could look at it as paving the way for more working mothers (and even working fathers) to have the opportunity to step off the workaholic path.

Neither the costs nor the benefits of alternative arrangements are minor: They strike at the core of what you want from being a professional and being a mother. Therefore, you should consider carefully. If the trade-offs are worthwhile, you can move on to thinking about how you would like to structure the arrangement. In all likelihood you'll find little guidance from your employer's policies and experiences, giving you the responsibility (and opportunity) to devise a creative, convenient arrangement. To help you, we review the various types of part-time arrangements. We also discuss alternatives to the traditional full-time job that do *not* involve a reduction in the number of hours you work, but rather shift some of your full-time hours either to your home or to earlier or later parts of the day.

Part-Time Arrangements

Coming up with a part-time arrangement is a bit like writing a business plan: You have to think about what you want, what other people want, and what has a reasonable probability of success. Then you have to experience it to see if you were right. There are numerous possible part-time arrangements, depending in part on how much you want to (or think you should) work. For example, if you decide to work 80 percent of your full-time job, you could work four regular days a week, or three long days, or every morning through midafternoon, or every afternoon. If you decide you want full days out of the office, the question becomes, which days? Obviously, there is no part-time arrangement that is right for everyone. However, there are certain factors everyone should ponder.

DEVISING A SCHEDULE

First consider the rhythm of the work week in your office. Do things have a habit of heating up on Friday—or slowing down? Are there regular Monday staff meetings? Do you call London from the east coast a lot, so that you need to be in the office in the mornings? These considerations will usually dictate the broad parameters of your part-time schedule.

Then you need to consider the nature of your work. Can you schedule your appointments or meetings so that you don't need to be in the office every day? Do you need long stretches of time to accomplish any given task? Can you take some of your work home, or do you have to do all of it at the office?

Just as important as the nature of your work is your *style* of working. For example, do you like to do a little bit on each project you are working on every day, or do you like to concentrate on one project at a time? Can you leave a project for a day or two without losing your stride? Do you need to take breaks during the day, or can you concentrate for long stretches? Do you mind writing detailed instructions for your secretary so he or she knows what to do on your days off?

Lastly, what do you want from your part-time schedule—at work and at home—and which goals are most important to you? Is it more crucial to minimize the appearance of working part-time by coming into the office every day or to spend an entire day with your children? Do you want to cut back significantly to, say, 50 percent of full-time, or will a smaller reduction satisfy you?

Scheduling for Style and Child

Paula Scott works four days a week. When she first returned from maternity leave she worked in the office Monday, Tuesday, and Thursday and at home on Wednesday, with Fridays off. Now she works in the office Monday through Thursday. She created that particular schedule because Mondays and Tuesdays are the days with the most meetings at the company, and she wanted to have three-day weekends to visit family. When she worked at home on Wednesdays, she would work while her baby napped. As she describes the arrangement: "I really loved this schedule, because it was such a terrific combination of working and being at home with my son. I was very productive during his nap, because it was very quiet and I knew what I needed to accomplish during that time. If I didn't finish what I wanted to accomplish, I would work an hour or two after my husband came home. I also accepted phone calls at home." Paula reluctantly agreed to go back to working in the office on Wednesday when her department lost two people. While she goes into the office on Fridays occasionally, she tries hard to maintain the boundary between work and home on that day.

Leslye Katz has worked part-time since her oldest child, Michelle, now eight, was nearly a year old. Leslye's original part-time schedule was Monday through Wednesday; it later became Monday through Thursday. Being the first financial professional at D & B to work part-time (as far as she knows), Leslye had to design her own schedule. She chose to work at the beginning of the week because it is usually busier than the end of the week.

Carol designed a schedule where she would be in the office from about 8:30 A.M. to 4 P.M. Monday through Thursday, with a target of billing about 60 percent of the annual budgeted hours for an associate. She chose that schedule for two reasons. First, she wanted to have a long enough stretch at the office so that she could get real work done. Carol thought that if she was in the office only a few hours every day, by the time she finished taking phone calls and reading the mail, the day would be almost over, and she would never get a chance to do the kind of work that required sustained thinking, reading, or writing. Second, and equally as important, she wanted to save an entire weekday to be with her baby, to preserve as much as possible that leisurely pace they had together. She envisioned devoting herself to her work without feeling too rushed when she was in the office and to Sarah without feeling the pressures of work hanging over her head.

She found that the schedule accomplished her goals. She was often able to work for a solid two hours in the morning before the rest of New York City started ringing the telephones. She also treasured the Fridays with Sarah, and later Sam, days which were completely free for leisurely visits to the park or unhurried errands around town. The down side was the stress of leaving the office at four o'clock. All too often, as Carol needed to run out the door, the partner she had been waiting to confer with finally got off the telephone. That created a rhythm of productive mornings and hectic afternoons that began to wear her down.

Scheduling for Perception

Two and a half years after Carol began her part-time schedule, Anne went part-time. Although Anne similarly targeted billing 60 percent, her schedule was completely different: 12:30 P.M. to 6:30 P.M. five days a week. She designed her part-time schedule with the primary goal of managing the partners' perception of her commitment to work. Anne felt that they equated "commitment" with being available and at their disposal at all times. While this attitude was justified in part, due to the nature of client demands for service, she also felt that this attitude camouflaged an unjustifiable fear that anyone who wanted to work part-time was not really serious about her career.

Rather than fight these perceptions, Anne took them into account in designing her schedule. She decided to work every day: This addressed the "she's not available" fear. Being in the office meant the partners did not have to worry about covering for her on any particular day if, for example, a client called with an unexpected demand. Anne also chose to work in the afternoon to address (in an admittedly superficial way) the "she's not serious" fear. Most of the partners arrived at the office between nine-thirty and ten, but stayed until six-thirty or seven. Her schedule gave her maximum "exposure," meaning that she was in the office when she was sure to be seen by all. She left the office around the same time that most of the partners left, creating the impression that she was working as hard as they were, even though she was not technically at her desk the same number of hours. Anne also felt that it would be easier to come in late than to leave early, having watched Carol fight the afternoon rush. Lastly, because she came in every day, Anne didn't have to worry about gaps in coverage or leaving the right instructions with her secretary. Her schedule meant there was one less list in her life.

Anne succeeded remarkably well at this "perception" game. It also worked well at home. She took her daughter Sarah to school and did errands with Matthew in the mornings. This freed up her time on the weekends, and she even joined a weekly morning mother-and-son play group. The group allowed her to meet some of the stay-at-home mothers in her neighborhood and gave both her and Matthew a new set of friends.

Anne's part-time schedule was not, however, without its disadvantages. For one thing, it had a lot of "transaction costs" due to the quick transitions from play to work to play that she had to make every day. She was constantly changing outfits: dressing in the morning for errands, then changing for work, then changing again when she got home. She also did not get home until at least seven-fifteen at night (because of her commute) and sometimes did not get home until much later. This meant that evenings were highly scheduled and often frenetic: As soon as she got home, she raced out of her work clothes and downstairs for dinner with the kids, who had waited for her. (Her husband, Don, made it home for dinner occasionally and for bedtime frequently.) As soon as dinner was over, it was time to get the kids ready for bed, which involved changing them, reading to them, singing to them, and finally tucking them in. Anne was constantly looking at the clock to see whether she was falling behind schedule. In the quasi hour remaining before she collapsed into bed, she would schedule the kids' after-school social life as well as her own. There was little, if any, "downtime" during the week when she and Don could just sit and talk to each other.

BEING FLEXIBLE

Whatever part-time schedule you design, flexibility is the key to making it work. Do not expect to stick to your schedule all the time; you will be sorely disappointed. Meetings run over; a client calls long distance ten minutes before your scheduled departure time; a presentation has to be finished and the word processing system breaks down. Besides "bad timing," you will experience the "creeping clock" phenomenon: No matter what hours you set, you will end up working longer hours. You should set up your schedule and your child care accordingly. Anne built a time gap into her schedule by setting her hours at 60 percent of full-time, knowing that she would be comfortable if she worked in the 70 to 75 percent range. She did.

On the other hand, you shouldn't bend so much that you end up breaking. Just as setting limits is important when you go back to work full-time, it is imperative when you reduce your hours. "I have to be very protective of my part-time schedule," says Leslye Katz, "because no one else is going to be. My boss is very supportive, but he is not going to protect my schedule. He isn't going to — and I don't expect him to — call people up and tell them to stop scheduling meetings on Friday. I am the one who has to be firm."

GETTING PAID

Schedule is not the only consideration in designing a part-time arrangement; compensation is another major item. Obviously, if you are not working full-time, you will not receive full pay. Instead, your compensation will be reduced in proportion to the reduction in your hours. For example, if you work three days a week, you should expect to get paid three fifths of your full-time salary. This seems simple enough. However, remember the creeping clock phenomenon: You will almost certainly work more hours than your schedule anticipated. The question then becomes whether — and how — you get compensated for the extra time.

We strongly advise that you try to get compensated for extra time for one basic reason: You will feel better about your part-time arrangement if you do, and it will therefore have a better chance of succeeding.

Consider these two stories. Paula Scott is supposed to work four days a week, but sometimes she cannot avoid working on her day off. Because she doesn't get paid when she does, it feels like a double imposition: She gets less time at home and no more money at work. In contrast, Leslye Katz, who also is supposed to work four days a week, gets paid for any extra days she works. Leslye feels comfortable offering her time to her company because she feels her flexibility and willingness to do what's necessary at work are acknowledged and compensated.

We have had similar experiences. Carol was the first to go part-time, and the issue of compensation for extra hours was not discussed. By the end of the first year, Carol had not only put in 30 percent more time than she was supposed to without getting paid for it, but she had also spent a fair amount of money paying her baby-sitter overtime. While getting paid for the time away from home was no *substitute* for that time, it at least would have made Carol feel that the firm appreciated her extra effort. Only after the second year, during which she worked closer to 80 percent rather than 60 percent of her full-time hours, did she have the courage and pent-up resentment to raise the issue with the firm. The partners expressed surprise at the disparity and agreed to pay her partial compensation for the additional time.

Having discussed this with Carol before negotiating her part-time arrangement, Anne made sure that the partners agreed in advance to pay for any time she worked over her 60 percent schedule.

Of course, benefits are an important part of your total compensation, and as we detail in our discussion of how to negotiate alternative arrangements, you can use them to be creative in putting together a compensation package.

Job Sharing

Job sharing means what it says: Two people share one job. This arrangement is more complicated to set up than an individual part-time schedule, because you have to find a partner who has a level of experience similar to yours and with whom you are compatible. (Unless your employer is one of the Enlightened

Ones, do not expect him or her to find this person for you.) One of the main advantages of job sharing over other part-time arrangements is that you are also less subject to the creeping clock phenomenon, because there are two bodies working on the same job. On the other hand, you have to deal with the stress of transition constantly, and you may have to address differing performance levels, as well as possible conflicts over benefits, vacations, and compensation.

Inevitably, stresses will emerge in working so intimately with a colleague. You have to be inside your partner's mind and vice versa. Your work styles may not be the same, which means you will have to adapt to each other. If you cover for each other when one is sick, you may begin to feel taken advantage of if your partner is out more often than you are.

CONVINCING THE BOSS

Harder than having a partner, however, is convincing your employer to allow a job-sharing arrangement. Job sharing seems to require even more imagination or openness on the part of management than part-time arrangements, so it is that much more dependent on supervisors' personalities and attitudes.

Mary Ellen Schoonmaker and her husband, Mike Hoyt, are both journalists and writers. When their first child was a year old, Mike was working at the copy desk at *Business Week* magazine part-time. He and Mary Ellen decided to approach Mike's boss about job sharing a full-time position. Even though their proposal was a "first" for the copy chief, his response was very positive. They job shared at the magazine for almost two years, dividing the work by shift.

Then Mike and Mary Ellen decided to apply for an editorial job at another magazine, again as a job-share team. This time, although the writing staff was enthusiastic, they met resistance in administration. As Mary Ellen explains: "One woman had a lot of ridiculous concerns, such as what would happen if the roof fell in and one of us got hurt and the other wanted to make a claim. She became a huge obstacle, because she couldn't visualize the option." The issue here was not whether the job-sharing team would work: Mary Ellen and her husband had already proven that. It was simply a question of, as Mary Ellen put it, vision. Ultimately, Mary Ellen and her husband got around this person's objections by working out a complicated "freelance" arrangement. Because the job involved editing one section of the bimonthly magazine, Mary Ellen and Mike split the job by alternating issues. Besides ensuring consistency within each issue, this arrangement also let both of them freelance during their off months.

Elizabeth Cheng Krist job shares the position of photography editor at a major business magazine. Her schedule is fairly typical of job shares: Her partner works Monday through Wednesday until lunch, and Elizabeth works Wednesday afternoon, Thursday, and Friday. She and her partner have lunch together on Wednesday to review the status of different projects; on Friday, Elizabeth prepares a status memo for her partner to read on Monday.

She found her partner in a friend at work, who was pregnant at the same time Elizabeth was. While on their maternity leaves, as they realized that they did not want to return to work full-time, they conceived of the job-share idea and proposed it to their boss.

At first, their boss resisted, raising a number of objections related to the nature of the job. As Elizabeth explains, "The photo editor works on a daily basis with the reporters, writers, and other editors who are assigned to the same stories. [Our boss] was worried that we might be confusing to others and that we might forget to tell her things." Elizabeth's partner, who took the lead in negotiating, pointed out that the photo department had always relied on freelance editors who created the same kinds of transition and communication issues that the supervisor was raising about the job share. The professionals in the department were, therefore, used to dealing with these issues. In addition, Elizabeth and her partner proposed that they would tell others up front that there were two editors working on the story. Since they had the same office and telephone number, anyone calling would always reach one of them.

Their boss decided to allow them to job share, and even went to bat for them to get approval from senior management. It has been going well ever since, partly because each partner tries to be sensitive to the other. "My partner used to be a very, very last-minute person," explains Elizabeth. "But her work habits have changed because she knows that, if she left things for the last minute, I would end up doing them." As far as Elizabeth is concerned, the principal disadvantage is that, because she works the second half of the week, there is no overlap with her partner before the weekend. Elizabeth must, therefore, spend part of every Friday writing the transition memo.

Sometimes a nominally part-time arrangement is actually a job share, though no one at the office calls it by such a trendy name. Laura Conway, a legal secretary, works for a partner in a law firm four days a week. To fill in for her on her day off, the firm at first had a "floater" who sat at her desk, and now has hired someone who is willing to work Mondays only. Laura doesn't regard this situation as a job share: "It's still my desk," she says. Nevertheless, she and her firm have devised a creative arrangement that satisfies everyone's needs.

Telecommuting

Telecommuting is a fancy word for doing your job from your home some of the time, or "substituting the computer for the commute," according to *PC/Computing* magazine. Telecommuting is the fastest growing type of alternative work arrangement, according to reports in the *Wall Street Journal* and the *New York Times*. Because you can telecommute whether you work part-time or full-time, the key feature of this alternative is the flexibility of *location* rather than time. Working from home instead of the office can be very valuable, especially if you have a significant commute. You not only eliminate the commute, but you also reduce a lot of other transaction costs, like having to get dressed for work in the morning and engaging in office chitchat. You can be more productive working from home, and can then use the "extra" time to take the kids to the doctor or attend the school play or even treat your kids to lunch.

LIMITS AND LIABILITIES

While a telecommuting arrangement may sound like the perfect solution to the quest for flexibility, you need to understand its constraints as well as its possibilities.

First, *do not* assume that since you will be home, you will not need child care. If you are going to be productive at home, you cannot at the same time take care of your children. The authors of *The Best Jobs in America for Parents* call working from home without child care "a formula for failure" and they're right. In fact, some companies require that you have child care before they will allow you to telecommute. You will need more than child care: You will also need the *willpower* to consistently close the door to your work space when your toddler comes running toward you wanting to play with blocks. You have to create the boundary between work and home *inside the house*, and stick to it, which is harder than it sounds.

Second, even though you may still be working your full-time job, you may lose status in the same way that part-timers do. To begin with, make sure that your company will not change your status from employee to independent contractor if you work from home. If your company labels you an independent contractor, it probably does not have to offer you the health insurance and other benefits it gives employees. In addition, independent contractors are rarely considered part of the internal advancement or promotion track.

Even if your status remains as an "employee," you may find your advancement harmed by a telecommuting arrangement, if your supervisor equates visibility with productivity (the "if I can see her at her desk, she must be working" style of management). Andrew Grove, chief executive officer of Intel Corporation, warns, in his column in *Working Woman* magazine, that "out of sight *does* mean out of mind" and recommends being in the office on a regular basis if you telecommute or have some other flextime arrangement. Small steps, such as coming into the office on Mondays or Fridays (so you don't have what appear to be long weekends every week), can help to avoid resentment among your colleagues, who may see your telecommuting as a special privilege rather than an alternative schedule.

Flextime

Flextime refers to an arrangement with your employer to work hours other than the traditional Monday through Friday, 9 A.M. to 5 P.M. For example, you may be able to arrange a schedule of four long days, instead of five days with regular hours, leaving you an extra day at home with the baby. Or you may set up a schedule where you begin work late in the day, so you don't start work until after you've taken the baby to day care in the morning. Or you may trade one weekday afternoon off for one weekend afternoon of work (at home or in the office), while your husband takes care of the children. Because flextime is a *shift* but not a reduction in hours, you gain flexibility without a loss in status or pay. Janet Grau works extended days Monday through Thursday so that she can take Friday afternoons off. At first she used that time to get a head start on errands such as grocery shopping; now she uses it for herself, exercising and taking it easy.

Negotiating an Alternative Arrangement

Because so few employers have official policies governing alternative work schedules, asking your boss feels a little like putting your life (or at least your job) on the line. A vice president for a major New York bank who has two small children says she did not ask for a part-time schedule until she felt she was willing to lose her job if they said no. She reasoned that her supervisor could interpret her request as a signal that she was not the same worker she used to be—and dismiss her altogether. Instead, her supervisor was extremely receptive and helped her design a job share with another working mother in the group.

♦ MANAGEMENT MISSES THE BOAT

Susan Hession was a store manager in a large retail clothing chain when she became pregnant in 1990. During her maternity leave, she proposed a part-time job for herself, assisting the overworked district manager with training and setting up sales meetings. The company wouldn't consider it, she was told. For part-timers, every hour had to "translate into dollars of sales," and a back-office job like the one she proposed was not seen as profitable. Not wanting to return to the long hours of managing a store, Susan left the company. Two years later the chain called Susan, offering her a part-time position as a store operations manager. The position, being in charge of hiring and training sales personnel at the larger stores, had been created recently within the company and was intended to improve the efficiency of the sales force. Susan rejected the offer graciously; by then, she was happily ensconced in a business that she started from home.

Unless your company has a flat-out prohibition against alternative work schedules, your request for an alternative arrangement will probably not be rejected immediately. Instead, you will probably encounter guarded willingness to consider the option—and a lot of questions or concerns. The better prepared you are to answer these concerns, the more likely your request will be granted. What follows are the issues you will likely encounter in negotiating your arrangement.

THE RADICAL FRINGE

If your firm doesn't have experience with part-time or alternative arrangements, the first concern (which may not even be stated explicitly) is that somehow your request is the first of its kind ever in your field or industry. There's an adage that, when it comes to being innovative, no company likes to be first, but they all want to be second. Therefore, part of your presentation (whether you are asked about this or not) should include a list of other firms or companies, preferably those which compete for talent with your company, that allow part-time or alternative arrangements. You may need to do some research. If you don't know anyone who is working an alternative schedule, start with your local professional or trade association, or call your friends who work for the competition and ask them to direct you to the women at their companies working alternative schedules. There are also organizations that collect information on alternative arrangements. A list of these groups is contained in Appendix B.

Working mothers on alternative schedules are usually willing, if not downright eager, to talk to other working mothers about their experience (unless they have been intimidated into secrecy by their employer's insistence on the "specialness" of their arrangement). Don't be shy: Find out the specifics of their arrangements, then ask them for additional leads. They invariably will know of others with similar schedules in other firms or companies. Not only will you gather invaluable information, you will also realize that you are not the only working mother in the world (or your business) who wants to work on an alternative schedule. This knowledge will encourage you to pursue your own desires.

THE BOTTOM LINE

Second will be the cost concerns: Will allowing an alternative arrangement cost the company? The answer can be quite complex. First you need to remember that losing you would cost the company both the investment made in training and the cost of replacing you.

Catalyst, an organization devoted to issues of women's advancement in the workplace, did a study at a major accounting firm to determine how women were faring. The study revealed that the firm had a "total absence of flexibility," and that, as a result, it lost a disproportionate number of high-performing women.[4] These results are consistent with the experience of other professional firms, leading to what the American Bar Association's Commission on Women in the Profession calls a significant "brain drain." On the other hand, at companies where a serious effort is made to treat alternative arrangements as part of the corporate culture, the number of female managers at the top has been steadily increasing.[5]

Beside losing valuable employees, employers should consider the cost of replacement. Large law firms, for example, spend hundreds of thousands of dollars on recruitment and training, not to mention the cost of time lost during transitions. Knowing how expensive it is to replace you should give you more confidence in seeking an alternative schedule.

On the other hand, allowing an alternative arrangement may actually create an economic (as well as a morale) benefit to your employer. Studies have shown that professionals who work part-time are more productive during their work hours than full-time professionals. When the city of San Diego instituted a telecommuting program in 1991 for professional as well as clerical staff, the city found that productivity and work quality remained the same *or improved.*[6]

Fixed Costs

However, most supervisors will not weigh your request against the long-term costs of replacing you and the somewhat amorphous benefits to morale and productivity. Rather, they'll be more concerned with immediate expenses associated with each employee, such as support, office space, and benefits. When

Carol met with the partners to discuss her part-time request, the discussion quickly came down to monetary concerns: A law firm bills by the hour, and hardworking associates are profit centers. By reducing her hours, they argued, Carol's revenues would pay for her own salary (as reduced) and for overhead (which stayed the same); the cream (their profit) would be cut off the top. When Anne asked to go part-time, the partners again raised the "overhead" argument: She would be less profitable to the firm because the overhead associated with her would become a greater portion of the revenues she generated.

Although no expert in law firm economics, Carol suggested that they consider that their calculations of profitability were not necessarily complete or accurate, especially considering the cost of turnover, as well as her expertise and efficiency. Anne pointed out that there were a lot of inefficiencies in the operation of the law firm. For example, the partners had yet to pick a phone system that automatically billed clients for long-distance calls, costing the firms thousands of dollars in unbillable phone expense. Why focus on the relatively small inefficiency caused by the fact that Anne was not in her office from nine to twelve-thirty? Although the firm agreed to both part-time arrangements, the partners clung to their notion that part-time schedules were costly.

Your proposal should include suggestions for economizing on fixed costs, such as sharing office space and secretarial support. Anne shared a secretary with four other attorneys: The secretary was able to work for so many attorneys because, in addition to the woman's fantastic skills, Anne did not use her for one third of the day.

Other employers similarly have found that part-time and other alternative arrangements can reduce fixed costs. Although sharing support staff is easier than sharing space, companies are experimenting with communal or shared offices, especially for employees who spend a significant amount of time out of the office servicing clients. A major accounting firm reduced its space requirement by seventy thousand square feet at its headquarters in Chicago by instituting shared office space for its auditors, the *New York Times* reported. A legal publishing firm saved thousands of dollars a year by having twenty telecommuters share office space, according to the *Wall Street Journal*. Job sharers usually can and want to share an office, eliminating the problem of "excess" space.

Benefits are another big concern among employers — and for good reason. Health, retirement, and other benefits can cost an employer up to 40 percent of a person's salary, and the total amount does not usually decrease when your hours do. If you are working only 60 percent of full time, the cost of benefits relative to salary can become very high. As a result, some employers try to drop part-timers or telecommuters from benefits altogether. Rather than going without, you can suggest that you stay on the company's plan but pay for some of the costs. If you job share, you can agree with your partner to take one full-time set of benefits and divide them between the two of you, or make some other equitable arrangement. Don't give up vacation or sick time unless forced to: You'll need it just as much when you're working part-time as when you were working full-time. However, if you job share, you and your partner can cover for each other during absences. Be sure to present this as one of the advantages of such an arrangement.

IT CAN'T WORK HERE

The "Floodgate" Fear

Even if you get past the cost arguments, you may still find resistance in debates over whether such arrangements can "work." These arguments come in several forms. For starters, there is the "floodgate" argument: If we let one employee work part-time, the entire work force will follow. Carol encountered this response when she went to the partners with her part-time request. One partner wondered what would happen if every woman at the firm wanted to do this when they had children. This partner seemed to be afraid that granting Carol's request would create a bias against hiring women in the future. Of course, not every woman wants to have children or work part-time. In fact, after allowing both of us to work part-time, the firm continued to hire women at a great rate. Only one went on to have a child and work part-time. Similarly, the experience of other companies that allow alternative arrangements is that not everyone wants to take advantage of them.

Clients, Clients, Clients

Concern or hesitancy can also be expressed as: "The clients expect us to be here whenever they need us." This is particularly prevalent in service businesses such as law and accounting. A part-time associate in a law firm in Portland, Oregon, heard this when the firm was discussing whether to allow part-time partners. The associate "chronicled how often [the partners] were inaccessible when [she] was looking for them"; she was promoted to part-time partner shortly thereafter, according to a report in the *New York Times*. Accountants can structure a part-time arrangement so that they work full-time during tax season but fewer hours the rest of the year.

Keeping Your Focus

Supervisors who have only known full-time work can have a hard time imagining how someone else can perform on a part-time basis. In our firm, the litigation partners thought part-time would work, but only for corporate and real estate attorneys. The corporate and real estate partners felt the firm could accommodate part-timers, but as litigation associates.

The result can be a change in the kind or quality of assignments you get once you switch to your alternative schedule. When Anne went part-time, she stopped getting litigation assignments, even though she had previously spent 30 percent of her time on such matters. She attributes this change in part to the fact that the partner responsible for work assignments was a (single, male) litigator who routinely put in very long hours. Anne felt that he could not imagine anyone doing what he did on a part-time basis. Because she did not realize what was happening in the beginning, she did not insist on litigation assignments. Eventually, she felt that her choices had been made for her—which she resented.

The key to combating this dynamic is to make clear when you are negotiating an alternative arrangement that you see no reason for the substance of your work to change when you go part-time; rather, the number of projects you are involved with at any one time should decrease. Remind your supervisor that it is in his or her interest, as well as yours, to have you build on your experience and continue to grow professionally. And be on guard against negative presumptions taking hold.

GIVE YOURSELF ALTERNATIVES

Sheila Nielsen, an attorney who worked part-time and now counsels attorneys looking for alternative arrangements, advises her clients to seek part-time employment outside their firm before they go to their current firm with a request. She reasons that, by going outside the firm, you will get experience negotiating an alternative arrangement, which will in turn make you more confident when you approach your current employer. In addition, you will realize that, even though employers rarely advertise part-time jobs, they exist—if you are willing to make the effort to find them. Knowing that there are other jobs out there cushions the feeling that you are risking your job when you approach your employer about an alternative arrangement. Lastly, it is always handy to have this "chip" in your pocket if you meet resistance from your boss.

Sheila's advice is sound. Yet, we also know how time-consuming it can be to interview while you're trying to get your job done and get home to see the kids. Just getting your resume in shape can put you over the edge. So, before you embark on this effort, evaluate whether you need the leverage that comes with it. If you are fairly confident your employer will be receptive to your proposal, then you may not need to have a backup plan.

Given the importance of how you are perceived, we recommend timing your request to coincide with the successful completion of a major project or similar accomplishment at work. If you decide during your maternity leave that you want an alternative schedule, wait to discuss it until you are feeling presentable enough to meet with your supervisor in person. Remember, this is a business deal, and you should treat it as you would any other business deal.

After all the arguments have been made and countered, ultimately, the success of an alternative arrangement will depend most on attitude: both yours and your employer's. You need to maintain a high degree of flexibility without resenting the intrusion into your home life this inevitably creates. Your employer needs to maintain a high degree of accommodation without penalizing you for changing the way work is performed and evaluated. These are precisely the attitudes that must be cultivated if working mothers are to be fully integrated into the workplace.

9

OTHER OPTIONS

Throughout this book we have repeated our sincere belief that each woman should be entitled to make her own choices about career and family, and each choice deserves equal respect. This chapter is for women who have decided to leave their jobs and either work at home, or not work (for pay), but rather devote their entire time to managing their households and being with their children. This last option, unfortunately, is a choice only for those women who have the financial means to make it, and fewer and fewer women do. However, having the choice does not automatically make it an easy one, nor are the dimensions of that choice always understood. Therefore, we discuss it along with other options.

Leaving the Workplace

Deciding to leave the workplace for an extended period of time (at least a year) is a complicated process, because it brings with it significant changes in crucial aspects of your life: your identity, your marriage, your environment, your daily rhythms. We don't kid ourselves into thinking that the work women do at home is any less demanding than the work women do outside the home. It is very different—with its own rewards and drawbacks. Of course, the largest reward is more time with your children. However, instead of finishing projects, attaining goals, and moving on, the way you did at work, you will spend a lot of time on tasks only to do them again—later that day, or that week.

Jim Cutler, a senior executive at Apple Computers, took several months off from work to be with his newborn and two older children. In an article in *M. Inc.* magazine, he says, "By the time I got [the kids] breakfast and then dressed and then to school and then shopping and then stopped at the cleaners and then paid the bills—just the things to manage the house had a kind of relentless feel to it. It required tremendous stamina. A lot of those things aren't self-invigorating the way things are at [work]."

While you will have more time with your kids, you may still find it difficult to get through a whole art project or read a whole book without being interrupted and distracted. Instead of daily interaction with colleagues and clients, you may go for days without having a meaningful conversation with an adult other than your spouse. And while you may have more time for your marriage, you may also find yourself feeling there is less common ground.

Who Am I Now?

All these changes happen at once. As a result, no matter how prepared you *think* you are, you will probably go through a transition period full of conflicting emotions. One friend who worked part-time for a couple of years, and then decided to stay home full-time, went through such an adjustment period—*even though* she was already spending two days a week at home. When Carol left her law firm to explore other options, she felt as if she had jumped off a cliff into an unknown world. It was not the same as maternity leave, because there was no predetermined end point. Definition seemed to be the key: She needed to be able to define (perhaps justify) why she was making this radical change.

Even if you plan to work at home, you will still have to deal with these issues. When Anne left her law firm to write this book, she was looking forward to lots of things: having more time with her children and more control of her time and working on a project that meant a great deal to her. What she did not anticipate was a perceived loss of identity and the loneliness she experienced at first, even though she had an exciting project to work on and was very friendly with the stay-at-home mothers from her play group.

Anne felt her identity go from one that was easily defined by the dimensions and accomplishments of her professional life to one that had no external markers to prove that she was still a working professional. Not traveling to an office made her new job invisible to those who were not familiar with her life. Other mothers in Matthew's and Sarah's classes thought that Anne had quit working, because she was in the children's school so much more and wore decidedly nonworking clothes. (The liberation from daily business dress was one change Anne embraced whole-heartedly.) The following fall, when Matthew and Sarah started in new classes with new teachers, they assumed that Anne didn't work. Somehow, this "invisibility" made it harder for Anne to think of herself in the same way as she had when she had been working at an office. It took nearly a year for her to be comfortable with her new identity.

WHY?

Both for your self-esteem and for your future plans, it helps to analyze carefully *why* you want to make the change. Think about what it is about your work that doesn't satisfy you: Is it the rigidity and demands of the workplace structure or is it the nature of the work itself? We have found that it is the former for many women with young children. If that's the case for you, you should recognize that you may want to return to your field (if not your old job) at some point, and should plan and act accordingly, by staying connected with the field and your contacts.

Staying in Touch

There are two parts to staying connected: keeping up with the changes in the field and keeping in touch with your colleagues. Take steps to do both: Subscribe to professional journals, attend conferences, have lunch with colleagues, and join committees. The next level of involvement may mean teaching a course at a local university or college, writing articles, or consulting part-time and working on special projects.

These steps all involve a commitment that goes beyond time:

You will need child care when you are away at those conferences or lunches and at home writing the articles or preparing for class. You will need to finance your involvement yourself (including paying fees that are set assuming that the money to pay them comes from a deep pocket).

NOT FALLING BEHIND

It is important to realize that if you leave your job—even if you do so thinking it will only be for a year or two—you may never catch up in the hierarchy of salary and prestige. Staying connected and involved in your field will not prevent that loss, but it helps you to reenter and may stem the backslide. It also helps you maintain your self-confidence (you can still "think like a lawyer," even if you spend your days carpooling) and keeps you from feeling isolated.

Finding Your Way

If you have left your job because you were not happy with the nature of the work itself, then staying connected is obviously not the right strategy. Instead, you will probably explore other options and try out other roles. One such role is full-time homemaker. Caring for children and managing a household is a full-time job, even though it's not compensated and is often misunderstood. Indeed, some women we talked to who had invested years in a profession considered it an "admission of guilt" that they enjoyed staying at home. There's nothing to feel guilty about. Indeed, with the freedom and possibilities for community involvement, it may suit your temperament better than any other work environment.

You may decide to change careers and pace that transition to coincide with your children's development. A commercial banker quit work after her second child was born and stayed home full-time until he was three. Then she began a part-time master's program in teaching. She will receive her teacher's certificate at the same time that her youngest enters school full-time. Another former commercial banker, who now has four children, is taking an evening course in landscape design to see whether this field interests her.

Our point is that we have a broad spectrum of choices

available to us. In some ways, women have a wider range of significant choices or roles than men in our society, even though society does not value each choice equally. (It is interesting to note that men who choose to stay home with their children probably enjoy even less support from the world at large than women who combine work and family.) If we value the choices we make for ourselves (as well as the choices that other women make), we have the ability to achieve a great deal of personal satisfaction by finding our own place in the spectrum.

Working for Yourself at Home

Small businesses are the fastest growing sector of the labor market, and the fastest growing segment of small businesses is among women starting their own out of their house.[1] Working for yourself has a lot of appeal. First, it gives you much more control over your schedule than working for someone else, while still providing some income. Working at home also gives you proximity to your children's schools, doctors, and the like. It is a lot easier to take an hour off for a school play if you can get to school and back quickly than if you have to commute an hour each way. Martha Stiven, a mother of two school-age children and a land-use consultant in Portland, Oregon, who works from her home, explains, "Working for myself enables me to do other things. It is a means to an end now. Working for somebody else cut off my options. Working for myself has enhanced my options."

Not only can working at home enhance your work life, it can also enhance your family life. "We treat my work more as a family function now: I sit the children down now and explain to them my deadlines. I will tell them I have a project due in two weeks and that it's going to be nuts," Martha says. "They're so involved in how the family is making it—and our attempt to balance work and family. They connect to my work so much better now that I'm doing it at home. They're also real proud of me. My husband's job is much more of a mystery." Anne similarly found that, once she started working at home, her children became more interested and involved with her work.

However, working at home is not all wonderful. It has its own demands and limitations, and you need to think about these carefully before striking out on your own. To begin with, starting your own business takes a tremendous amount of time and energy, not to mention financial risk. So, while not impossible, it is difficult and needs to be planned with care.

YOU *STILL* NEED CHILD CARE

The first step is finding child care. Because of the effort involved, working at home is *not* a substitute for child care: You absolutely will need child care to conduct your business. Whenever you see a picture in a magazine or newspaper of a mother working at her desk at home while her baby rests contentedly on her lap, remember that this scene probably didn't last much longer than the time it took to photograph it! It may be possible to work at home without child care for the few months after you have recovered from delivery and before your baby starts to crawl, but you simply cannot care for a baby or toddler and work at the same time. (Working at home *without* child care is feasible only if all your children are in school full-time and if you can call it a day when school gets out.)

DRAWING THE LINE

You will also need to separate yourself from your child and her care-giver—and maintain this separation consistently. When Susan Eilertsen was expecting her second child, she decided to move her business out of the house. "I knew that with two children I could never keep enough separation between my kids and my work," she says. It helps if your home office is physically separate from the living spaces of your house. Anne's office is in the basement; when she is in her office, she cannot hear what goes on upstairs.

When Anne first stopped going to the office, her younger son Matthew was only two and a half years old (Sarah was in first grade and out of the house). He went to preschool three mornings a week, and napped in the afternoons, but Anne needed to work more hours than that. Even though a baby-sitter whom Matthew adored came to the house, Anne knew that he would clamor for her attention if he knew she was nearby. So she simply didn't tell him that she was working at home, making sure to go

---

◆ CLOSING THE DOOR

Physical separation alone is not enough. Sheila Nielsen's office is off her bedroom at home. She "trained" her children to respect her work time by showing them her office and the phone and telling them that they *cannot* talk to her at all when she is on the phone in her office. She also tries to keep set hours, from 9 A.M. to 2 P.M. In the morning she leaves the family area as if she is going to work, saying, "Bye, I'm going to work."

---

downstairs when he was upstairs, and sneaking out for lunch or errands from the basement exit. As far as Matthew was concerned, when Anne went to work, she went out of the house to an office. He did get a little suspicious because Mom had stopped wearing "office clothes." However, Anne explained that she had changed jobs and that her new job did not require her to dress up anymore. He was satisfied with that explanation.

Looking back on this deception, Anne realizes that it was more for her sake than for Matthew's; she didn't want to deal with drawing the line every day. And, gradually, Anne let Matthew realize that she worked at home, and taught him that she can't play with him while she is working. As long as Anne remains firm in her position, Matthew is willing to go along. But it is a line that Anne has to draw constantly.

. . . For Your Husband

Your children are not the only ones who will need to be trained to respect your work space and time. Your husband may need to be educated as well. Once you are home during the day, it may be hard for him to resist asking you to run the errands (the dry cleaner seems to be a favorite) that he used to do on Saturdays when you were both working outside the home. Gently remind him that you are working and cannot be expected to be available to do his chores at a moment's notice. Martha Stiven goes so far as to schedule an occasional meeting for five in the afternoon that could have been scheduled for eleven that morning, because a five o'clock meeting means her husband has to come home early. It is a subtle way to remind him that she is working, too.

. . . and *Your Friends*

Then there are your friends. Working at home can create two different problems with respect to friends. The first is isolation. Even if your work involves being on the phone a lot, it is no substitute for the spontaneous discussions that occur in office halls and the time spent talking over lunch with colleagues. It's a lot harder to have casual interaction once you are working alone in your basement or spare bedroom.

Having left her position as store manager at a retail clothing chain after her son was born, Susan Hession started a crafts business about a year later. She makes fabric-covered frames and albums and dried flower arrangements while the baby is napping or in the evening. "I really miss being in the store, the responsibility and control . . . and the social contact," she admits.

If you live in an area where most of the women work outside the home, the potential for isolation only increases. On the other hand, if you live in an area were many mothers don't work, you may have the opposite problem. Rather than loneliness, you may find yourself having to tell them not to call during your work hours.

START-UP NEEDS

Working from home has certain start-up issues and costs. We've already mentioned the "home office": You will need to designate some space in your home. If you cannot give up a room, then take a corner of a room where you can put a desk and some file cabinets. You will also need some equipment: at the very least an answering machine, probably a computer, and possibly a fax machine. Even if you don't have a fax, it is tremendously helpful to have a separate phone line for your business. A different line automatically separates business calls from personal ones. This allows you to answer business calls in a professional manner (perhaps by stating your name rather than simply saying "Hello") and to hook up an answering machine to take your business calls when you are not available.

Not only must you be set up to do work, but you must also be able to create and maintain a professional image. Besides a phone line, you should have letterhead and business cards. You must also be willing to spend money to attract business, such as taking people out to lunch, which can involve the cost of the lunch and also transportation.

SETTING YOUR SCHEDULE

Working from home doesn't necessarily guarantee you the perfect work schedule, either. A lot depends on what you do and the relationships you have with your clients. Because Susan Hession makes craft items, she can do it on her own schedule, working as much or as little as she wants. Susan Eilertsen had recently started her home-based public relations business when she got pregnant. "I had very personal clients to whom I gave very personalized service," she says. "Because of this relationship, I did not feel any anxiety telling them I was shutting down the business for four months to be home with the baby."

When Carol Barrett and her family first moved to Austin, Texas, from Annapolis, Maryland, she went to work for herself as a urban planning consultant. She found that the more success-ful her business became, the more her clients looked to her for help in emergencies and work "crunches." Her hours became increasingly erratic and hard to predict. "Working for yourself is no good if you cannot predict your schedule," she says. Carol decided to look for a job, because she felt that even longer hours were easier to handle than unpredictable hours.

CAN IT WORK?

Finally, there is the issue of viability. The bottom line is that working for yourself (at home or anywhere else) works if you can make it work financially. While we don't want to scare you, you should know that more than half of all small businesses fail within the first four years of operation. Before you take this as a sign that you should not even try, decide what financial success means to you. Does it mean simply having extra spending money, or does it mean making the equivalent of your old salary? How long can you afford to "invest" in start-up time, during which your income flow may be a trickle? You also need to consider carefully whether you have the temperament to start your own business at home. Susan Eilertsen describes that temperament as someone who is very self-initiating and resourceful. (Of course, it never hurts to have a specific expertise and lots of contacts.) As we discussed above, you need to be able to draw firm lines and stick to them—with yourself, your children, your husband, and your friends.

Without these characteristics, you may find yourself miserable and floundering. In her book *Women and Home-based Work,* Kathleen Christensen tells the story of an investment banker who tried to start her own business after the birth of her first child:

> Despite her success and experience in the business world [the investment banker] possessed little of the savvy or confidence needed to start her own business. [She did not have] the typical psychological profile, capital, or business vision characteristic of entrepreneurs.

As Professor Christensen points out, many working mothers become home-based entrepreneurs "by default, backing into it as a solution, rather than pursuing it as an ambition." This can lead to a lot of frustration and, ultimately, failure.

You do not have to start a business completely by yourself— nor should you. There are organizations that help women build and maintain their own businesses. The Small Business Administration can provide some support as well as a favorable interest rate for loans. It runs a Women's Entrepreneurial Training Network that links experienced women business owners with those starting out. In addition, American Women in Enterprise Development Corporation runs training programs and has a hotline to answer business questions. A list of these organizations and resources available for women starting their own businesses is contained in Appendix B.

As with part-time arrangements, working at home will not make work/family conflicts disappear magically. However, if you set realistic goals for your business and expectations for yourself as a mother and spouse, then working at home can be a positive experience for everyone.

Reentry after an Extended Absence

Reentering the work force after an extended leave is like climbing a mountain without any safety ropes. You put your ego on the line, as you try to explain to prospective employers why years at home have made you a better worker. If people think that childbirth and maternity leave can turn a woman's brain to scrambled eggs, they are certain that several years out of the work force ensure that those eggs can't be unscrambled.

The first step toward successful reentry is deciding *why* you are going back to work. If you are returning for financial reasons, the answer is easy. However, if this is only part of the motivation, make sure you know whether you really want to work or whether you *think* you want to work because everyone else tells you (or sends you signals) that you should be working. As we've discussed before, society both reveres motherhood and belittles women who decide to make motherhood their full-time occupation by failing to recognize this work. On the other hand, professional women seem to have prestige, even if they are criticized as unfeminine. Add to these stresses the pressure toward career achievement that starts in college and continues through graduate school. Though gone are the days when university deans would openly say that women are simply taking up a "man's place," many women still believe this secretly, and believe that others do too. Deciding to pull out of the work force just proves this point—to themselves and to others. You need to separate yourself from these pressures and decide that you want to return to work because it's the right choice for you.[2] Leading a balanced life means finding your own balance.

Returning to work requires the rest of your family to make adjustments that may not be easy at first. Many women reentering the work force experience tremendous guilt at having chosen to work, and respond to this guilt by trying to do everything at home they used to do, thereby minimizing the impact of their choice on other family members. But this strategy is doomed to fail. As we said earlier, taking care of children and a home can be a full-time job, and you can't bear all of those responsibilities if you have a job outside the home as well. Your family is probably comfortable with the routines you established when you were home full-time (and may even take them for granted). It will take time, perseverance, and flexibility to develop new routines that you can all live with.

10

WHAT THE FUTURE
CAN BE

In the previous chapters we have described the choices available
to working mothers and their possible professional, financial, and
emotional consequences. Our goal has been to help you make the
choices best suited to you. Supported and spurred on by the
modern feminist movement, women have gained access to univer-
sities, corporations, bureaucracies, and even political parties that
our mothers and grandmothers would not have thought possible
when they were young. But women have come to learn that
access alone is not enough. While we are now being let into the
workplace, we are not truly part of the club. The choices we have
are not sufficient, and the price for making them is too high.

The basic problem is that, no matter how women decide to
structure their work and family lives, they do so in the absence
of genuine, fundamental social support. American society has yet
to recognize the need for support because its expectations for the
workplace and the home are based on separate, sex-based images
of success. The dominant image of professional success is male
and is made possible by a particular family structure. In every
profession we can name, career advancement is modeled on a
standard male life-story: He goes to school, he does his professional apprenticeship, he works like a maniac developing expertise and building a clientele, and he finally wins accolades and
serves on boards and committees. All the while, he can have a
family, because his wife is taking care of the home and raising

the children. Conversely, the culture clings to a single image of parenthood that is based on "the good mother" model of success: The mother willingly sacrifices her personal aspirations and ambitions to service the needs of her family.

Working mothers have been trying to fit our experience into both of these models at the same time, and it doesn't work. The professional model doesn't apply. Our childbearing years collide with the traditional path to professional success, virtually guaranteeing that we will have our children just as the men around us are working the hardest. And we don't have a "wife" at home.

Yet our lives don't quite match the motherhood model either. "Motherhood" isn't old-fashioned or unimportant, nor is a woman not working when she is taking care of the children and running the household. The problem with the traditional motherhood model is that it allowed for only one role: mother. Many of us aspire to play other roles as well, and these ambitions don't vanish the instant we give birth.

Having been raised in this society, we have, of course, absorbed *both* the professional and motherhood models. As a result, we are measuring ourselves against unrealistic standards of performance and achievement. Time and time again, working mothers told us that they worry that they aren't doing a good enough job at work or at home. Rather than recognizing the need to change the standards, working mothers see only their failures to meet them.

The first step in creating new expectations that conform with our experiences and aspirations is to stop blaming ourselves. We need to recognize that we're hobbled by models which do not truly fit our experiences or the expectations we would like to cultivate—in ourselves, in our marriages, in our workplaces, and in our children.

Advocating for Change in the Workplace

But we must go further than simply letting go of the guilt. We must also advocate for change in the workplace, so that women's choices are whole choices, and women are no longer penalized for their gender. Government must provide incentives for employers to develop progressive policies for working parents and must promote quality child care for all working parents, regardless of income. Employers must not only provide choices but must stop punishing women for making them. They must not only offer maternity leave, but must make it a real option, by providing some income replacement during leave. They must not only allow part-time arrangements but must stop requiring that full-time work be accomplished on a part-time schedule and for part-time pay. Women who take advantage of these options should not be denied the rewards of their work. As a result, the paths to success will multiply and the definition of and possibilities for success will expand.

These are not small changes. Society has resisted them and will continue to do so. Change is uncomfortable and threatens the perceived self-interest of those running the workplaces and making the laws. One way to overcome their resistance is to help them see that it is actually in their interest to make these changes. Working mothers represent a significant segment of workers and have enormous talent and experience. The workplace suffers when their talent is stifled and their experience wasted.

Unfortunately, we cannot rely solely on employers seeing that it is in their self-interest to change the workplace. Since the benefits of family-friendly policies are long-term, they may not be immediately visible or quantifiable; companies tend to look for success in the bottom line. On a deeper level, we are asking those in power to change the rules by which they themselves succeeded and with which they identify. Even rigorous cost-benefit analysis may not be enough to shake traditional notions of success.

Another strategy: Involve others in your struggle. If policymakers, employers, and fathers understood from personal experience what it means to combine work and family, they would recognize the need for the support. For example, in Oregon, supporters of a bill to guarantee unpaid family leave appealed successfully to legislators by invoking the experiences of their daughters and granddaughters. At John Hancock Financial Services, top management has been behind the company's numerous child care and family benefits from the beginning. They were given the business reasons for these programs, but Katharine Hazzard, Hancock's work/family coordinator, believes that personal experience also played a role.

"Our former chairman outlined his life in a speech a couple of years ago," says Hazzard. "He had a mother who was eighty-nine and an aunt who was eighty-eight; he had daughters in their thirties and forties with children of their own, and he had a baby-boomer wife and an eight-year-old child. So he had personal experience with work and family issues. I think that made a difference in top management's attitudes."

As our husbands participate more in caring for the family and the household, they will be more supportive of their colleagues who are working mothers.

Still, cultivating empathy is not a cure-all. There will always be people who can't, or refuse, to understand. And even someone who tries to empathize cannot fully appreciate the consequences of another's choices.

Ultimately, we have to depend on ourselves to advocate for and create a multiplicity of choices. It is easy to feel frustrated and tired, but one way to overcome the sense of defeat is to give ourselves credit for our ongoing achievements. Every time someone says to you, "I don't know how you do it," remind yourself that you are in fact "doing it." Congratulate yourself, and recognize that you are not alone. Make yourself visible to other working mothers so that they feel less alone. As we feel more confident in our success at combining work and family, the world will reflect our concerns and be shaped by our experiences, as workers and as parents.

The Making of a Working Father: Redefining the Roles

As we have discussed throughout the book, most of us assume the roles of mother and father without being explicit with our spouses about what these roles mean to us. "Couples don't talk out what being a parent means to each of them: What their expectations are for themselves as well as for each other," says Dr. Elliott Rosen, a psychologist who has counseled many working couples. "Instead, they adopt a range of assumptions about what ought to happen. They know that having children involves a lot of work, but they don't think in terms of negotiating with each other over the roles."

The forces that push working couples toward assuming traditional patterns of dividing child-rearing and housework responsibilities are very intense—and come from both inside and outside ourselves. As we discussed in Chapter 1, the idea that women are better nurturers than men and therefore should be responsible for child *and* home is a deeply ingrained social assumption. As women raised in our society, there is a certain comfort—an automatic sense of dominion and achievement—that comes with taking control of the domestic sphere. For many professional working mothers, already swimming against the tide by their very decision to work, giving up some of this control is difficult.

♦ WHO'S IN CHARGE HERE?

"Women tell their husbands that they want them to be more involved in the child rearing. But he dare not, because if he does, she may start to feel devalued," explains psychologist Elliott Rosen. "Working mothers experience real pain when their spouses are perceived as the primary or significant care-givers. They feel compromised, they feel their role as a mother is demeaned."

It's not easy to share your child's adoring gaze. "Because my husband and I split everything fifty-fifty, including the baby's feedings, baths, getting dressed, and playtime, I don't get to be Number One," says Janet Grau, a city planner in Milwaukee. "My son, Peter, may even like my husband a little better than me. Peter is also very attached to his baby-sitter. . . . I periodically have to fight my Parent Number Three complex, whether it's true or not."

It took Diana Manning, an industrial real estate developer and mother of two, years before she gave up cleaning the house and hired a cleaning service. Now she's struggling over whether to continue to do the laundry—or let the person cleaning the house do that too. "It's funny how hard it is to let go of things like that," muses Diana.

"I do all the housework on Fridays during Danny's nap time and over the weekends," says Paula Scott, a marketing manager for a large food company. "I would love to have a cleaning woman, but I haven't done anything about it. I've always cleaned my own home, so I think I still have to do it."

If women are programmed to want control over the family

sphere, men are programmed to see themselves as being financially responsible for the family. "As men, we learn early on that a 'good' man gives his family what they need and what they want," says Rosen. "When we have children, this provider drive intensifies. This is not based on a practical assessment of financial needs. It's based much more on the internal map that men have about what they are supposed to be."

♦ THE MAN IN THE MIRROR

For twenty years, the [Yankelovich] Monitor's pollsters have asked its subjects to define masculinity. And for twenty years, the leading definition, ahead by a huge margin, has never changed. It isn't being a leader, athlete, lothario, decision maker, or even just being "born male." It is simply this: being a "good provider for his family."[1]
—Susan Faludi, *Backlash*

Compounding this strong "provider" pull away from family obligations is a marketplace mentality about how domestic responsibilities should be allocated. "One of the most common unspoken assumptions of marriage [is], the more money a partner makes the more power they should have to do what they want," explains Kathleen Christensen in *Women and Home-Based Work*. "The corollary to this is that the less money a partner makes the more they should do what the other doesn't want to do."

"Even the most professionally savvy women frequently accept an unfair division of housework because they earn less than their husbands," Christensen continues. "In effect, they feel that they are somehow required to buy themselves out of these responsibilities. . . . By accepting the assumption that money and power in a relationship are linked in this way, they allow the rules of the marketplace to define the dynamics of their intimate relationship."[2]

The strength of these internal forces, reinforced as they are by myriad external signals, makes them hard to fight. "The real crunch in relationships comes because neither the father nor the mother feels safe enough to give up that area of control which feels necessary to them in defining their roles," says Rosen. Instead, many women adopt the Superwoman mentality. "They think they'll just continue to do it all," explains Rosen. But the stress and work/family conflict that inevitably come with holding on to control over the domestic sphere force many of us to let go—albeit reluctantly. While we may all fantasize about being Superwoman, actually trying to be Her extracts too high a toll on us and our relationships.

You should establish patterns of shared responsibility early on, because your husband will be most adaptable then. There is also another reason: Much as we are loath to say this, because of its antifeminist implications, we know from our experience and that of others that as your children get older, they probably will look to and lean on their mothers more than on their fathers. (This may be in part because, as they get older, they are more aware of the different roles that people play, and our culture clearly sends signals that a mother's role is to nurture.) Diana Manning's husband had primary responsibility for their two young children for almost two years while he earned his master's degree. "The kids still usually come to me first when they have something to say or confess, though," she says. "On the surface, he looks busier than I do; but in fact he isn't any busier than I am. We both manage a lot of people and have a lot of responsibility. We both have a more-than-full-time position. But it's easier for him to push aside casual time with the kids, and it's not so easy for me to do that. My ears are always ready to hear things that aren't urgent. He is always ready to hear something that is important, but I think he's less ready to hear things that aren't important. That's the reality."

Mary Ellen Schoonmaker, who job shared with her husband for many years, echoes these thoughts. "Mike and I made a far greater effort than ninety-nine percent of the people I know to split things evenly," she says. "Mike made some tremendous sacrifices to be home with Emma and Georgia. He still does fifty percent of the cooking and housework. But a lot of the psychological stuff still falls on me. I think men can disassociate themselves from the psychological dynamics of the family more easily than women can. Or maybe we just fall into it more readily than they do."

Given the force of this almost gravitational pull of children toward their mothers, if you set up your marriage so that your husband is not involved in the children's day-to-day life and activities when they are very young, it becomes difficult, if not impossible, to change or even *move* toward shared parenting as your children get older.

As you work toward getting your husband to take more responsibility, do not expect any support—let alone help—from the outside world. To begin with, some people may actually think there is something wrong with you if your husband is the one baking the birthday cake or scheduling the play dates. Even if they don't think negatively of you, people will tend to make a *big deal* when fathers perform tasks traditionally relegated to mothers.

"When we first had children, my wife was commuting to Wall Street and I was in graduate school," says Elliott Rosen. "I was the one who took the kids to school and the playground. I was the only father doing those things, and I got all kinds of applause for it. It was humorous."

When Carol's son, Sam, was two, he started a nursery school program that required parent participation. Carol had just started her full-time teaching job, so, although the "Helping Parent" schedule listed only mother's names, she drafted Rob for the task. Rob dutifully took his turn as "Helping Parent," and Carol didn't hear the end of it from Sam's teachers: Rob was such a *terrific* helper. Perhaps the teachers had never had a "Helping Dad" before. This kind of excessive praise lets men think they are doing something special, instead of simply what they ought to be doing.

Sometimes these messages are not so subtle. Tina Bailey and her husband had already adopted three children when the adoption agency asked Tina and her husband to adopt a fourth. At that time Tina was working as a full-time professor and was up for tenure. When the agency called, she froze.

"I asked the agency whether I still had to take six months off after the adoption, and they said yes," recalls Tina. "I told my husband [who is also in academics] that I could not take six months off and jeopardize what I had spent four years working to achieve. He agreed with me and said, 'This is disgusting. I can take paternity leave.' We called the adoption agency and they agreed to this arrangement."

"But, in all honesty, I have to say that the form that his paternity leave took was quite different from my previous maternity leaves," Tina admits. "For the first time, the agency allowed us to have our fourth child in child care half-days. So all my husband had to do was take a [partial] leave for six months. I also think the agency treated him differently. He got more mileage out of taking his leave than I ever did taking six months off full-time. Part of this was changing mores, but part was also that the agency was willing to be more accommodating to my husband's career than to mine. That was almost ten years ago, but I would not be surprised if things were pretty much the same today."

The decisions involved in the making of a working father are extremely personal and are therefore different for each family. One thing is clear, however: Where husbands truly share the work, working mothers are more than willing to acknowledge their husbands' contributions.

♦ CREDIT WHERE CREDIT IS DUE

"It is very, very hard to be a successful scientist. It is very, very hard to be a good mother. To do both is very, very, very, very hard! And impossible without a supportive husband," says an assistant professor living in the Northwest.

"I couldn't do my job—especially with the travel—without my husband sharing with the child care. My husband and I go to great lengths to see that my work does not suffer due to being a parent," says a manager in a manufacturing company in the Northeast.

It is our sincere belief that teamwork at home is an integral and significant part of the new family structure that must and will emerge in response to the permanence of mothers in the workplace.

We are all entitled to lead balanced lives—and to discover our balance. By redefining the "professional success" and the "good mother" models, working mothers will expand the range of options available to everyone. If we can manage to do this, we will be doing a great service, not just to ourselves and other women, but to society.

♦ SEND US A CARD

The journey of working motherhood is a varied one. Please keep us posted as you travel it and let us know if there are issues we haven't addressed. You can do so by writing us in care of Doubleday, 1540 Broadway, New York, New York 10036. We look forward to hearing from you.

APPENDIX A

Summary of State Parental, Family, or Medical Leave Legislation

Prepared by Families and Work Institute, April 1993

As of April 1993, some form of leave legislation was pending in nine states: Kansas, Massachusetts, Nevada, New York, North Carolina, Ohio, Pennsylvania, South Dakota, and Utah. Several states have employment policies for their own employees related to family leave, including: Arizona, Colorado, Kansas, Maryland, and New York.

The Massachusetts Employment Leave Insurance Bill is exemplary, as it would establish temporary insurance to provide income to workers on family and medical leave. This bill covers all employees for up to twenty-six weeks for personal medical leave or to care for a sick family member (defined as any "person living in the immediate household of the employee") and covers employees for sixteen weeks of parental leave, which can be taken on a full- or part-time basis.

State (effective date)	Employer Size (number of employees)	Employees Covered	Maximum Length of Leave (weeks)	Provision	Must Employer Continue to Contribute to Preexisting Health Benefits?	Job Guarantee	Comments
ALASKA (Jan. 1, 1992)	> 21	All	18 (over 24 months for family leave/ over 12 months for pregnancy or child care leave)	Birth/adoption Family illness	Yes	Same or comparable position	

CALIFORNIA (Jan. 1, 1992)	≥ 50	All	16 (over 2 years)	Birth/adoption Family illness (includes spouse if over age 65) Foster care	No	Same or comparable position	
CONNECTICUT (July 1, 1990)	≥ 75	All	16 for private; 24 for state employees (over 2 years)	Birth/adoption Family illness Personal illness	State employees — yes; employee contributes portion of premium that employer would have contributed had employee not taken leave. Private employees — no	Same or comparable position	
DELAWARE (July 20, 1984)		State employees who are adoptive parents	6	Adoption	No explicit provision	No explicit provision	
DISTRICT OF COLUMBIA (Oct. 3, 1990)	≥ 50; Phase down to ≥ 20 in 1994	All	16 (over 2 years)	Birth/adoption/ placement of foster child Family illness Personal illness	Yes — employer must maintain employee's health insurance under same conditions as if employee had not taken leave.	Same or comparable position	"Family care" includes anyone with whom employee maintains committed relationship.

State (effective date)	Employer Size (number of employees)	Employees Covered	Maximum Length of Leave (weeks)	Provision	Must Employer Continue to Contribute to Preexisting Health Benefits?	Job Guarantee	Comments
FLORIDA (Oct. 1, 1991)		State employees	24 (over 2 years)	Birth/adoption Family illness	No	Same or comparable position	
HAWAII (July 1992)		State employees; for private employees (≥100), begins in 1994	4 (over 2 years)	Birth/adoption Family illness	No	Same or comparable position	
ILLINOIS (Sept. 1983)		Eligible state employees	52	Birth/adoption Family illness	No—employer must continue health insurance, but employee pays full premium.	Same or comparable position	"Family care" includes any member of employee's family or household.
IOWA (1988)	≥ 4	All female employees except for household, domestic	8	Pregnancy, childbirth, related medical conditions	No	No provision	This leave is to be used when employee has no other leave or has insufficient time under sick leave, temporary disability, or health plan.

State	Employer size	Coverage	Weeks	Reasons	Benefits	Reinstatement	Other
KENTUCKY (July 15, 1982)	≥ 1	Only adoptive parents	6	Adoption of child under age 7	No explicit provision	No explicit provision	
LOUISIANA (1987)	≥ 26	All female employees	16	Pregnancy, childbirth, related medical conditions	No	No provision	
MAINE (Aug. 4, 1988)	≥ 25	All	10 (over 2 years)	Birth/adoption Family illness Personal illness	No	Same or comparable position	
MARYLAND (July 1, 1988)		All state employees in executive branch	12	Birth/adoption/foster care Family illness	No	Same or comparable position	Leave is dependent on supervisor approval.
MASSACHUSETTS (Jan. 1, 1989)	≥ 6, except for nonprofit social clubs and fraternal associations	All female employees with 3 consecutive months of full-time employment with the same employer	8	Birth/adoption	Employer must provide same benefits as are provided to all other employees on leave of absence. Employer may also offer paid leave.	Same or comparable position	

State (effective date)	Employer Size (number of employees)	Employees Covered	Maximum Length of Leave (weeks)	Provision	Must Employer Continue to Contribute to Preexisting Health Benefits?	Job Guarantee	Comments
MINNESOTA (Aug. 1, 1987)	≥ 21	All	6	Birth/adoption; Allows employees to use accrued sick days to care for sick child.	No — employer must continue to make insurance coverage under its group rate available to employee but can require employee to pay the entire premium.	Same or comparable position	Also allows employees 16 hours of unpaid leave each year to attend school conferences or classroom activities.
MONTANA (Jan. 1, 1988)	≥ 1, except fraternal, charitable, or religious nonprofit associations	Female employees in private sector	"Reasonable" leave of absence	Pregnancy	No	Same or comparable position	
NEW JERSEY (May 1, 1990)	≥ 75; phase down to ≥ 50 in 1993	All	12 (over 2 years)	Birth/adoption Family illness	No	Same or comparable position	

NORTH DAKOTA (Jan. 1, 1990)		All state employees	12 (for full-time workers) 8 (for part-time workers)	Birth/adoption/foster care Family illness	No—employer must provide continued coverage but is not required to pay costs of coverage.	Same or comparable position	
OKLAHOMA (Aug. 25, 1989)		All state employees	Not explicit	Birth/adoption Family illness (for child or any dependent adult)	No—employee can continue state group insurance if she or he pays full premium.	Same position	
OREGON (Parental leave: Jan. 1, 1988) (Family care leave: Jan. 1, 1992)	≥ 25 for parental leave; ≥ 50 for family care leave (employee must work for 180 days before being eligible)	All	12 (over two years)	Birth/adoption Family illness	No	Same or comparable position	If at least one parent works for a covered employer, the two parents must split the 12 weeks granted by statute into non-concurrent parts unless their employers agree to other terms.

State (effective date)	Employer Size (number of employees)	Employees Covered	Maximum Length of Leave (weeks)	Provision	Must Employer Continue to Contribute to Preexisting Health Benefits?	Job Guarantee	Comments
RHODE ISLAND (July 1987)	≥ 50	All	13 (over 2 years)	Birth/adoption Family illness Personal illness	Yes—employer must maintain its contribution to employee's preexisting health benefits. However, before taking leave, employee must pay employer a sum equal to the premium required to maintain employee's health benefits. Employer will return this payment to employee within 10 days after returning to job.	Same or comparable position	

State	Size	Coverage	Length	Reasons	Benefits	Reinstatement
SOUTH CAROLINA (1986)		All state employees	5 days of paid accrued sick leave (over 2 years)	Family illness	No explicit provision	No explicit provision
TENNESSEE (Jan. 1, 1990)	≥ 100	All female employees with 12 consecutive months of full-time employment with the same employer	16	Pregnancy, childbirth, nursing of infant	Employer must continue to pay benefits only if they are provided to other employees on leaves of absence.	Same or comparable position, assuming proper notice had been given to employer
VERMONT (Sept. 1, 1991)	≥ 10	Female employees in the private sector with 12 consecutive months of employment at an average of 30 hours per week for the same employer	12	Pregnancy, childbirth	No—employer must continue to provide benefits but may require employee to pay entire cost of benefits.	Same or comparable position

State (effective date)	Employer Size (number of employees)	Employees Covered	Maximum Length of Leave (weeks)	Provision	Must Employer Continue to Contribute to Preexisting Health Benefits?	Job Guarantee	Comments
WASHINGTON (Sept. 1, 1989)	≥ 100	All	12 (over 2 years); employee's accrued sick leave may be used to care for sick child	Birth/adoption Child's illness	No	Same or comparable position	Employer may limit or deny leave to up to 10% of work force that is designated as key personnel, or highest paid 10% of its employees.
WEST VIRGINIA (July 7, 1989)		All state employees	12	Birth/adoption Family illness	No — employer must continue group health insurance, but employee pays full premium.	Same or comparable position	

WISCONSIN (April 25, 1988)	≥ 50	All	6 (parental); 2 (family care); 2 (personal medical); no more than 8 weeks over 1 year for a combination of reasons related to family and medical leave	Birth/adoption Family illness Personal illness	Yes—employer must maintain its contribution to employee's preexisting health benefits. If health insurance coverage is provided, the employer may require that the employee pay the full premium for 8 weeks of coverage into an interest-bearing escrow account.	Same or comparable position

APPENDIX B
Organizations and Resources*

General Information: The following organizations are good sources of information on working mothers as well as work and family issues generally.

> **Families and Work Institute**
> **330 Seventh Avenue**
> **New York, NY 10001**
> **(212) 465-2044**

The Families and Work Institute conducts research and develops policies and programs for balancing the changing needs of families with the continuing need for workplace productivity. The institute operates a national clearinghouse of information on work and family life, advises business, government, and community organizations, and conducts management training on work and family issues. Among its many publications are the *Corporate Reference Guide to Work-Family Programs*, which contains a unique "Index of Family-Friendliness" and ranks 188 companies, and the *State Reference Guide*, which parallels the corporate guide for state employees. The institute also runs the Fatherhood Project, which looks at the changing role of the father in the family and how that affects the workplace, and does research in the areas of child care and elder care. While it does not provide services on an individual basis, the institute is an excellent source of information on work and family issues.

> **National Association of Commissions for Women**
> **Reeves Center, Room N-354**
> **2000 14th Street, NW**
> **Washington, DC 20009**
> **(800) 338-9267 or (202) 628-5030**

Most states and some municipalities have independent, government-funded commissions on women whose mission it is to improve the status of women. The National Association of Commissions for Women is the umbrella organization for these commissions that facilitates communication among them and serves as their presence in Washington. Work and family issues

---

*By offering this list, the authors are not making any representations regarding its completeness or the quality of the services offered by the organizations listed.

are on the agenda of many of these commissions, and the National Commission can get you in touch with the appropriate commission in your area.

Wellesley College Center for Research on Women
Wellesley College
Wellesley, MA 02181-8259
(617) 283-2500

The Wellesley College Center for Research on Women conducts research on and develops programs for improving the status of women in a range of settings—from the workplace to the home to the classroom. In the work and family area, the center has done research on how women handle multiple roles, as well as how multiple roles affect families, and on child care issues such as school-age child care. Anyone can become an associate of the center by paying dues; as an associate, you receive discounts on the center's publications, invitations to center events, and the center's newsletter, *Research Report*.

Women's Bureau, U.S. Department of Labor
200 Constitution Avenue, NW
Washington, DC 20210
(202) 219-6652 (number to call to order publications)

The Women's Bureau investigates and reports on the status of women in the workplace. It publishes statistics on such issues as the wage gap between men and women, women business owners, and booklets on various topics, including one on employers and child care. It also publishes a "Work and Family Resource Kit," an introduction to work and family issues such as dependent care options and alternative work schedules directed at employers. The Women's Bureau has ten regional offices beside the office in Washington and runs the Work and Family Clearinghouse, described under Chapter 6 below.

The following organizations deal with the topics and issues raised in the respective chapters.

CHAPTER 1

MOTHERS IN THE WORKPLACE

American Bar Association
Commission on Women in the Profession
750 North Lake Shore Drive
Chicago, IL 60611
(312) 988-5668

The American Bar Association established its Commission on Women in the Profession in 1987 to promote the full integration of women into the profession. The commission has gathered statistics on women in the legal profession, held hearings, and published various materials, including *Lawyers and Balanced Lives: A Guide to Drafting and Implementing Workplace Policies for Lawyers* (see Suggested Reading). The commission also publishes a biannual newsletter and an annual directory of associations of women lawyers. Anyone can order commission publications by writing or calling.

Catalyst
250 Park Avenue South
New York, NY 10003
(212) 777-8900

Catalyst promotes the advancement of women in business by working with corporate management (through human resource managers, for example) to analyze existing barriers to women's advancement and recommend ways to eliminate those barriers. Concerned primarily with professional and management-level women, Catalyst looks at a wide range of issues, including work and family issues. In this area, Catalyst has developed a "Corporate Guide to Parental Leaves" (1988) and a report on "Corporate Child Care Options" (1987). Catalyst also publishes a national directory of career resource centers that counsel individuals. Catalyst's corporate supporters have access to its information center and receive discounts on publications; however, anyone can order its publications.

Center for Policy Alternatives
1875 Connecticut Avenue, NW
Suite 710
Washington, DC 20009
(202) 387-6030

The Center for Policy Alternatives is a policy advocacy organization that works exclusively at the state level with state and local legislators and public officials on a number of different policy areas, including work and family. In the work and family area, the center has focused on promoting family and medical leave legislation as well as child and elder care policies.

Center for Women Policy Studies
2000 P Street, NW
Suite 508
Washington, DC 20036
(202) 872-1770

The Center for Women Policy Studies is a policy research and advocacy organization that seeks to advance the status of women by doing research and developing programs in the areas of education, health, employment, and violence against women. At the core of each of the center's programs is the premise that sex and race bias must be addressed simultaneously. In the work and family area the center is working on how women of color define and experience work and family issues. The center has published research reports, which are available to the public for sale. The center also has associates who pay an associate's fee and receive a discount on center publications.

> **Institute for Women's Policy Research**
> **1400 20th Street, NW**
> **Washington, DC 20036**
> **(202) 785-5100**

The Institute for Women's Policy Research conducts research into a variety of women's issues, focusing primarily on women and children in poverty. In 1989 the institute did a study on the costs to working women and to taxpayers of the lack of parental leave. The study, entitled *Unnecessary Losses: The Costs to Workers of the Lack of Family and Medical Leave,* was used by women's advocacy organizations to lobby for the Family and Medical Leave Act.

> **Women's Legal Defense Fund**
> **1875 Connecticut Avenue, NW**
> **Suite 710**
> **Washington, DC 20009**
> **(202) 986-2600**

The Women's Legal Defense Fund is a public policy advocacy organization that works to improve the status of women in the workplace, among other issues. It started the Women, Work & Family Action Council, a coalition of organizations and advocates concerned about work and family issues, and led the lobbying effort in favor of the Family and Medical Leave Act. The fund files amicus briefs in cases of major significance to women but does not represent individual clients or bring its own cases.

CHAPTER 3
MATERNITY LEAVE AND OTHER BENEFITS

> **National Women's Law Center**
> **1616 P Street, NW**
> **Washington, DC 20036**
> **(202) 328-5160**

The National Women's Law Center's mission is to advance the status of women through law, using both litigation and legal advocacy, through testimony and the filing of friend-of-the-court briefs. While the center litigates cases that it thinks will have a broad impact, it does not normally represent individuals with complaints against a specific employer. However, the center will respond to requests for legal representation by discussing your rights and referring you to attorneys across the country who specialize in sex discrimination law. In addition, the center runs an annual nationwide "Child Care Tax Credits Outreach Campaign" to educate parents and child care providers about the credits. The center publishes a newsletter that is free of charge to anyone who requests to be put on the center's mailing list (once on the list, however, you will receive solicitations for contributions to the center).

9 to 5, National Association of Working Women
238 West Wisconsin Avenue, Suite 700
Milwaukee, WI 53203
(414) 272-7795

9 to 5 is an educational and advocacy organization dedicated to improving the status and treatment of working women, primarily office workers. It runs a hotline (the "800" number listed above) that you can call with questions regarding whether your employer's parental leave policies comply with the law. In addition, as a member you can consult with 9 to 5 regarding possible legal action. 9 to 5 offers its members other benefits, such as low-interest credit cards, loans, and discounts on prescription drugs as well as on the organization's publications.

NOW Legal Defense and Education Fund
99 Hudson Street
New York, NY 10013
(212) 925-6635

The NOW Legal Defense and Education Fund works on cases defending (and sometimes creating) women's rights in a variety of areas. While NOWLDEF does not provide legal representation to individuals, it has developed "legal resource kits" that explain laws in general terms to those who think they may have a suit. One such publication is the "Employment-Pregnancy and Parental Leave Kit."

CHAPTER 5

THE CHILD CARE DECISION

American Council of Nanny Schools
Delta College, Room A-67
University Center, MI 48710
(517) 686-9417

The American Council of Nanny Schools is the umbrella organization for accredited nanny schools across the country. The council keeps a registry of all the graduates from the schools that belong to the council.

Child Care Action Campaign
330 Seventh Avenue
New York, NY 10001
(212) 239-0138

The Child Care Action Campaign is a public education and advocacy organization whose goal is to increase the supply of quality, affordable child care. It has developed a series of excellent information guides on child care issues, from what benefits corporations provide, to how to find in-home care, and the tax and other obligations of employers of in-home care-givers. The campaign also advises companies, primarily small businesses, on child care benefits, and has published a report on the subject called *Not Too Small to Care*. You can join the campaign as a member and receive its newsletter, called *Child Care Action News*, as well as other benefits.

Child Care Law Center
22 Second Street, Fifth Floor
San Francisco, CA 94105
(415) 495-5498

The Child Care Law Center is a legal support center providing legal training, technical assistance, and advocacy support to legal services attorneys and others who work on child care issues. The center works primarily on child care issues faced by low-income families in California. However, the center also provides assistance to family day care providers, parents, policymakers, government agencies, and employers throughout the country. The center publishes a quarterly newsletter on child care law, to which anyone can subscribe.

Children's Defense Fund
25 E Street, NW
Washington, DC 20001
(202) 628-8787

The Children's Defense Fund is a research and advocacy organization that focuses primarily on issues affecting low-income families and children. While not a source of information on child care availability, the fund is a good source of information on the federal and state laws dealing with child care standards, credits, and the like.

International Nanny Association
P.O. Box 26522
Austin, TX 78755
(512) 454-6462

The International Nanny Association is an educational organization whose members are either in-home child care providers or those who employ, place, or train such providers. Members receive a bimonthy newsletter, a biannual membership directory, discounts to INA programs and publications, and assistance with locating competitively priced health insurance for in-home providers. The INA also publishes an annual directory of agencies and training programs for in-home care providers that can be ordered by writing the organization.

National Association of Child Care Resource and Referral Agencies
1319 F Street, NW
Suite 606
Washington, DC 20004
(800) 424-2246 or (202) 393-5501

The National Association of Child Care Resource and Referral Agencies operates a hotline, called Child Care Aware (the "800" number listed above), which helps parents (and others) across the country locate child care resource and referral agencies in their area. These local agencies list legal child care providers of all kinds, from day care centers to nanny placement services. The association has also published a book, *The Complete Guide to Choosing Child Care,* and provides other useful information to those seeking child care. A membership organization for child care resource and referral agencies, the association also services these agencies through a quarterly newsletter, national and regional conferences, and other programs.

National Association for the Education of Young Children
1509 Sixteenth Street, NW
Washington, DC 20036-1426
(800) 424-2460

The National Association for the Education of Young Children, a membership organization for child care professionals, runs an accreditation program for day care centers similar to the program run by the National Association for Family Day Care (see next entry). While primarily a resource organization for those in the child care field, the association provides some referral services to parents—it refers parents to the association's accredited day care centers, for example—and has brochures and other materials on how to choose day care and on other, similar topics.

National Association for Family Day Care
1331-A Pennsylvania Avenue, NW
Room 348
Washington, DC 20004
(615) 834-7872

The National Association for Family Day Care is a membership organization consisting of providers, family day care associations, corporations, and parents who are interested in improving the quality and availability of family day care. The association runs an "800" information line, publishes a bimonthly newsletter and the annual *National Directory of Family Day Care Associations and Support Groups,* and runs an accreditation program. The accreditation program recognizes providers who go beyond state standards in providing high quality family day care. Send inquiries to the address above; the phone number is for the association's accreditation program.

National Council of Jewish Women
National Family Day Care Project
53 West 23rd Street
New York, NY 10010
(212) 645-4048

The National Family Day Care Project of the National Council of Jewish Women, a membership organization with over ten thousand members, works to increase the supply of high quality family day care by addressing employers, providers, and parents. It has published *Employers and Family Day Care* (1991), a guide to employer-sponsored family day care programs, as well as *Choosing Family Child Care* (1990), a pamphlet for parents interested in family day care. The project has also developed innovative approaches to issues such as zoning obstacles to family day care and materials for family day care providers, such as guides to licensing and marketing their services.

> **Working Parent Resource Center**
> **Town Square, North Central Life Tower**
> **445 Minnesota Street**
> **St. Paul, MN 55101**
> **(612) 293-5330**

The Working Parent Resource Center, funded and managed by the St. Paul Public Schools, provides parenting education and information to working parents. Located in downtown St. Paul, the center offers: classes on such topics as preparing your school-age child for self-care and handling guilt as a working parent; a lending library; and free individual consultations on specific problems. Any parent, not just those with children in the public school system, can use the center.

CHAPTER 6
CHILD CARE BENEFITS:
GETTING YOUR EMPLOYER TO CARE

> **Child Care Action Campaign**
> **(See entry under "Chapter 5" above.)**

> **Families and Work Institute**
> **(See entry under "General Information" above.)**

> **Initiatives: Center for Workforce Diversity**
> **Horsham Business Center**
> **300 Welsh Road, Building 4**
> **Horsham, PA 19044**
> **(215) 659-5911**

Initiatives is a corporate consulting firm that provides an array of services on work/family issues, from workshops for employees at the workplace on balancing work and family, to management training programs, to resource and referral services.

> **Minnesota Vocational Education**
> **Work & Family Institute**
> **Hennepin Technical College**
> **1820 N. Xenium Lane**
> **Plymouth, MN 55441**
> **(612) 550-7155**

The Work & Family Institute, operating through the Minnesota technical college system, provides seminars to employees at their workplace on work and family issues, such as time and energy management, handling guilt as a working parent, and team building at home and work. The institute contracts with companies to determine which topics are of most interest and will be of most use to their employees and customizes its presentation accordingly. The institute has trained seminar leaders throughout Minnesota and in twenty other states, working through various kinds of educational institutions, such as community colleges and adult education programs.

National Council of Jewish Women
Work/Family Project
53 West 23rd Street
New York, NY 10010
(212) 645-4048

The Work/Family Project of the National Council of Jewish Women focuses on helping employers assist their employees with work and family issues. For example, the project helps employers understand the range of child care benefits that they can offer employees—and choose the right mix of benefits for their situation. The project's programs are run through the local NCJW sections throughout the country. The project has published *Working with Employers and Other Community Partners: A Work/Family Guide* (1992).

Work and Family Clearinghouse
U.S. Department of Labor, Women's Bureau
200 Constitution Avenue, NW
Washington, DC 20210
(800) 827-5335 or (202) 219-4486

The Work and Family Clearinghouse is a national database of information on all kinds of child and elder care programs, as well as on alternative work arrangements. By calling the clearinghouse, you can get information on the kinds of programs currently offered by employers across the country, what factors to consider in deciding to set up a specific program, and bibliographical information and referrals to organizations (nonprofits only) and state agencies involved in child/elder care issues and services. While the clearinghouse is used primarily by employers, it has also helped employees prepare proposals on dependent care programs to take to senior management. It is an excellent place to begin such an effort.

Work/Family Directions
930 Commonwealth Avenue West
Boston, MA 02215-1212
(617) 278-4000

Work/Family Directions is one of the oldest consulting companies in the work and family area. It offers a wide array of services to companies, including workplace surveys, work and family labor force planning and strategy development, and management training programs on how to handle work/family issues. In addition, it offers a service called "The Family Resource Program," whereby a company can contract with Work/Family Directions to be available to the company's employees when they have work and family questions on a wide range of issues, such as child and elder care referrals, and school achievement issues. IBM was one of Work/Family Directions' first major clients to use this service: It uses Work/Family Directions to provide child care resource and referral services throughout the country.

Workplace Options
109 South Bloodworth Street
Raleigh, N.C. 27601
(800) 874-9383 or (919) 834-6506

Workplace Options is a corporate consulting firm that specializes in helping employers design and deliver work and family benefits. Workplace Options offers employee and management training workshops, needs assessment, a customized "work/family" newsletter, and resource and referral services. Working mostly in the Southeast, Workplace Options also manages on-site child care centers.

CHAPTER 8
ALTERNATIVE ARRANGEMENTS

Association of Part-Time Professionals
Crescent Plaza, Suite 216
7700 Leesburg Pike
Falls Church, VA 22043
(703) 734-7975

The Association of Part-Time Professionals is a membership organization that provides workshops, seminars, networking events, and counseling on issues relating to seeking, structuring, and maintaining part-time jobs. The majority of its members and meetings are in the Washington, DC, area. However, the association's monthly newsletter, sent to members, has a somewhat wider geographic scope, and it reports on national and other developments in the area of part-time and flexible work arrangements.

New Ways to Work
149 Ninth Street
San Francisco, CA 94103
(415) 552-1000

New Ways to Work is an educational and advocacy organization devoted to promoting flexible work arrangements. Started over twenty years ago, NWW is a recognized leader in the field. It serves as a clearinghouse for information, has an extensive publications list, and offers seminars and training to companies. Annual membership benefits for individuals include direct mail access to the NWW library, a subscription to the NWW quarterly *Work Times,* and invitations to seminars and other events.

CHAPTER 9
OTHER OPTIONS

American Woman's Economic Development Corporation
71 Vanderbilt Avenue
New York, NY 10169
(212) 688-1900 or (800) 222-2933 (outside NYC)

The American Woman's Economic Development Corporation helps women who are starting their own businesses. AWED offers extensive (often year long) courses on starting your own business and managing its growth. In addition, AWED has a hotline service (the "800" number listed above) that will answer specific questions for up to ten minutes for ten dollars, a more general telephone counseling service, and a business counseling service run out of its office in New York. AWED's sister organization, American Women in Enterprise, is a membership organization that offers its members a newsletter and discounts to AWED conferences and seminars.

Mothers' Home Business Network
P.O. Box 423A
East Meadow, NY 11554
(516) 997-7394

Mothers' Home Business Network is dedicated to helping mothers work at home. The network offers its members a newsletter, *Homeworking Mothers,* and discounts on publications such as *Mothers and Managing a Typing Service at Home.*

National Association for Female Executives
127 West 24th Street
New York, NY 10011
(212) 645-0770

The National Association for Female Executives is a membership organization that offers several services to women business owners, including access to capital through a Venture Capital Fund and a credit line; group insurance coverage, including medical and dental insurance; and discounts on travel, car rentals, and the like. Members also receive a bimonthly newsletter and invitations to association workshops, conferences, and evening programs.

National Association of Women's Business Advocates
c/o Ohio Department of Development
P.O. Box 1001
Columbus, OH 43266-0101
(614) 466-4945

The National Association of Women's Business Advocates is a network of women's business advocates throughout the country. Most such advocates are employed in a state's economic development or small business department. However, twelve states have created a separate formal position of "women's business advocate." By contacting the association, you can learn who is the advocate in your state. That person, in turn, can refer you to resources and services for women's business owners in your state.

National Association of Women Business Owners
1377 K Street, NW
Suite 637
Washington, DC 20005
(301) 608-2590

The National Association of Women Business Owners is a membership organization whose purpose is to promote and support women business owners. Through its national headquarters and fifty chapters, the association provides networking and leadership training. In addition, its chapters tailor programs and services to their membership. For example, a chapter with many members who have home-based businesses runs programs geared to that group. By joining the national association, you receive a monthly newsletter and quarterly bulletin, as well as invitations to the national annual conference.

Small Business Administration
Office of Women's Business Ownership
409 Third Street, SW
Washington, DC 20416
(202) 205-6673

The Small Business Administration, through its local offices in every state, runs programs and offers services to small business owners generally, and women business owners in particular, including workshops that educate women business owners in the procedures of federal procurement. In addition, the SBA runs the Women's Entrepreneurial Training Network, which links established women business owners with those starting out. The Office of Women's Business Ownership also provides financial assistance in the form of loans to women business owners.

APPENDIX C

A Checklist of Essential Questions to Ask When Seeking Good Child Care*

Use the following checklist, in conjunction with our advice in Chapter 5, when evaluating family day care providers or child care centers.

Instructions for Using the Checklist

♦ Plan to visit each program for at least one hour.
♦ Complete the checklist during the observation. Write "Y" or "N" on the line to indicate "yes" or "no." If you wish, jot notes on the back of your list to help you remember details.
♦ As part of your visit, make an appointment to talk with the care-giver for about fifteen minutes after you've had time to observe the program.
♦ Keep in mind that the best time to visit is in the morning. Try to include drop-off time in your observations so you can see how the children, parents, and care-givers interact.

---

*adapted from *Child Care Action Campaign Information Guide 19*

CARE-GIVERS: HOW MANY CHILDREN IS EACH CARE-GIVER RESPONSIBLE FOR?

☐ **1.** The staff is the most important factor in the quality of care. Optimal staff/child ratios vary by age and type of care. The Child Care Action Campaign recommends the following ratios:

Family Day Care:
    1 adult: 5 children, including the care-giver's children. There should be no more than two infants.

Child Care Centers:
    Infants and toddlers: 1 adult to 4 children
    Two-year-olds: 1 adult to 4–6 children
    Three-year-olds: 1 adult to 7–8 children
    Four-year-olds: 1 adult to 8–9 children
    Five-year-olds: 1 adult to 8–10 children
    School-age children: 1 adult to 10–12 children

☐ **2.** The total group size should be about two times the staff/child ratio.

☐ **3.** Care-givers should have some training in child care, child development, or early childhood education. They continue to learn about children by reading books and articles, taking courses, and/or belonging to a professional organization.

☐ **4.** Care-givers have good character references. A background check has been done if your state requires one.

☐ **5.** Care-givers are warm, affectionate, and seem to enjoy being with children.

☐ **6.** Care-givers pay attention to the children and interact with them, rather than chatting with other care-givers or attending to personal things.

☐ **7.** Care-givers use a pleasant tone of voice and talk a lot to the children, including babies and toddlers.

☐ **8.** Care-givers change their style of supervision to suit the age and abilities of the child—very close supervision for infants and toddlers, more independence for three- and four-year-olds. Children are never left unsupervised.

☐ **9.** Care-givers seem to be easy to talk to and work with.

☐ **10.** Care-givers are energetic, in good physical health, and able to keep up with the children.

☐ **11.** Care-givers have had a physical examination within the past two years.

☐ **12.** Many of the care-givers have been working at the center for an extended period of time and plan on staying in the child care profession.

EMOTIONAL DEVELOPMENT AND DISCIPLINE

☐ **1.** Reasonable discipline is maintained through careful supervision, clear limits, age-appropriate explanations, and use of "time out." No spanking or corporal punishment is ever used, nor is harsh discipline such as shouting, shaming or withholding of food.

☐ **2.** Care-givers avoid conflicts between children by listening and watching carefully so that they can step in early—before the situation escalates.

☐ **3.** Care-givers appropriately use praise and attention to encourage cooperation and helpfulness. They call attention to children who are being good more often than those being bad.

☐ **4.** There is a pleasant, generally happy tone in the group much of the day. Care-givers show warmth and affection by smiling, talking to, and hugging children. Infants and toddlers are held often.

☐ **5.** Care-givers are patient when annoying and unanticipated events happen, such as spills at the table or accidents with toileting.

☐ **6.** Care-givers are able to talk with parents about discipline methods and are willing to work with parents and other staff to find ways to solve a child's problems.

PLAY ACTIVITIES

☐ **1.** Toys are organized so that they are easy to find and easy to put away.

☐ **2.** Children—including babies and toddlers—have easy access to some safe toys kept for them on open shelves or in organized boxes.

☐ **3.** There are age-appropriate toys and games to build eye-hand coordination, such as grasping toys for infants; nesting cups for toddlers; and puzzles, small building toys, and safe scissors for older children.

☐ **4.** Safe and easy-to-use art materials, such as nontoxic crayons, paints, and play dough, are provided so that children can create their own work as soon as they are able.

☐ **5.** Records for listening, singing along, and dancing to—as well as musical toys and instruments—are available. The care-giver sings simple songs with children of all ages.

☐ **6.** Building toys, such as blocks, are available; toy people, cars, and other accessories are added to enhance imaginary play.

☐ **7.** Soft toys and dolls, toy dishes, and dress-up clothes are available for imaginary play.

☐ **8.** Clean sand and water are available for play outdoors—and sometimes indoors.

☐ **9.** Infants and toddlers have many age-appropriate toys to use (soft toys, musical toys, balls, etc.), and there is enough safe crawling space to encourage their exploration of the environment.

☐ **10.** Challenging materials, such as scissors or toys with many pieces, are introduced—with supervision—as children are ready for them. A care-giver stays with the children while they use such materials.

☐ **11.** Space is provided for children to play alone or in small groups, protected from the pressure and competition of other children.

☐ **12.** There are rugs and soft, comfortable furniture for the children to relax on.

☐ **13.** Colorful pictures of everyday things are hung at the child's eye level without the use of sharp objects such as tacks.

☐ **14.** Children's artwork is displayed where it is visible to children.

FACILITY OPERATION AND POLICIES

☐ **1.** Substitute care-givers with whom the children are familiar, and who are knowledgeable about the program, are available when the main care-giver is absent.

☐ **2.** The indoor care-giving area is large enough for the group and is clearly organized, so that children know where different activities take place and where they can get toys and put them away.

☐ **3.** The children play outdoors in a safe area every day, except in bad weather.

☐ **4.** There is a schedule that covers the basic care routines and play periods (both indoors and outdoors), including some daily planned activities, like story time for preschoolers or singing time for babies. An alternative activity is available for children who do not want to join the group activity.

SAFETY

☐ **1.** Electrical outlets and heaters are covered and stairs have safety gates.

☐ **2.** Equipment is maintained to ensure safety, and there is enough space for active physical play outdoors (and to some degree, indoors) for all age groups.

☐ **3.** Cleaning fluids, medicines, and other harmful substances are stored in locked cabinets out of the reach of children.

☐ **4.** The outdoor play area is fenced and cleared of debris and poisonous plants.

☐ **5.** The outdoor area is protected from animal contamination, including covering the sandbox when not in use.

☐ **6.** There are fire extinguishers in the building and an adequate number of working smoke detectors.

☐ **7.** Emergency numbers for the fire station, rescue squad, police, poison control, etc., are posted near the telephone.

☐ **8.** There is an emergency exit plan so that the care-giver can get all the children out quickly. Fire drills are held monthly, so that children and care-givers know what to do in case of an emergency.

☐ **9.** Safety restraints and seats are used every time a child is in a car, bus, van, or other moving vehicle.

HEALTH AND NUTRITION

☐ **1.** Telephone numbers of parents and another relative or friend are recorded and are easily accessible for contact in an emergency.

☐ **2.** Parents are told immediately about any accident that a child has; they are also told about any contagious illnesses in the group.

☐ **3.** Care-givers wash their hands with soap and water each time they change a diaper or toilet a child, and before they prepare or serve food, in order to prevent the spread of germs.

☐ **4.** At least one care-giver has had first aid and CPR training within the past two years.

☐ **5.** The care-giver will give the child medicine only with a parent's permission and precise written instructions.

☐ **6.** Wholesome, nutritious meals and snacks are served daily, on a suitable schedule.

☐ **7.** If a care-giver provides food, weekly menus are posted where parents can see them. Care-givers also discuss a child's eating habits with parents and make note of any allergies or other special food needs.

☐ **8.** Babies are held while being bottle-fed. Babies and toddlers are not put to bed with bottles (this can cause tooth decay and ear infections).

☐ **9.** Care-givers supervise a suitable nap/rest time and provide each child with a cot or bed with clean linen. Quiet activities are planned for nonnappers.

MANAGEMENT POLICIES

☐ **1.** Parents are welcome to visit any time of the day.

☐ **2.** The facility is registered or licensed if required.

☐ **3.** The operating policies covering fees, hours of operation, procedure if a child becomes ill, vacations, and meals are available in writing.

☐ **4.** Information about the program, including discipline methods used, the children's schedule of activities, and weekly menus is available to you in writing.

☐ **5.** The care-giver will report to you regularly about your child's activities and interests while at the center or child care home.

WARNING SIGNS OF POOR CHILD CARE

☐ **1.** Parents are not allowed to drop in unannounced at all times of the day. You are required to call before visiting or coming to pick up your child at a different time.

☐ **2.** Parents must drop off the child in the office and may not come into the care-giving areas.

☐ **3.** After several months, your child continues to be unhappy about going to the child care facility, or your child suddenly becomes unhappy after she or he seems to have adjusted. This may or may not be a danger sign, since children often have problems with separation, but it should be attended to.

☐ **4.** Your child talks about being afraid of or disliking a particular care-giver or seems quiet and fearful in her presence.

☐ **5.** There is frequent staff turnover and you notice unfamiliar people caring for the children when you drop off or pick up your child.

☐ **6.** The care seems lax and indifferent. You see children being made to wait for long periods of time or left to play unattended indoors or outdoors.

☐ **7.** Your child has an excessive number of injuries that the care-giver cannot explain adequately.

☐ **8.** The care-giver's voice or manner seems harsh, rude, or indifferent toward any of the children.

☐ **9.** There are insufficient toys for the children to play with or few interesting activities. Toys may be put on display but are not used regularly by the children.

☐ **10.** When you express any concerns, the care-giver becomes upset or defensive and cannot discuss the matter rationally with you.

☐ **11.** You feel uneasy about the care, are not confident about the care-givers, or worry about how your child is doing. A visit to spend time with your child and observe what her life in care is like should reassure you.

APPENDIX D

List of Children's Books With a Working Mother Character*

Blaine, Marge. *The Terrible Thing that Happened At Our House.* Illustrated by John Wallner. New York: Macmillan, 1975.

---

*compiled by Once Upon a Time, a children's bookstore in New Rochelle, New York, May, 1993.

Bauer, Caroline. *My Mom Travels a Lot.* Illustrated by Nancy Parker. New York: Penguin, 1985.

Berenstain, Stan, and Jan Berenstain. *The Berenstain Bears—Mama's New Job.* New York: Random House, 1984.

Carlson, Nancy. *Take Time to Relax!* New York: Viking, 1991.

Hazen, Barbara. *Mommy's Office.* Illustrated by David Soman. New York: Macmillan, 1992.

Hest, Amy. *The Mommy Exchange.* Illustrated by DyAnne diSalvo-Ryan. New York: Macmillan, 1988.

Hines, Anna Grossnickle. *Daddy Makes the Best Spaghetti.* New York: Clarion, 1986.

Holabird, Katharine. *Alexander and the Magic Boat.* Illustrated by Helen Craig. New York: Crown, 1990.

Komaiko, Leah, and Kids. *A Million Moms and Mine.* New York: Liz Clairborne,° 1992.

Levine, Abby. *What Did Mommy Do Before You?* Niles, IL: A. Whitman, 1988.

Merriam, Eve. *Mommies at Work.* Illustrated by Eugenie Fernandes. New York: Simon & Schuster, 1989.

Steig, William. *Brave Irene.* New York: Farrar Straus & Giroux, 1986.

Williams, Vera B. *A Chair for My Mother.* New York: Greenwillow, 1982.

Ziefert, Harriet, *Where's Mommy's Truck?* Illustrated by Andrea Baruffi. New York: HarperCollins, 1992.

°available through Liz Clairborne Foundation, 141 Fifth Avenue, New York, NY 10010.

NOTES

Introduction

1. Dynerman, Susan Bacon, and Hayes, Lynn O'Rourke, *The Best Jobs in America for Parents*, at page 21. New York: Rawson Associates, 1991.

Chapter 1

1. Bureau of National Affairs, *Pregnancy and Employment, The Complete Handbook on Discrimination, Maternity Leave, and Health and Safety*, at page 107. Washington, D.C.: Bureau of National Affairs, 1987.

2. Bureau of National Affairs, *101 Key Statistics on Work and Family for the 1990s: BNA Special Report #21*, at page 30. Washington, D.C.: Bureau of National Affairs, 1989 (hereafter *BNA Report #21*).

3. Flating, Sonja, *Child Care: A Parent's Guide*, at page 104. New York: Facts-on-File, 1991.

4. Friedman, Dana, "Linking Work-Family Issues to the Bottom Line," at page 27. New York: The Conference Board Report Number 962, 1991. See also Flating, *Child Care: A Parent's Guide*, at page 10.

5. Even the *New York Times*, which seems to relish stories about women dropping out of the work force, admits that "[c]ontrary to a flurry of news reports that women are leaving the work force to raise children, [the Bureau of Labor Statistics is] not seeing any dropping out on account of kids." Nasar, Sylvia, "Women's Progress Stalled? Just Not So," *Sunday New York Times Business Section* 1:1, October 18, 1992.

Chapter 2

1. Bureau of National Affairs, *Pregnancy and Employment: The Complete Handbook on Discrimination, Maternity Leave, and Health & Safety*, at page 3. Washington, D.C.: Bureau of National Affairs, 1987. A 1980 study reported that "41 percent of pregnant women in white-collar jobs worked into their ninth month of pregnancy." By the early 1990s, 50 percent of all pregnant women in the work force worked into their third trimester. Hughes, Kathleen, "Pregnant Professionals Face Pressures at Work as Attitudes Toward Them Shift," *Wall Street Journal*, February 6, 1991, Section B, 1:4.

2. Hughes, "Pregnant Professionals Face Pressures at Work as Attitudes Toward Them Shift."

3. Friedman, Dana, "Linking Work-Family Issues to the Bottom Line," at page 7. New York: The Conference Board Report Number 962, 1991.

4. As Felice Schwartz says, "Women are expected to quit," especially after they have children. Schwartz, Felice, *Breaking with Tradition: Women and Work, the New Facts of Life*, at page 56. New York: Warner, 1992.

Chapter 3

1. Bureau of National Affairs, *Pregnancy and Employment: The Complete Handbook on Discrimination, Maternity Leave, and Health & Safety*, at pages 11–12 (describing *California Federal Savings and Loan v. Guerra*). Washington, D.C.: Bureau of National Affairs, 1987.

2. A study performed in 1989 in Connecticut showed that 35 percent of companies surveyed did not comply with the state's maternity leave laws. Shellenbarger, Sue, "Work & Family Column," *Wall Street Journal*, September 18, 1992, Section B, 1:1. On a positive note, a woman won a pregnancy discrimination suit by arguing that the employer had violated state law, which required companies to offer equivalent or comparable jobs to women returning from leave, by giving her a different job when she returned to work which was much less secure than her original job. *Johnson v. Goodyear Tire & Rubber*, 790 F.2d 1516 (E.D. Wash. 1992).

3. "FaxPoll," *Inc.* January 1992, at page 22.

4. Schwartz, Felice, *Breaking with Tradition: Women and Work, the New Facts of Life*, at page 91. New York: Warner, 1992.

5. Brown, Harriet, "Beyond the Mommy Trap," *Vogue*, September 1991, at page 506.

6. Friedman, Dana, "Linking Work-Family Issues to the Bottom Line," at page 26. New York: The Conference Board Report Number 962, 1991.

7. Dynerman, Susan Bacon, and Hayes, Lynn O'Rourke, *The Best Jobs in America for Parents*, at page 68. New York: Rawson Associates, 1991.

8. American Bar Association, *Lawyers and Balanced Lives: A Guide to Drafting and Implementing Workplace Policies for Lawyers*, at page 6. Chicago: American Bar Association, 1990.

9. Friedman, Dana, "Linking Work-Family Issues to the Bottom Line," at page 12.

10. National Council of Jewish Women's Center for the Child, "Accommodating Pregnancy in the Workplace," November 1987 Summary. New York: National Council of Jewish Women, 1987.

11. A male teacher successfully challenged as discriminatory a provision in his collective bargaining agreement that allowed women but not men to take a one-year "childrearing leave." *Schafer v. Board of Public Education of the School District of Pittsburgh*, 903 F.2d 243 (3d Cir. 1990). At the same time that this case was decided, the Equal Employment Opportunity Commission, the federal agency responsible for enforcing and interpreting the Pregnancy Discrimination Act, issued a policy guide that, consistent with the *Schafer* case, advises companies to offer child care leave—as opposed to pregnancy disability leave—to parents of both sexes. Pulliam, Lynn, "Pregnancy Disability and Child Care Leave: What Does Title VII Require?" 17 *Employee Relations Law Journal*, at page 511 (Winter 1991–92).

Chapter 5

1. Noble, Barbara Presley, "Making a Case for Family Programs," *Sunday New York Times Business Section*, at page 25. May 2, 1993, reporting on two studies on the benefits of work/family programs. See also Luxenberg, Stan, "All Work and No Playtime," *Scholastic Update* September 6, 1991, describing a working mother's experience at Stride Rite Corp.; Williams, Monte, "Oh Baby: On-site Childcare Coming Out of the Dark Ages," *Advertising Age* February 25, 1991, describing a working mother's experience at Marriott Corp.

2. Galinsky, Ellen, "What Really Constitutes Quality Care?" *Exchange*, September 1986, at pages 41–42.

3. Modigliani, Kathy, *Choosing Family Day Care: A Handbook for Parents*, at page 2. New York: National Family Day Care Project of the National Council of Jewish Women, 1990.

4. Rowland, Mary, "Strategies for Stay-at-Home Moms," *Sunday New York Times Business Section*, at page 18, August 23, 1992, describing a study by Laurence Levin and Joyce Jacobsen on the economic impact of stepping out of the work force; see also Wadman, Meredith, "Mothers Who Take Extended Time Off Find Their Careers Pay a Heavy Price," *Wall Street Journal*, July 16, 1992, Section B, 1:1.

Chapter 6

1. Friedman, Dana, "Linking Work-Family Issues to the Bottom Line," at page 12 (emphasis in original). New York: The Conference Board Report Number 962, 1991.

2. Wheatley, Meg, and Marcie Schorr Hirsch, *Managing Your Maternity Leave*, at page 152. New York: Houghton Mifflin, 1983.

3. Friedman, Dana, "Linking Work-Family Issues to the Bottom

Line," at page 30 (emphasis added). New York: The Conference Board Report Number 962, 1991.

4. Crosby, Faye, *Juggling: The Unexpected Advantages of Balancing Career and Home for Women and their Families*, at page 8. New York: The Free Press, 1991.

5. Shellenbarger, Sue, "Child-Care Setups Still Fall Apart Often," *Wall Street Journal*, September 26, 1991, Section B, 1:1.

6. Dynerman, Susan Bacon, and Lynn O'Rourke Hayes, *The Best Jobs for America for Parents*, at page 13. New York: Rawson Associates, 1991. One study of parents who rely on their children taking care of themselves (after school, for example) found that:

> [while] the average American worker typically misses somewhere between seven and nine days a year, mothers with self-care arrangements [children taking care of themselves] miss approximately 13 days a year while fathers miss 13.4 days.

Galinsky, Ellen, "Child Care and Productivity," Bank Street College paper prepared for the Child Care Action Campaign, March 1988, at page 6.

7. Newsday, "Smart Money/Working" column, February 2, 1988, at page 49.

8. Hyland, Stephanie, "Helping Employees with Family Care," *Monthly Labor Review*, September 1990, at page 22.

9. Friedman, Dana, "Linking Work-Family Issues to the Bottom Line," at page 13. New York: The Conference Board Report Number 962, 1991.

10. Ferguson, Trudi, and Joan Dunphy, *Answers to the Mommy Track: How Wives & Mothers in Business Reach the Top & Balance their Lives*, at page 157. Far Hills, N.J.: New Horizon Press, 1991.

11. Friedman, Dana, "Linking Work-Family Issues to the Bottom Line," at page 28. New York: Conference Board Report No. 962, 1991.

12. Veum, Jonathan, and Philip Gleason, "Child Care: Arrangements and Costs," *Monthly Labor Review*, October 1991, at pages 10–11.

13. Galinsky, Ellen, "Child Care and Productivity," Bank Street College paper prepared for the Child Care Action Campaign, March 1988, at page 8.

14. Besides making child care expensive, its labor-intensive nature makes cost-cutting strategies hard to implement. Ewing, Stephen E., "Nourish Thy Children: Investing in Child Care to Nourish Corporate Productivity," *Vital Speeches*, June 15, 1990, at page 517.

15. The Child Care Law Center in San Francisco and the Child Care Project of the National Council of Jewish Women in New York have done innovative work in creating solutions to the zoning problem. Their approach is to involve local government, community organizations, child care providers, and parents. For information on these organizations, see Appendix B.

16. Galinsky, Bank Street paper, at page 14.

Chapter 7

1. Friedman, Dana, "Linking Work-Family Issues to the Bottom Line," at page 18. New York: The Conference Board Report Number 962, 1991.

2. Crosby, Faye, *Juggling: The Unexpected Advantages of Balancing Career and Home for Women and their Families*, at page 122. New York: The Free Press, 1991.

Chapter 8

1. As Barney Olmsted and Suzanne Smith report in *The Job Sharing Handbook*, New York: Penguin, 1983, at page 169:

> The 1980 White House Conference on Families conducted a Gallup Poll which indicated that 54 percent of the people surveyed identified flexible hours, including job sharing, as a number-one priority. In 1981, the General Mills national study, "Families at Work: Strengths and Strains," observed that "part-time work with full benefits emerged as the benefit with the greatest breadth and depth of support." In 1982, Better Homes and Gardens magazine conducted a readers' survey that indicated that 66 percent of the 32,500 respondents wanted more flexible work hours and 29 percent specifically desired job sharing.

Similarly, a poll of over one thousand career professionals found that "82 percent of the women would choose a career path with flexible full-time hours and more family time but slower career advancement over a fast-track career with inflexible hours." Aburdene, Patricia, and John Naisbitt, *Megatrends for Women*, at page 100. New York: Villard, 1992.

2. As of 1990, 25 percent of all women in the workplace worked part-time. "At the management level, 9 percent of women and 4 percent of men work part-time. Of professionals, 22 percent of women and 8 percent of men work part-time," says Felice Schwartz in *Breaking with Tradition: Women and Work, The New Facts of Life*, at page 138. New York: Warner, 1992.

3. According to the American Bar Association's Commission on Women in the Profession, women across the country report that the prevailing assumption is "that women who seek an alternative schedule are not serious about the practice of law." ABA Commission on Women in the Profession, *Lawyers and Balanced Lives*, Part II, at page 5. Chicago, Ill.: American Bar Association, 1990. As Susan Bacon Dynerman and Lynn

O'Rourke Hayes, authors of *The Best Jobs for Parents in America*, New York: Rawson Associates, 1991, at page 85, point out:

> The Catch-22 of flexibility is this: women need it, but, right now at least, flexibility will slow them down professionally. If they cut back their hours, women are perceived as less committed. If they take time off, they may suffer career setbacks.

4. Schwartz, Felice, *Breaking with Tradition: Women and Work, The New Facts of Life*, at page 181. New York: Warner, 1992.

5. Shellenbarger, Sue, "Work & Family: Averting Career Damage from Family Policies," *Wall Street Journal*, "Work & Family" column, June 29, 1992, Section B, 1:6.

6. Cweren, Helene, "City of San Diego Launches Telecommuting Program for Its Employees," Current Municipal Problems Vol. 19, page 82, 1992–93. The program was initially established to comply with air pollution control requirements but has generated significant benefits in other areas as well.

Studies of part-time lawyers show the same results. According to the American Bar Association's Commission on Women in the Profession, the "ratio of billable hours to hours worked is reported to be higher for attorneys on alternative work schedules than for full-time attorneys." ABA Commission on Women in the Profession, *Lawyers and Balanced Lives*, at pages 22–23. Chicago, Ill.: American Bar Association, 1990.

Likewise, a study of a part-time program at the Boston Department of Public Welfare instituted in the early sixties showed that "half-time workers were 89 percent as productive as full-time employees." Schwartz, Felice, *Breaking with Tradition: Women and Work, The New Facts of Life*, at page 78. New York: Warner, 1992.

Chapter 9

1. See American Women's Economic Development Corporation's *Inbusiness* newsletter, at page 1, September/October 1992, citing a 1987 study funded by the federal government. See also Patricia Aburdene and John Naisbitt, *Megatrends for Women*, at page 65 (reporting a study done by the National Foundation for Women Business Owners that indicates that more people are employed by women-owned businesses than by Fortune 500 companies) and page 229 (reporting a study showing that "the number of self-employed women working full-time at home tripled between 1985 and 1991, from 378,000 to 1.1 million). New York: Villard, 1992.

2. For a detailed approach to reentering the work force, see Eleanor Berman, *Re-entering*. New York: Crown, 1980. While much of her advice does not apply only to mothers who are reentering the work force, she never loses sight of the emotional context surrounding their job search, particularly the low self-esteem many mothers have when they begin the process. Berman counsels:

> Under no circumstances should you be apologetic about the years you've been away from the work force. They've given you a wider perspective, a knowledge of human nature, the ability to get along with people, a sense of responsibility. You've had the opportunity to organize and supervise and counsel and pursue myriad interests that might not have been possible within the confines of a nine-to-five job. If you know this *and truly believe it,* you should be able to convince your prospective employer that your maturity is a tremendous advantage. (Emphasis added.)

Chapter 10

1. Faludi, Susan, *Backlash: The Undeclared War Against American Women,* at page 65. New York: Crown, 1991.

2. Christensen, Kathleen, *Women and Home-Based Work: The Unspoken Contract,* at page 138–39. New York: Henry Holt, 1988.

SUGGESTED READING

Chapter 1

Crosby, Faye. *Juggling: The Unexpected Advantages of Balancing Career and Home for Women and their Families.* New York: The Free Press, 1991. A sociological look at the women who balance work and family, including an extensive review of the research and literature on working mothers.

Faludi, Susan. *Backlash: The Undeclared War Against American Women.* New York: Crown, 1991. Forceful analysis of the manifestations of and reasons for antifeminism, including attitudes that perpetuate the "glass ceiling" and other workplace obstacles for women.

Friedman, Dana. "Linking Work-Family Issues to the Bottom Line," New York: The Conference Board Report Number 962, 1991. Comprehensive and in-depth review of the impact that work/family conflict has on the bottom line and the effect, including how to measure it, of various programs. Using findings from over eighty studies, this report conveys "most of the information that a company would need to determine the appropriateness of creating a work-family agenda."

Schwartz, Felice. *Breaking with Tradition: Women and Work, The New Facts of Life.* New York: Warner, 1992. In-depth analysis of the way managers view professional women in general, and working mothers in particular, and arguments for changing these views to make the workplace more accommodating to working mothers.

Sekaran, Uma, and Frederick T. L. Leong, eds. *Womanpower: Managing in Times of Demographic Turbulence.* Newbury Park, CA: Sage, 1992. Deals with various aspects of women in the workplace, including a section on legislation that has helped, and hindered, women's advancement, and a chapter on corporate policies and practices regarding work and family.

Zuckerman, Harriet, Jonathan R. Cole, John T. Bruer, eds. *The Outer Circle: Women in the Scientific Community.* New York: W. W. Norton, 1991. Essays about the status of women in science and in-depth interviews with three women scientists.

Chapters 2 and 3

American Bar Association. *Lawyers and Balanced Lives: A Guide to Drafting and Implementing Workplace Policies for Lawyers*. Chicago: American Bar Association, 1990. Practical, straightforward manual for legal employers on the work and family issues lawyers confront and the reasons to adopt and implement policies on parental leave and alternative work schedules. (The guide also contains a section on sexual harassment.) The manual contains excellent model policies, annotated to explain the reasons behind each section of the policies. The arguments and model policies are applicable to service firms other than law firms.

Barrett, Nina. *I Wish Someone Had Told Me: Comfort, Support and Advice for New Moms from More Than 60 Real-Life Mothers*. New York: Fireside, 1991. Honest account of the good and the bad moments of becoming a mother, including a chapter on the decision to go back to work.

National Research Council. *Work and Family: Policies for a Changing Work Force*. Washington, D.C.: National Academy Press, 1991. This report contains information on the inadequacy of current employer responses to parental leave and child care and recommendations regarding the kind of leave and other family-related benefits employers should offer.

Wheatley, Meg, and Marcie Schorr Hirsch. *Managing Your Maternity Leave*. New York: Houghton Mifflin, 1983. Practical advice on issues ranging from being pregnant on the job to returning to work.

Women's Bar Association of the District of Columbia. *Guidelines on Family and Medical Leave and Alternative Work Schedules*. Washington, D.C: The Women's Bar Association of the District of Columbia, 1991. Provides a model family and medical leave policy and a model policy on alternative work schedules in the context of the legal workplace. Each model provision is followed by an explanation and rationale.

Women's Bureau, U.S. Department of Labor. *A Working Woman's Guide to Her Job Rights*. Washington, D.C.: U.S. Department of Labor, 1992. Brief descriptions of rights afforded under a number of federal statutes, such as the Occupational Safety and Health Act, the Americans with Disabilities Act, and the Pregnancy Discrimination Act, federal tax provisions relevant to women (such as the child care tax credit), and general description of state laws.

Zigler, Edward, and Meryl Frank, eds., *The Parental Leave Crisis: Toward a National Policy*. New Haven, Conn.: Yale University, 1988. The book compiles pieces by leading experts in the field of child development, labor economics and policy, and law advocating for a national parental leave policy that is more generous than currently available (even under the Family and Medical Leave Act).

Chapter 4

Berg, Barbara J. *The Crisis of the Working Mother: Resolving the Conflict Between Family and Work.* New York: Summit, 1986. Based on interviews of working mothers and on 750 responses to questionnaires distributed by *Savvy, Parents,* and *Homemaker* magazines, the book is about what it feels like to be a working mother. The book places a good deal of emphasis on the guilt working mothers feel—why we feel guilty and what we can do about it.

Brazelton, T. Berry. *Working and Caring.* Reading, Mass.: Addison-Wesley, 1985. About and for working parents, this book is structured around the stories of two couples and a single mother. Although anecdotal in nature, the book also contains some policy suggestions and a chapter on evaluating day care.

Hochschild, Arlie. *The Second Shift.* New York: Viking, 1989. Through in-depth accounts of how a dozen two-paycheck couples deal with child rearing and housework, this book demonstrates how stubborn traditional gender lines are at home. As a result, working mothers end up working at their domestic tasks—the "second shift"—an extra month of twenty-four-hour days a year.

Chapters 5 and 6

Binswanger, Barbara and Betsy Ryan. *Live-In Child Care.* New York: Dolphin/Doubleday, 1986. Very practical guide to the various live-in arrangements and how to decide what kind of arrangement makes sense for you.

Brazelton. *Working and Caring.* See listing under Chapter 4.

Buhler, Danalee. *The Very Best Child Care and How to Find It.* Rocklin, Calif.: Prima, 1989. Book focuses primarily on day care centers, including health and safety features to look out for and what to ask day care center workers.

Families and Work Institute. *The Corporate Reference Guide.* New York: Families and Work Institute, 1991. A detailed look at the types of family-friendly policies that companies can implement, including a "family-friendly" index by which to measure a corporation's receptivity to developing such policies as well as its ability to implement them.

Flating, Sonja. *Child Care: A Parent's Guide.* New York: Facts-on-File, 1991. A useful, honest guide to making a child care decision, from what it feels like to how to look for the type of child care you decide is best for you.

Galinsky, Ellen, and William H. Hooks. *The New Extended Family: Day Care that Works.* New York: Houghton Mifflin, 1977. Reviews different forms of child care as they were emerging in this country in the late 1970s.

Morgan, Hal, and Kerry Tucker. *Companies That Care: The Most Family-Friendly Companies in America — What They Offer, and How They Got That Way.* New York: Fireside, 1991. In-depth profiles of sixteen companies and shorter descriptions of over eighty other companies and their family-friendly policies and attitudes.

Muscari, Ann, and Wendy Wardell Morrone. *Child Care That Works: How Families Can Share Their Lives with Child Care and Thrive.* Garden City, New York: Doubleday, 1989. Book focuses on what it feels like to find and live with child care and useful information about different options.

Spaide, Deborah. *The Day Care Kit: A Parent's Guide to Finding Quality Child Care.* New York: Birch Lane, 1990. Matter-of-fact, concise book on child care options, focusing on day care centers.

Women's Bureau, United States Department of Labor. *Work and Family Resource Kit.* Washington, D.C.: United States Department of Labor, 1993. Directed at employers, the Kit contains information on child care benefits and programs, as well as alternative work schedules and a list of further resources and references.

Chapters 7 and 8

Canape, Charlene. *The Part-Time Solution.* New York: Harper & Row, 1990. General advice and encouragement for working mothers who are interested in working part-time. While interesting and helpful, the book tends to downplay the disadvantages of the part-time solution.

Christensen, Kathleen, Ph.D. "Flexible Staffing and Scheduling in U.S. Corporations," New York: The Conference Board Research Bulletin No. 240, 1989. Results of survey of over five hundred large companies on their current and projected flexible staffing and scheduling policies.

Dynerman, Susan Bacon, and Lynn O'Rourke Hayes. *The Best Jobs in America for Parents Who Want Careers and Time for Children Too.* New York: Rawson Associates, 1991. Flexibility in the workplace. Part I covers the kinds of jobs that exist and where they are; Part II covers how to negotiate and manage these flexible jobs; and Part III profiles twenty-five flexible companies and their policies and contains a guide to resources.

Ferguson, Trudi, and Joan Dunphy. *Answers to the Mommy Track: How Wives & Mothers in Business Reach the Top & Balance their Lives.* Far Hills, N.J.: New Horizon, 1991. Book is based on in-depth interviews with numerous women who have been highly successful and have children.

While interesting because of the women it profiles, the book obscures, rather than illuminates, how they managed to reach the top and balance their lives.

Gordon, Gil. *Telecommuting Review: The Gordon Report*, published by Gil Gordon Associates, is a newsletter on telecommuting issues to which anyone can subscribe. Current subscription price is $157/year and is available from Telespan Publishing, 50 West Palm Street, Altadena, CA 91001.

Lee, Patricia. *The Complete Guide to Job Sharing*. New York: Walker and Company, 1983. Extended pamphlet (with bibliography and forms) regarding job sharing.

National Research Council. *Work and Family: Policies for a Changing Society*. See entry under Chapter 3 for description.

Nollen, Stanley, D., ed. *New Work Schedules in Practice*. New York: Van Nostrand Reinhold, Work in America Institute Series, 1982. A technical, research-based look at work patterns in this country.

Norris, Gloria, and Jo Ann Miller. *The Working Mother's Complete Handbook*. New York: New American Library, 1984. The book covers every aspect of being a working mother—from what it's like at work to taking care of the house, the kids, your husband, and you. While the book is very comprehensive as a result, each subject gets treated in a rather superficial way.

Olmsted, Barney, and Suzanne Smith. *The Job Sharing Handbook*. New York: Penguin, 1983. Authors are the founders of New Ways to Work, a nonprofit that consults with employers and people seeking alternative work arrangements. Book is a detailed, in-depth treatment of how to job share.

The Women's Bar Association of the District of Columbia. *Guidelines on Family and Medical Leave and Alternative Work Schedules*. Washington, D.C.: The Women's Bar Association of the District of Columbia, 1991. See entry under Chapter 3 for description.

Chapter 9

Berman, Eleanor. *Re-entering*. New York: Crown, 1980. Based on the materials and curriculum of the Ellen Morse Tishman Memorial Seminars for Re-entering Homemakers sponsored by the Hunter College Career Counseling and Placement Office, as well as interviews with career counseling professionals across the country and reentered homemakers, this book is an anecdotal and practical guide to going back to work after an extended absence.

Christensen, Kathleen. *Women and Home-Based Work: The Unspoken Contract*. New York: Henry Holt, 1988. Based on fourteen thousand responses to a *Family Circle* survey and one hundred in-depth interviews, the book reviews the pros and cons of working from home. It provides a very honest and therefore useful assessment of what it takes (both from a personal and a logistical perspective) to make working from home successful.

Kahn, Sharon, and the Philip Lief Group. *101 Best Businesses to Start.* Garden City, New York: Doubleday, 1988. Very matter-of-fact book on what it takes to start a business, the pros and cons of doing so, and three- to five-page descriptions on the best kinds of businesses to start.

Sanders, Darcie, and Martha Bullen. *Staying Home: From Full-Time Professional to Full-time Parent.* New York: Little, Brown, 1992. Based on interviews and a survey, this book deals primarily with the emotional aspects of leaving the workplace to be a stay-at-home mother.

In addition there are various sources of up-to-date information on work and family issues, including the *Wall Street Journal*'s "Work & Family" columns; *Working Mother* magazine's annual "100 Best Companies for Working Mothers" report; the *National Report on Work and Family* (a biweekly publication published by Business Publishers, 951 Persing Drive, Silver Springs, MD 20910. Subscription rate: $481.96/year); and the Work/Family Roundtable (a survey of work/family practitioners, consultants, and corporate coordinators published four times a year by the Conference Board, 845 Third Avenue, New York, NY 10022). Lastly, many of the organizations listed in Appendix B publish newsletters, brochures, information guides, and other materials on work/family issues.

INDEX

229

ANNE C. WEISBERG and CAROL A. BUCKLER both graduated from Harvard Law School and worked for a law firm in New York. Weisberg is an advocate for women's rights in the workplace, and lives in Scarsdale, New York, with her husband and three children. Buckler is an associate professor at New York Law School, and lives in Larchmont, New York, with her husband and two children.